SATHER

The Peoples of
Borneo

The Peoples of South-East Asia and The Pacific

General Editors
Peter Bellwood and Ian Glover

Each book in this series will be devoted to a people (or group of associated peoples) from the vast area of the world extending from Hawaii in the north to Tasmania in the south and from Fiji in the east to Cambodia in the west. The books, written by historians, anthropologists and archaeologists from all over the world, will be both scholarly and accessible. In many cases the volumes will be the only available account of their subject.

Already published
The Peoples of Borneo
Victor T. King

In preparation

The Melanesians
Matthew Spriggs

The Vietnamese
Jeremy Davidson

The Malays
A. C. Milner

The Bugis
Christian Pelras

The Maoris
Atholl Anderson

The Fijians
Nicholas Thomas

The Khmers
Ian Mabbett and David Chandler

The Peoples of the Lesser Sundas
James L. Fox

The Balinese
Angela Hobart, Urs Ramseyer and Albert Leeman

The Lapita Peoples
Patrick Kirch

The Javanese
Stuart Robson

The Peoples of Borneo

Victor T. King

BLACKWELL
Oxford UK & Cambridge USA

First published 1993

Blackwell Publishers
108 Cowley Road
Oxford   OX4 1JF
UK

238 Main Street, Suite 501
Cambridge, Massachusetts 02142
USA

British Library Cataloguing in Publication Data
A CIP catalogue record for this book is available from the British Library.

Library of Congress Cataloging-in-Publication Data
King, Victor T.
The Peoples of Borneo / Victor T. King.
p.   cm.
Includes bibliographical references and index.
ISBN 0-631-17221-1 (alk. paper)
1. Borneo. I. Title.
DS646.3.K5   1993
959.8′3—dc20   92-34994
CIP

Typeset in 11 on 12½pt Sabon by Acorn Bookwork, Salisbury
Printed in Great Britain by T.J. Press Ltd, Padstow, Cornwall

This book is printed on acid-free paper

Contents

List of Plates

List of Maps, Tables and Figures

Maps

Tables

Figures

Preface

When I was asked by Dr Ian Glover whether I would be
interested in writing a book on the peoples of Borneo, I
eagerly accepted. I did not anticipate what an arduous task
it would be. As I began to read through the literature prior to
putting pen to paper I realized how little I knew, and yet I have
had a professional academic interest in the island and its
cultures for the past 20 years.

The reader will have to accept the imperfections. I write as
an anthropologist and as someone interested in the sociology
of modernization and development. But I was commissioned to
write a multidisciplinary account of the peoples of Borneo,
their social and cultural evolution and their relationships with
surrounding people through time. The informed reader will
note that some of my chapters, especially those on prehistory
and early history, are highly derivative. I am on stronger
ground in later chapters where I have been able to use some
of my own research material.

In compiling a general book on Borneo I was conscious of
two further problems. First, I did not wish to burden the
reader with a large number of references. Much has been
written on Borneo, and it was tempting to demonstrate how
much I had read by providing a long list of authors. I resisted
the temptation, and I have tried to keep to key texts and those
books and articles which I have found particularly useful or
interesting. Even so, I have ended up with a substantial bibliography. Second, it was difficult to decide, in some cases, what
to put in and what to leave out. There are large gaps in our

knowledge of Borneo, but on some topics and issues one is
overwhelmed with material. In any general text on Borneo
some writings are indispensable and one does not need to
spend too much time deciding whether one should include or
eliminate them. However, I have also been very much guided
by my own interests and knowledge. Some readers may be-
moan the fact that I have not covered certain subjects in
sufficient detail, or, sadly, that I have missed some out altogether. All I can say is that I have tried, given my own
limitations and my particular academic interests, to present
as well-rounded a study as I can.

I should also say that I have concentrated especially on the
Dayak peoples of Borneo; in other words, the non-Muslim,
non-Malay natives. Some might call them the 'tribal groups'.
But as I explain in the text, for various reasons I also consider
the Muslim coastal populations and the Islamic states of
Borneo, though in less detail.

I am afraid I have decided not to acknowledge anyone,
except the two series editors who read the manuscript and
made many helpful suggestions, and who presumably thought
that I was adequate to the task. All those scholars of Bornean
societies with whom I have corresponded, collaborated or
argued over the past 20 years will know who they are, and
that I am indebted to them. I could not begin to single some
out for special praise, but perhaps most worthwhile of all have
been those who have been critical of me. In the course of my
studies, I have made ethnographic errors, several of them,
changed my mind on occasion and got some analyses and
interpretations hopelessly wrong. I hope I have learned something from these experiences.

Finally, I should record my thanks to the University of Hull,
which granted me six months' leave in 1991 to write the book.
Without the breathing space I could not have completed the
text. I just wish I had been left alone completely within that
period, but such is the situation in British universities today. I
am thankful for small mercies.

Hull
October 1992

1

The Island of Borneo: General Perspectives

Population

It is a straightforward matter to describe the island of Borneo in demographic terms. It is something else to capture the diversity of its peoples and cultures and their historical development. Let us therefore start with the simple in this first chapter and progress towards the complex. Borneo is a geographical unity; it is the third largest island in the world after Greenland and New Guinea, covering some 746,000 square kilometres (km^2). It is located at a pivotal point in the region which we call South-East Asia, which in turn lies mid-way between the heavily populated continental land masses of China and India (Fisher 1967: 220). Borneo is one of the numerous islands in the humid tropics of Asia which are scattered around the southern and eastern rim of the South China Sea (map 1); it is part of the Sunda continental shelf along with other important islands such as Java and Sumatra. Much of Sundaland is submerged beneath the shallow South China and Java Seas. Borneo comprises mainly weathered sedimentary rocks, tectonically stable with no recent volcanic activity, except on a minor scale in south-eastern Sabah.

A most important fact, which is a legacy of European colonialism and which we shall examine in detail in chapter 5, is that Borneo is divided politically (map 2). These political and administrative boundaries commonly cut across cultural

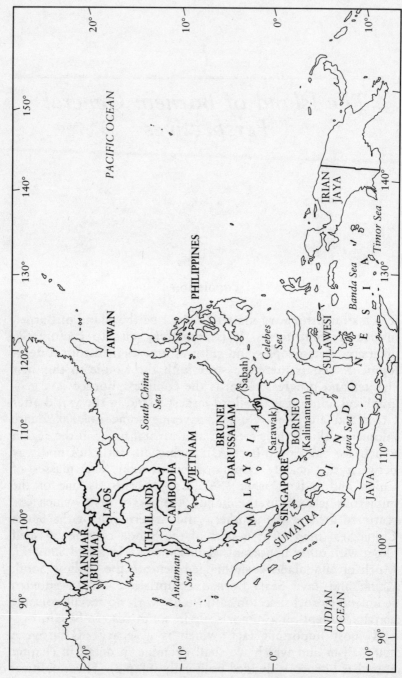

Map 1   Borneo in South-East Asia

Map 2   Borneo: main political and administrative divisions

groupings and relations. The largest, southern part, about 540,000 km² in extent, is referred to as Kalimantan (table 1). It belongs to the Republic of Indonesia, which, until it formally received its independence from the Dutch in December 1949, was known as the Netherlands East Indies. Kalimantan comprises almost one-third of the total land area of the Republic and it is divided into four administrative units or provinces: Kalimantan Barat (West), Kalimantan Tengah (Central), Kalimantan Selatan (South) and Kalimantan Timur (East).

Much of northern Borneo, about 200,000 km², is the territory of the Federation of Malaysia, comprising the states of

Table 1   *Political and administrative divisions of Borneo*

Division	Area (km^2)
Kalimantan Barat	146,670
Kalimantan Tengah	152,600
Kalimantan Selatan	37,660
Kalimantan Timur	202,440
Kalimantan (total)	**539,370**
Sarawak	124,967
Sabah	76,115
East Malaysia (total)	**201,082**
Brunei Darussalam	**5,765**
Borneo (total)	**746,217**

Sources: *Statistik Indonesia. Statistical Yearbook of Indonesia* (various issues)
Annual Statistical Bulletin, Sarawak (various issues)
Annual Bulletin of Statistics, Sabah (various issues)
Brunei Statistical Yearbook (various issues)

Sarawak and Sabah. Formerly they were both British Protectorates from 1888 until the Japanese Occupation. They became British Crown Colonies in 1946 and remained so until 1963, at which time they were granted independence and were brought together with the Federation of Malaya, which had gained its independence from Britain in 1957, to form the new Federation of Malaysia. Sabah was known as British North Borneo prior to independence. Both states are commonly referred to as the Malaysian Borneo territories, or sometimes as East Malaysia, to differentiate them from Peninsular or West Malaysia, the former Malay or Malayan Peninsula.

A small remaining enclave of land in north-western Borneo, surrounded on all its landward sides by Sarawak, is the oil-rich Muslim Malay sultanate of Brunei Darussalam. Like Sarawak and North Borneo, Brunei received British Protectorate status in 1888, but it only became fully independent from Britain on 1 January 1984; it had decided to remain outside the Federation of Malaysia.

Despite the fact that Borneo is a considerable land mass, it has a small overall population. Kalimantan's population, for example, is only 4.56 per cent of Indonesia's total population.

Table 2   Population figures, 1980 and 1990

Division	Population 1980	1990 (estimates)
Kalimantan Barat	2,486,100	3,057,100
Kalimantan Tengah	954,400	1,309,500
Kalimantan Selatan	2,064,600	2,503,400
Kalimantan Timur	1,218,100	2,087,500
Kalimantan (total)	6,723,200	8,957,500
Sarawak	1,308,000	1,667,000
Sabah	1,011,000	1,479,000
East Malaysia (total)	2,319,000	3,146,000
Brunei Darussalam	185,200	241,400
Borneo (total)	9,227,400	12,344,900

Sources: *Statistik Indonesia. Statistical Yearbook of Indonesia* (various issues)
Annual Statistical Bulletin, Sarawak (various issues)
Annual Bulletin of Statistics, Sabah (various issues)
Brunei Statistical Yearbook (various issues)

In 1980 the whole of the island provided a home to just over 9 million people (table 2). It is estimated that in 1990 Borneo's population was still at most only about 12.5 million in total. The island is therefore relatively sparsely populated in relation to its land size. In 1980 the population density averaged about 12 persons per km^2, and in 1990 it was still only approximately 17 persons per km^2. Of course, densities do vary, between about 66 per km^2 in Kalimantan Selatan through to 43 persons per km^2 in Brunei Darussalam to as little as 8 or 9 persons per km^2 in the interior province of Kalimantan Tengah. The population is quite heavily concentrated on certain parts of the coast, and along the main rivers, so that in some remote forested regions of the hinterland densities may be as low as 1 person per km^2.

In the Malaysian territories the main centres of population are, in Sarawak, in and around Kuching, the state capital, extending eastwards and north-eastwards along the coast to Sibu, the second most important town, and then to Bintulu and Miri near the border with Brunei (Jackson 1968: 38; Jones 1966: 4). Kuching is the administrative, industrial and commercial centre of Sarawak; Sibu is a port town, exporting especially saw-logs and timber-based products. Bintulu and Miri are foci of the oil and gas industry. In Sabah, the bulk of the population is found in the western coastal districts centred on the state capital, Kota Kinabalu, with some relatively important settlements on the east coast at Sandakan and Lahad Datu, serving the large oil palm plantations and the timber industries there (Chatfield 1972: 57ff.; Lee 1965: 53ff.).

In Brunei the small population of about 250,000 is found in two main coastal locations – in the capital, Bandar Seri Begawan and the Brunei-Muara district in the east, and in the oil and gas field areas of Seria and Kuala Belait to the west (Zaharah 1976: 1ff.).

In Kalimantan the population is principally located in the four provincial capitals – Banjarmasin (450,000 approx.) on the south coast, Pontianak (400,000 approx.) in the west at the delta of the Kapuas river, Samarinda (300,000 approx.) on the east coast, and the only inland administrative seat, Palangkaraya (100,000 approx.) in Central Kalimantan (Sellato 1989a: 17). A further 400,000 people approximately dwell in and around Balikpapan, the oil capital of East Kalimantan, north of Samarinda. These five cities account for about one-fifth of Kalimantan's population, and the Samarinda-Balikpapan coastal conurbation is especially important as a centre for the oil, gas, timber and plantation industries.

These concentrations demonstrate a historical continuity with earlier centres of economic and political activity, which were invariably located along the coasts of Borneo. Particularly during the first millennium AD various port sites in Borneo became increasingly involved in maritime trade in the region and with India, China and countries beyond. Apart from the suitability of these locations for regional and international commerce, they point to another major feature of Borneo's social, economic and natural history. Much of the island is covered, or at least it has been until recently, with dense equatorial rainforests. These and the difficult terrain of the interior have presented enormous problems for economic development and human settlement there. Prior to the beginning of the neolithic period in Borneo, some 4,500 years ago, there was virtually no possibility that stone-using hunting and gathering populations could tame the forests, and even during the first millennium AD, when the use of iron tools became more widespread, the size of the population dwelling in and exploiting the tropical forest environments of the hinterland must have been very small indeed. We shall return to these issues in subsequent chapters because human–environment relations constitute one of the most significant themes in this book. Any general text on Borneo peoples could hardly ignore the influence of the rainforest on human social, economic and cultural development.

West and East: popular images of Borneo peoples

Aside from the dominant role of the rainforest environment in the island's history, the relations between Europe and the Orient have also helped shape the societies and cultures of Borneo. In chapter 5 I shall pay considerable attention to the course of European colonialism and some of its consequences for indigenous Borneo peoples. This exercise also requires a discussion of continuities and transformations in Borneo societies, economies, cultures and political systems prior to European contact. In chapters 3 and 4 we shall consider the innovations introduced into Borneo as a result of Austronesian settlement of the island commencing in the mid-third millennium BC, and then the changes resulting from the incorporation of coastal Bornean communities, and to a lesser extent inland peoples, into far-flung networks of trade and commerce particularly from the middle of the first millennium AD. Apart from the increasing economic links with India and China, it was not until the establishment of Muslim trading states in Borneo, mainly from the early sixteenth century, and the gathering pace of conversion of natives to Islam, that we begin to witness considerable changes in the social, economic, cultural and political organizations of Bornean peoples, which had begun to take shape with Austronesian settlement some 4,000 years before.

Nevertheless, it was not until Europeans began to establish a firm political and economic presence in Borneo in the nineteenth century that we witness marked transformations among the village societies of the interior. Once they were drawn into the wider imperial systems of the British and Dutch the rate of change accelerated, and this has, if anything, further increased since political independence. Indonesian Kalimantan has now experienced over 40 years of independence, and East Malaysia nearly three decades, and, although the Sultanate of Brunei was not granted its full independence until recently, it too could scarcely have remained unaffected by the processes of decolonization and modernization which had been set in motion in Asia following the end of the Pacific War and the defeat of Japan.

As one might expect, the long period of change in Borneo from the time when the island was first populated by Austronesian speakers (Bellwood 1978, 1985) has given rise to an increasing diversity of socio-cultural and economic forms. Internal variations and adaptations along with external influences have produced a complex human mosaic, which we shall begin to examine in chapter 2. But there are also clearly recognizable similarities and linkages between many Borneo peoples, which have their origins in the distant past and which, despite the changes especially during the last 1,500 years or so, have persisted from earlier times.

Although I emphasize the importance of European contact, I do not wish to give the impression that Bornean peoples were merely passive playthings of the powerful forces which were emanating from Europe. Local communities also moulded and directed their own destinies, and even when Europeans were expanding and consolidating their territorial hold over Borneo, locally generated changes and processes continued, just as they had done prior to European intervention. Be that as it may, much of our general knowledge of early Borneo societies and cultures before the great changes of the late nineteenth and the twentieth centuries comes from the writings of Western observers, and these tended to create particular perceptions of the island and its peoples. Ever since Europeans first came to the islands lying across the great seaways between India and China from the beginning of the sixteenth century, Western popular images of Borneo have remained remarkably constant, and these were reinforced in the nineteenth century when Europeans came into closer and closer contact with the interior natives, resulting in an increasing number of publications by travellers, explorers, scientists, administrators and missionaries for a European educated lay readership.

A number of well-known Europeans also constructed, or had constructed for them by biographers and official historians, reputations as intrepid adventurers, bringing civilization to the savages of the tropical jungles. The Englishman, James Brooke, the first 'White Rajah of Sarawak', as he was popularly known, who carved out for himself his own personal domain on the north-west coasts of Borneo, became surrounded by a romantic and exotic mythology. Sylvia Brooke, the wife of the third Rajah, Sir Charles Vyner Brooke, also helped add to the aura of the Brooke name in her autobiography, suitably entitled *Queen of the Headhunters* (1972). The tone of her writing is clear. As she says at one point,

The Dyaks were at one time the fiercest of all the Bornean tribes; and it stands to the credit of the administration of three generations of Brookes that these turbulent people have now given up their ancient and violent customs. (p. 84)

Indeed, there was some truth in the stories of the adversities and excitement faced by Europeans in Borneo. Probably one of the most famous incidents was the murder of Charles Fox and Henry Steele, officers of the Sarawak Government, in 1859, at the hands of natives in Kanowit on the Rejang river (Tuton Kaboy 1965: 207ff.). In Dutch Borneo, the celebrated explorer, and representative of the East Indies Government, Georg Müller, was also killed by Dayaks in the upper Kapuas region in 1825 (Veth 1856, ii: 396), and James Erskine Murray, on an abortive expedition to open up the southern regions of Borneo to British commerce, was killed in February 1844 in an engagement with Malay and Bugis boats at the mouth of the Mahakam river (Saunders 1986: 109). Yet despite these real dangers, there was a strong element of imaginative creation of the savagery and brutality of Bornean peoples.

Invariably early European attention focused on such matters as coastal piracy, slave-raiding and tribal headhunting, and these elements were to be found both in scientific texts and in works of popular fiction. Probably one of the most widely known Victorian stories based on Borneo material is James

Plate 1   'Reuben Davidger and Tom Cox approach the Pirate Village'

Greenwood's *The Adventures of Reuben Davidger* (1869), which weaves a tale of excitement and derring-do around the themes of piracy, headhunting and life in the forests. The illustrations to the story are especially evocative, and those by H. S. Melville of the approach to the pirate village (p. 105) and the Dayak head dance (p. 117), capture the European-perceived violence, danger and primitiveness of Oriental societies (plates 1 and 2). It is therefore not surprising that Europeans often saw Borneo natives as living in a state of nature, closely in tune with their natural environment. In some cases, the European imagination merged humans and animals. It was probably the Englishman, Captain Daniel Beeckman, following his visit to southern Borneo, who was the first to portray the forest ape, the *orang utan* (*Pongo pygmaeus*) as a

Plate 2   'The Dyak Head Dance'

creature of fable (T. Harrisson 1955) (plate 3). Beeckman notes that

The Natives do really believe that these were formerly Men, but Metamorphosed into Beasts for their Blasphemy. (1718: 37)

From then the mythical 'Wild Men of Borneo' emerged. In the 1870s T. Skipwith published a short piece entitled 'Men with Tails' in a small book of Sarawak stories edited by W. M. Crocker (1875), and Captain Mayne Reid in his *The Castaways. A Story of Adventure in the Wilds of Borneo* (1892 [1870]) continues the theme of 'Man or Monster?': the *orang utan*, half-man, half-animal. The following gives one a flavour of the image Reid created for European audiences:

It was the *tout ensemble* of this strange creature in human shape – a man apparently covered all over with red hair, thick and shaggy, as

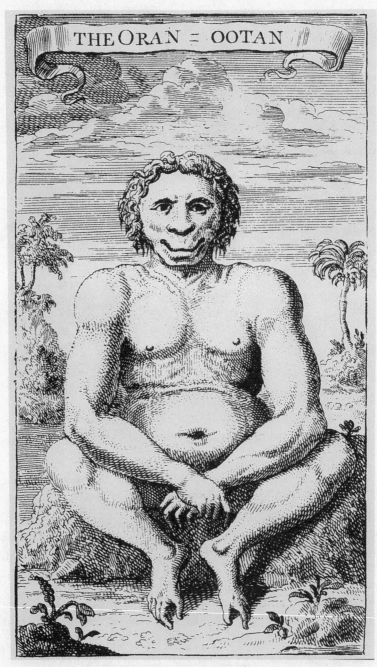

Plate 3 'The Oran-ootan'

upon the skin of a wolf or bear; bright red over the body and limbs, and blacker upon the face, where it was thinnest – a creature, in short, such as neither boy nor girl had ever seen, and such as was long believed to exist only in the imagination of the ancients, under the appellation of 'satyr'. (p. 173)

The search for these mythical human–animal creatures also occupied some European scientific observers. Carl Bock, the late-nineteenth-century Norwegian naturalist and explorer, was one who indulged in the sensational and exotic (1881: 143). During his travels in central Borneo he was to dwell on the story of men with tails: and, both explicitly and implicitly, contrasted Western civilization with Bornean savagery, rationalized and explained in terms of Victorian theories of evolution. Bock was clearly in search of the 'missing link': living creatures with combined human and animal characteristics. Furthermore, this preoccupation with primitive savagery also resulted in his conviction, based only on rumour, that not only were Borneo natives headhunters, but some were also cannibals. Bock refers to his meeting with the supposed 'cannibal chief' Sibau Mobang (plate 4), and, in terms which well illustrate Bock's perceptions and motivations, says

I was hardly prepared to see such an utter incarnation of all that is most repulsive and horrible in the human form. (p. 134)

Even such scholarly texts as Alfred Russel Wallace's *The Malay Archipelago* (1869) has as its frontispiece illustration an imaginative depiction of human and animal confrontation – typically again the *orang utan* ('the man of the forest') pitched against loinclothed Dayaks armed only with spears and axes (plate 5).

Some recent popular travel books continue to promote these sorts of images. Two of the most outstanding examples of sensationalism are Wyn Sargent's *My Life with the Headhunters* (1976) with, among other things, its description of native 'witch-doctors', and Jean-Yves Domalain's *Panjamon* (1974), preoccupied yet again with exotic customs: headhunting, tattooing and initiation. Even Andro Linklater, in what is otherwise an interesting, amusing and informed account of his experiences in Sarawak, entitles his book *Wild People* (1990). There is clearly irony here since Linklater explains that those

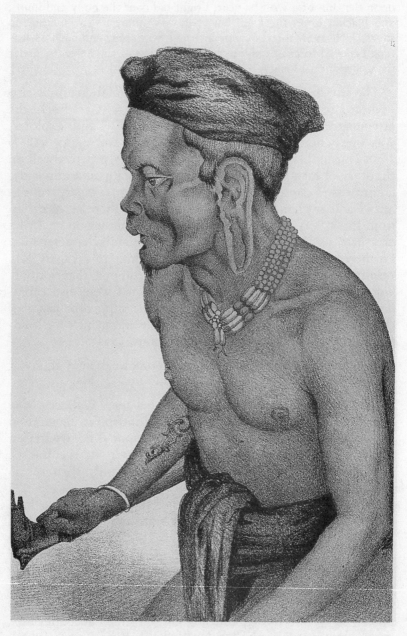

Plate 4 'Sibau Mobang, Chief of the Cannibals'

Plate 5 'Orang utan attacked by Dyaks'

natives whom he met hardly lived up to that reputation. But the immediate allusions to wildness associated with Western expectations about jungle peoples help sustain the deep-rooted images of the 'Wild Men of Borneo'.

Of course, alongside the more far-fetched accounts of tribal life, there were the sober texts of such scholar-explorers and scientists as Carl Lumholtz (1920), Charles Hose (1926) and Hendrik Tillema (1938/1989), who recorded as sympathetically and accurately as they could native cultures, lifestyles, world-views and temperaments. Nevertheless, they too were working in the context of Western imperialism and European percep-tions of their moral responsibility for native welfare and deve-lopment. It is not surprising therefore that some of the most committed of scientists wrote in a paternalistic way, and found it difficult to disguise their prejudices and their evolutionist assumptions. After all, for these observers too the natives of Borneo were objects of investigation, enquiry and speculation. They were appropriated as elements in theories of evolution, cultural diffusion or acculturation; they had to be sorted into categories and classified on the basis of cultural traits or language or presumed origins.

These images and descriptions which, in my view, tended to promote a general view of Borneo and its peoples as other-worldly, unknown, dangerous, close to nature and primitive, need to be placed in the context of the unequal relations between the West and the East. My historical examination of these relations in this book is designed to demonstrate these inequalities and their consequences, and the detailed consid-eration of Borneo ways of life and cultures in chapters 6 to 9 will provide some insights into the characteristics of traditional political institutions, including piracy, slavery and raiding, and into religious beliefs and practices which include the taking of heads and their ritual treatment. In addition, I shall consider the close relationships between human societies and cultures and the tropical rainforest environment. Popular European myths exaggerated this relationship into one which tended to merge man and nature. What I shall endeavour to do is to demonstrate the ways in which Bornean societies have adap-ted to and used what is after all a difficult environmental setting. This preoccupation with human–environment relations assumes an even greater importance when we examine the processes and effects of modernization in Borneo in chapter 10, especially commercial logging, forest clearance, land development and resettlement.

One of the major issues facing the modern world is the appropriate human use and maintenance of the environment, and nowhere is the crisis of the exploitation and destruction of natural resources so immediate as in the equatorial rainforests. Despite the popular myths of Borneo, another perception of the island has very recently begun to be cultivated among Western audiences, and that is of long-established ecosystems under threat. Only by considering rainforest-based economies and traditional modes of adaptation to the complex environments of this part of the world can we begin to appreciate just how daunting and uncertain are the future prospects for the indigenous populations of Borneo. I shall examine the range of human adaptations to the environment in chapters 3 and 6, and subsequently consider the ways in which these are being transformed by external pressures.

The name of Borneo

It was as a result of European contacts that the island received its popular name (Avé and King 1986: 20–1). The term 'Borneo' is a Western corruption of the local word 'Burni', which was used to refer to a powerful sixteenth-century Muslim trading state on the north-west Borneo coast; and because the state laid claim to extensive territories outside the port capital, then the name 'Burni' or 'Borneo' was also used to embrace the whole island (Low 1848: 2). It was therefore not surprising that the important trading empire of 'Burni', which began to be described by such European writers as Tomé Pires and Antonio Pigafetta in the first decades of the sixteenth century, and which indeed had far-flung territories around the coasts of Borneo, should provide the island with its now accepted name. In these early Western texts numerous variants of the name appear – Burni, Burney, Burny, Borny, Borney, Burneo, Bornei, Bruneo, Porne and Borneu. To the Chinese it was early on in the ninth century referred to as P'o-ni (or Foni, or P'o-li). The now accepted term for the Sultanate which traces its descent from the noble kingdom of Burni is 'Brunei'. Apparently this latter name was not popularized until the mid-nineteenth century, and it was probably given currency by the first Rajah of Sarawak, James Brooke. Prior to his use of the term to refer to the capital of the Sultanate and its outlying territories, it was called simply 'Borneo' or 'Borneo Proper' by Europeans.

However, it is as well to note that even before the European commercial contacts of the sixteenth century, the island was known by yet other names, and these can be confirmed because of references to the island as the source for the most excellent quality camphor (see chapter 4). It was known by medieval European cartographers as Java Major (or Java the Great). In early Arabic sources from the twelfth and thirteenth centuries it was called Muja, with its capital of Kamrun; and in the fourteenth century as Sribuza – the Arabic rendering of Srivijaya (Nicholl 1980).

There is yet another name which presently competes with that of 'Borneo' for general acceptance and that is 'Kalimantan'. The Indonesians use it specifically to refer to the southern two-thirds of the island, but it is also widely accepted in Indonesia as a general name for the whole island. The association of the term 'Borneo' both with the non-Indonesian Sultanate of Brunei and with Western corruptions of a local name must have played a part in its rejection by the strongly nationalistic Indonesians. But the word Kalimantan was also known by some European travellers in the early nineteenth century. Hunt's celebrated text *Sketch of Borneo or Pulo Kalamantan* appeared in 1812, and in the 1830s Domény de Rienzi referred to Borneo as Kalémantan (1836). Apparently the name 'Kalimantan' originates from the word 'Kalamantan', meaning 'the land of the *lamanta*' (raw sago). This referent certainly draws attention to a most important element of the tropical vegetation of Borneo, and we shall consider the economic importance of sago in chapters 3 and 6. But it is said that the Javanese transformed the name to 'Kalimanten', meaning for them 'river(s) of precious stones'. This was felt by the Javanese to be a fitting descriptive term to be applied to the many parts of the island which were known for their supplies of gold and

valuable gems such as diamonds. Indeed, the Javanese have
had long-established political and economic links with Borneo, which were at their most intense during the period of
the Javanese empire of Majapahit in the fourteenth and fifteenth centuries (see chapter 4).

Be that as it may, Indonesian sensibilities have not prevailed;
the generally accepted name for the island remains Borneo,
and it is the term which I shall continue to use in this book.

Borneo: a neglected island?

It might be expected that, at the present time, Borneo would
occupy a more important economic and political position in
South-East Asia than it does. It has a geographically central
location in the Indonesian-Malaysian archipelago, and is the
pivot of this long chain of islands which runs from the
Malayan Peninsula through to eastern Indonesia (Fisher
1967: 220–1). It is also rich in natural resources, and has a
long history of mercantile contacts with other regions. Yet the
main centres of population and political and economic control
lie elsewhere, in such places as Java to the south and Peninsular Malaysia to the west. With the exception of Brunei
Darussalam, Borneo is divided between the nation-states of
Malaysia and Indonesia, and constitutes the peripheral, less
developed frontierlands of these countries.

The main reasons for this marginal position are to be found
in environmental circumstances. The coastal regions of Borneo
are particularly uninviting. Large areas are covered by man-
grove, nipah and sago palm swamp forests; soils are commonly
of heavy peat. Certain swampy, waterlogged tracts stretch
inland for some distance. These areas are difficult to drain
and cultivate intensively, and travel is not easy except by boat.

Furthermore, until recently, when large-scale commercial
logging began, the interior of the island was covered by dense
equatorial rainforest, with a canopy some 30 to 50 metres in
height, mainly comprising mixed *dipterocarp* forest (Mac-
Kinnon 1975). As Bellwood has said, these forests are 'ever-
wet, hard to clear and burn with simple equipment' (1985: 12).

Apart from the more extensive low-lying areas of the west

and south of the island, and some relatively substantial river basins, the terrain is difficult, and, in many places hilly or mountainous, cut by fast-flowing rivers with rapids and water-falls in upstream regions (plate 6). The main chain of uplands is located roughly in the centre of the island, rising to over 4,000 metres in Mount Kinabalu in the north-east (plate 7) (map 3). Although rivers themselves can present obstacles to travel in the interior, given the rapid rise and fall in water-levels and large-scale flooding following sudden torrential tropical downpours, they have been the most obvious form of inland transport. The rivers radiate out from the central upland chain like the spokes of a wheel; the main ones are: in the west, the Kapuas, which is the longest river in Borneo at 1,010 kms; in the north-west, the Rejang; in the east, the Kayan and Mahakam rivers, the Mahakam being 715 kms in length; and in the south the Barito, some 650 kms long, the Kapuas and the Kahayan. Most villages are located along water-courses, and while communities are often linked by pathways and there are land-routes across watersheds, travel

Plate 6   Negotiating the rapids along the Kayan river, East Kalimantan

Plate 7 '*Kina Balu from the lower Tampasuk*'

by land has invariably been slow and difficult. In some parts of the island the lack of good stone for infill has made road-building extremely problematical, and in the wet season roads become quickly waterlogged and can be easily swept away.

Despite the luxuriance of the rainforest, the soils of Borneo are generally of very poor quality, comprising mainly yellow-red latosols, acidic, heavy clay forms which contrast markedly with the rich volcanic soils of Java and Bali where intensive agriculture can be supported. Early European visitors to the island assumed mistakenly that the rainforests were nourished by fertile soils (Fisher 1967: 50). Instead nutrients and minerals are mainly stored in the vegetation and not so much in the soil. High temperatures of 25°C to 35°C on average, very high annual rainfall, which is especially heavy during the monsoonal periods, of between 2,500 mm. and 5,000 mm., and high humidity mean that processes of decay and decomposition are very rapid, and animal and vegetable matter is quickly broken down on the forest floor and taken up by the vegetation. The forest acts as a protective covering for the thin soils and as a giant sponge absorbing the heavy rainfall and releasing it slowly back into the atmosphere. Once the trees are felled and cleared the delicate ecological balance begins to break down and rapid surface run-off and soil erosion may result, especially on steeply sloping terrain (Spencer 1966).

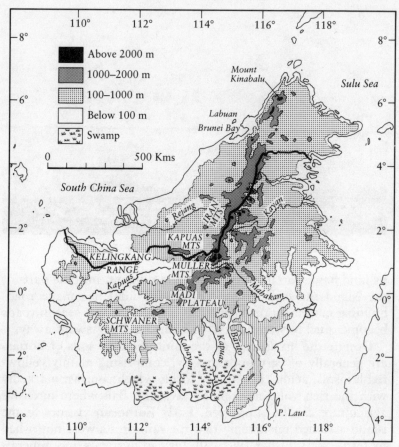

Map 3   Borneo: relief

It is difficult to establish intensive, continuous forms of cultivation in this environment, and the recent large-scale logging of the forest, road-building and the expansion or resettlement of communities have set in motion processes of environmental deterioration. There are limited areas of the island where irrigated agriculture is possible; it is undertaken in some river valleys, coastal regions and interior tablelands, but even here heavy rainfall and sudden flooding make cultivation precarious and require substantial investment in drainage works and flood control. Estate agriculture, based on oil palm, cocoa and rubber is also practised; it provides good ground cover and is now expanding rapidly with government encouragement. Tree crops such as rubber and cocoa are grown both on plantations and in smallholdings and are well-suited to indigenous farming systems. We shall consider the prospects and difficulties of large-scale commercial land development in chapter 10, but we should note here that it has not always proved to be the best solution to Borneo's development problems.

Of course, clearing the forest does not immediately or automatically result in environmental damage. Local farmers have developed systems of shifting or swidden cultivation – popularly referred to as 'slash-and-burn' agriculture – which permit the opening of the forest and its use for growing crops such as hill rice, without doing irreparable damage to the soils and to the prospects for vegetational regrowth. Although clearing the forest and burning it for agriculture obviously requires the disturbance of the forest, the important element in this system is the practice of the rotation of fields. After farming, the land is usually left fallow for several years so that the forest can regenerate and is then eventually available for future cycles of cultivation and fallowing on a long-term basis (Spencer 1966: 24ff.). Shifting cultivation as traditionally practised was also supplemented by such activities as hunting, forest gathering and fishing.

Aside from these farming communities, some small native groups rely almost exclusively on the resources of the rainforest, and do not grow crops. Living a relatively mobile existence, they exploit wild sago, hunt forest animals and birds, collect wild fruits, tubers, vegetables and other products and disturb the forest very little. In addition, there are coastal settlements, mainly those at the confluences of major rivers, which rely mainly on trade and the control of the movement of goods by water. Some also depend heavily on fishing and gathering in the coastal swamp forests. Certain peoples there specialize in the cultivation of coastal sago palms.

All these long-established economic forms have experienced rapid changes more recently, especially arising from government-directed development programmes, but also simply as part of the general processes of modernization. From production systems which did not usually lead to significant environmental degeneration, we are now witnessing the rapid spread of forms of exploitation of Borneo's natural resources which are unlikely to be sustainable in the longer term, given the delicate nature of the island's environment.

Apart from the limited concentrations of population along trade routes and at major strategic coastal and riverine locations, the generally extensive traditional forms of resource use, mainly to meet subsistence needs and well adapted to the difficult Bornean environment, have meant that overall population densities have been and are low. Communities are scattered, many of them in the remote interior. In comparison with the heavily populated rice-bowl areas of mainland South-East Asia, and the islands of Java and Luzon, Borneo's population is small. Thus, labour supplies for any sustained economic development, or, in the past, for the construction of palaces, monuments and public works in the court capitals of the trading states, were lacking. Even when Europeans established small concentrations of plantation agriculture in, for example, the eastern coastal regions of North Borneo from the late nineteenth century, labour had to be imported from such places as Java (Gudgeon 1981; Tregonning 1965: 85). The second Rajah of Sarawak, Sir Charles Brooke, also brought in farmers from south-eastern China to develop the lands of the lower Rejang river for rice farming and cash-crop agriculture (Crisswell 1978: 138).

These inadequate population and agricultural resources also help explain the relatively unstable nature of the traditional large-scale political organizations of Borneo, and perhaps it is worth dwelling a little on this matter here before taking it up in more detail in chapters 4 and 7. It was trade, tribute, tax and toll collection and not agriculture which provided the *raison d'être* for the emergence and expansion of state formations in Borneo (Warren 1981: xxii–xxvi). Such states as Brunei and Banjarmasin became important port centres; they established themselves in the trade in forest products from the interior and as nodal points in international networks of commerce, which linked Borneo to other regions of Asia and beyond. Nevertheless, Borneo still lay on the margins of the main India–China trade routes through the South China Sea and those to the spice islands of eastern Indonesia through the Java Sea and the Straits of Makassar.

These Borneo states were also dependent on attracting mobile sea-farers such as the Bugis of southern Sulawesi and the Bajau of the southern Philippines to anchor and do business in their markets. These traders by sea often shifted their activities and interests between ports, if commercial advantage dictated, and they did not form a permanent, stable urban population. What is more, the wealth and power of the coastal polities also relied on the maintenance of relations with agriculturalists and hunters-gatherers in the interior, who supplied luxury tropical forest goods sought-after in overseas markets, and basic foodstuffs and other materials for the port centres (Healey 1985: 16) (see chapter 4). As with the mobile sea people, the interior tribes could also transfer their allegiance between competing states and rulers when circumstances demanded.

The coastal states never established firm and extensive political control over many of the scattered populations of the inhospitable and relatively inaccessible hinterland, and given their lack of agricultural resources and the distance of Borneo from the main India–China trade routes through the Malacca Straits, the Borneo states never achieved the political and economic status of either the mainly agricultural-based empires of Java's Majapahit and Khmerian Angkor in Cambodia, or the great Muslim trading emporium of Malacca on the Malayan Peninsula (King 1990: 110ff.). Usually situations of uneasy alliance and tension existed between upriver tribes and downriver states; the coastal peoples were too weak politically and militarily to dominate the interior, and, as Rousseau says,

the interior groups, who had the manpower, had neither the political organization nor the desire to control the coastal areas. (1990: 299)

Given these circumstances, states such as Brunei had decentralized administrations. Warren uses the term 'segmentary' to characterize their structure. He says,

Pyramidal in form, a segmentary state is comprised of sub-units which are structurally and functionally equivalent at every level of the political system. (1981: xxii)

In other words, it consisted of a relatively loose network of river-mouth entrepots focused on certain prominent trading locations such as at Brunei Bay and the Sarawak river delta (see chapter 4). This gave some access to and control of trade goods, but rarely did political and administrative authority extend into the interior or into areas away from the main rivers. The representatives of the coastal rulers were granted rights to tax and tribute in the domains attached to their office, in return for their administrative services, allegiance and political support. If they were established local leaders in their own right, and not merely administrative appointees of a ruler, then they also commonly had their hereditary domains independent of the ruler. They were thus vassal states, similar in form to the dominant state, and linked to it by tributary relations, alliance and clientship. In this situation there was constant competition among local leaders and between them and the ruler to increase their own control over trade and, if possible, village communities, at the expense of others.

This competitive environment provided for the official sponsorship of piracy (Tarling 1963). Far from coastal piracy being an illegitimate form of activity, a symptom of Oriental decadence and the decay of political authority, as it was perceived by early European observers, it was used by competing rulers to establish, maintain or increase their respective control over the flow of trade goods (Healey 1985: 18ff.). In other words, it was an accepted element, given the decentralized nature of Bornean state formations, of political activity and institutionalization. Importantly, not only were the ships and cargoes of one's competitors a target of piratical raids, but also men, women and children, who were taken as slaves: these latter provided a vital source of labour in a labour-scarce economy, and they could be sold or exchanged for other goods. It was also the sea-faring Bugis and Bajau, and various sea peoples of the Sulu archipelago such as the Illanun and Balangingi, who were used in the pirate crews of the Malay rulers.

Aside from piracy and slaving, headhunting and inter-village feuds were a widespread expression of political relations between tribal communities in the interior. With its scattered populations, interior political units were usually small-scale and subject to alternative processes of fission and fragmentation on the one hand, and fusion and amalgamation on the other. These processes contributed to the complexity of the ethnic mosaic in Borneo. Until the establishment of British and Dutch territorial and administrative control from the second half of the nineteenth century, many communities were physically mobile and were commonly in persistent relations of hostility and feud with their neighbours. Sometimes raiding, as undertaken by the aggressive and migratory Iban peoples of western and north-western Borneo, took place over long distances, though it was usually conducted between communities in adjacent river basins, much more rarely among related populations along the same river.

Trade and tributary relations had existed between coastal states and hinterland populations from at least the middle of the first millennium AD, and it was not the case that headhunting always operated in a separate political sphere from piracy. Some of the headhunting tribal groups, and especially the Ibans, were recruited as mercenaries by Malay coastal raiders (Pringle 1970: 45ff.). This involvement in sea piracy earned the Ibans the early name 'Sea Dayaks', given to them by the Brooke regime in Sarawak. The Ibans were also an important element in the complex political relations which existed within and between the various constituent units of the eighteenth- and nineteenth-century Sultanate of Brunei. One means of state control was by playing off or forming alliances with one tribal group against another. Iban mercenaries were in pursuit of goods as well as heads, both of which were important in their own socio-political organization, partly based as it was on the competition for prestige (King 1976b).

It was not surprising then, given the environmental, demographic, economic and political conditions of Borneo, that Europeans did not establish a firm presence there until the nineteenth century. Nor did Borneo yield much in the way of valuable trade goods saleable in Chinese or European markets. Even when the Europeans did attempt to become involved in the affairs of the coastal states prior to the nineteenth century, they found it extremely difficult to sustain their foothold. Indeed, in their first real efforts to extend their administrative control of the island they resorted to the same kinds of political and military methods used by the native coastal rulers. They recruited tribal headhunters as mercenaries, and they played one local ruler off against another. The

Brookes in Sarawak continued to employ punitive expeditions, comprising 'friendly' and pacified natives, against recalcitrant upriver 'rebels' until the first decades of the twentieth century (Pringle 1970: 210ff.).

However, despite the relative neglect of the island by Europeans, and despite the fact that their main commercial and economic interests were focused in other parts of the South-East Asian island world, once European administrations were established, the transformations which took place, such as the elimination of headhunting and piracy, had far-reaching consequences for the social organizations of the inhabitants of the island.

I shall take these issues up again in detail in chapter 5, but I trust that the main themes are now clear. All the time we have to keep in mind the vital importance which the environmental context, especially the constraints of the rainforest and coastal swamplands, has played in the formation and development of Bornean peoples and cultures. For a long time much of Borneo remained at a distance from European interest and administration – a neglected and relatively unknown island. It entered European thought and writing as a hostile place: inhospitable, dangerous, barbarous and difficult to govern. Pirates, headhunters, primeval jungles were the main elements of European myths and legends. Let us now turn to consider the major categories of population which constitute the complex ethnic mix of Borneo, and from which these European images were created.

2

The People

Introduction

As one might expect, the fact that the native population of the island is small in numbers and generally dispersed has been a major reason for the rich ethnic diversity of the peoples there. Separate groups have progressively differentiated from each other over a long period of time. However, there are certain broad categories and associated ethnic nomenclatures which have been used to classify the peoples of Borneo. Those considered to be the native inhabitants of the island are usually referred to collectively as 'Dayaks'; alternative forms are 'Dyak', 'Daya' or 'Dya'. This rather imprecise term covers a diverse collection of tribal groupings such as the Ibans, Kayans, Bidayuhs, Kendayans, Malohs or Tamans, Lun Bawangs and others, with their own distinctive languages and cultures. But it is used specifically to designate the non-Muslim, non-Malay natives of the island. Generally the Dayaks live in the interior, though there are communities found close to the coasts, and, as a result of migration, some natives have more recently settled in the coastal towns.

There is some dispute about the derivation of the term 'Dayak'. Its use became especially common from the nineteenth century when it was increasingly employed by Europeans to refer to the pagan indigenes. Dutch and German scholars regularly used the term to cover all non-Malay natives (Hudson 1967b: 24–8; King 1978a: 1–3). But English writers tended to restrict it to the so-called Land Dayaks (or

Bidayuhs as they are now called) in the western areas of
Sarawak inland from Kuching, and the Sea Dayaks (Ibans).
The latter are found widely in Sarawak; at the time of the
establishment of Brooke rule they were expanding rapidly
eastwards and north-eastwards into Sarawak, and, in the
company of Malays, were engaged in coastal piracy from the
Skrang and Saribas areas in the lower Batang Lupar. The label
'Dayak' was certainly known by the Dutch as far back as the
mid-eighteenth century and was used even then as a general
referent for 'inland' or 'interior' people (Pringle 1970: xviii).

The term apparently had pejorative connotations, meaning
something akin to 'rustic', 'yokel' or 'bumpkin' (Mallinckrodt
1928: 9–10). At first sight this suggests that it was a referent
created for natives by outsiders. Certainly Europeans adopted
it for convenience, and Hans Schärer proposes that

[t]he name *Dayak*, probably derived from the Malay *aja*, means
'native' and is very likely a designation applied by immigrant Malays settled on the coast to the pagan population of Borneo. (1963: 1)

There is also some suggestion that it might be derived from the
Central Javanese language, referring to the act of behaving in
ways considered to be inappropriate or improper. Yet, there
are words in various Dayak languages too which could have
been the source of the term 'Dayak', and which mean quite
simply 'person' or 'interior/inland person'. Natives in north-
eastern Sarawak and western Sabah, who were commonly
designated 'Murut' by coastal peoples, call themselves '"Lun
Dayeh" with a historical connotation of "interior people like
us"' (Crain 1978: 124). The Land Dayaks of the Sadong area
of Sarawak refer to themselves as '*Bidayuh*' or 'people of the
interior' (Geddes 1954: 6), and, in certain Kenyah dialects the
word *daya* means 'upriver' (Whittier 1973: 12–13). It is possible that an indigenously derived term was adopted by coastal
'outsiders' and given a condescending connotation. Despite
this circumstance, more recently the non-Muslim natives of
Sarawak have also begun to use the term 'Dayak' in a political
sense to demarcate themselves generally and decisively from
Muslim communities, and it has been incorporated into the
name of an indigenous political party in Sarawak (Jayum
1990: 148). This practice occurred much earlier in Indonesia

where the Serikat Dajak, an association with political objectives, was established in 1919 (Avé and King 1986: 112).

There is a further difficulty with the label 'Dayak'. Commonly it is used to refer to all non-Muslim indigenes, including the forest nomads, although sometimes it is employed specifically for the settled agriculturalists, and the separate designation 'Punan' is used for hunters-gatherers (Hoffman 1983; Rousseau 1990: 20; Sellato, 1989b: 7, 15). This distinction is obviously based on economic and ecological criteria (that is, between farmers and nomadic hunters-gatherers), because culturally and historically the Punan are not distinct; they are Austronesian speakers like the agriculturalists and are of the same physical stock. In my discussion, I shall include the forest nomads in the general category Dayak. What is more, the term 'Punan' itself covers a quite culturally diverse range of peoples, and although it is the most common general name for them, there are other ethnic terms which are also used to designate hunters-gatherers (see below).

Both terms 'Dayak' and 'Punan' are contrasted categorically with 'Malay' (Avé et. al. 1983). One of the most important distinctions in Borneo is between those who are Muslims and those who are not. The main defining characteristic of Malayness is the Islamic religion, although Malays are also delimited by their language and certain customary practices. Nevertheless, the Malays too comprise a heterogeneous population. The majority originated from those of the autochthonous peoples of Borneo who converted to Islam. Gradually over time religious conversion would result in a reclassification of the Dayak converts as Malay; the local Malay term for this process is *masok Melayu* ('to become Malay' or 'to enter Malaydom') or sometimes *turun Melayu* ('to come down [and become] Malay') (Sellato 1989a: 20). Brunei Malays, for example, originated largely from the early pagan population inhabiting these north-west coastal regions; it was such communities as the Lun Bawangs and Dusuns (Bisayas) (see below) there who converted to Islam and became Brunei Malay. Even in interior West Borneo there are numerous examples of local Dayaks of Kendayan, Bidayuh and Maloh origin embracing the Muslim faith and eventually identifying themselves as Kapuas Malays. Rousseau also informs us that the Bulungan Malays of eastern

Borneo appear to be descended from Islamized Kayans (1990: 283). Although the term 'Malay' is used as the general referent, more specific identifications are designated by using a locational prefix, such as Banjar Malay, Brunei Malay or Sarawak Malay (plate 8).

The Malay population of Borneo has also been augmented by Muslim outsiders from Java, Sumatra, Sulawesi and the Malayan Peninsula, and it is likely that some Malay communities in Borneo did owe their establishment to limited early immigration of Muslim traders from the western parts of the archipelago. Malays live mainly by small-scale trade, sea and inland fishing, rice agriculture (usually swamp rice cultivation), coastal gathering and more recently, commercial agriculture. They live predominantly in coastal regions, along the main rivers, and in the main trading and market centres. Some residents of the old court capitals of the sultanates were also involved in a range of manufacturing activities, particularly in brass-, silver- and iron-working (King 1988a). Luxury products were designed for the palace, while everyday wares were usually traded upriver to Dayak communities, as well as serv-

Plate 8   Saribas Malays of Sarawak

ing the needs of ordinary citizens in the capital (see chapter 4).

Over time other Muslim peoples have also settled in Borneo. Some intermarried with Borneo Malays, but others came in larger numbers, sometimes with their women, and retained a separate identity. There are now significant numbers of Bugis from south Sulawesi, who have settled especially in the coastal districts of western, eastern and south-eastern Borneo. As a result of their military prowess they also controlled for a time or even founded certain coastal states such as Mempawah in West Kalimantan.

The Muslim Javanese are found all over Borneo. Their settlement certainly dates back to the fourteenth and fifteenth centuries, during the golden age of the East Javanese kingdom of Majapahit, which claimed sovereignty over parts of Borneo at that time. However, it is likely that Javanese traders had settled in small numbers in Borneo even before then. The Javanese population in Kalimantan specifically has increased dramatically during the last two decades as a result of government-sponsored large-scale resettlement (or transmigration) of communities from overcrowded Java to the less populated regions of Borneo (see chapter 10).

The Muslim Madurese from the island of Madura to the south are found in various parts of Kalimantan, often dwelling in towns and working as casual labourers and pedicab drivers (Avé et al. 1983: 7–8). They are also estate workers, fishermen and cattle traders. Then there are the Bajaus, the famous 'sea-gypsies' or 'nomads' from the southern Philippines, who have settled around the eastern and north-western coasts of Sabah. Though some are still fishermen, strand collectors and small-scale traders living mainly on boats and at anchorages, others have turned to land-based activities such as farming and cattle-raising (Nimmo 1972; Sather 1975). The numbers of Muslims in Sabah have also been augmented by other traders and sea people coming in from the Sulu islands of the southern Philippines and settling particularly along the east coasts.

It is extremely difficult, if not impossible, to give any precise indication of the size of population by ethnic group in Borneo since this information is often not provided by governments. However, very roughly I would suggest that all the Muslim groups of Borneo probably constitute some 60 to 65 per cent of the total population of the island, which would mean a figure of about 7.5 million people.

Aside from the Dayak and Malay populations, as well as the Muslims from neighbouring islands, there are also other immigrants from within the region, some long settled, others of more recent origin. Hindu Balinese have, like the Javanese, been resettled to sites in Kalimantan under the Indonesian government's 'transmigration' programme. Christian Indonesians from such eastern islands as Timor and Flores have migrated to Malaysian Borneo as estate and agricultural labourers.

Finally, there are communities in Borneo which are derived from migrations from much further afield, particularly India and China. There are small pockets of Indians, some of whom are descended from settlers who came to Borneo many centuries ago as cloth merchants and traders. In the former British-protected territories of northern Borneo more recent small-scale Indian immigration into such places as Brunei and Sarawak was the result of colonial connections (Deen 1989; Komarusamy 1989). Most Indian settlers were Muslims, and some did marry into local Muslim society. In addition to the Muslim Indians there are even smaller numbers of Middle Eastern Arabs who came to Borneo as traders and over time merged into Malay communities.

Last but not least, a very significant immigrant Asian population in Borneo is the Chinese, who are found especially in the trading and commercial sectors (Chew 1990; Chin 1981; Lee 1976). Many are urban-based (plate 9). Like the Indians, the ancestors of the Chinese in Borneo arrived to pursue their interests in trade (see chapter 7). Some communities are long-established, although the bulk of the settlement has occurred during the last 200 years or so. For example, Chinese settlers began to populate parts of western Borneo as gold-miners from the latter part of the eighteenth century (Jackson 1970). With the gradual exhaustion of the deposits over the next century, some miners moved into the goldfields of western Sarawak such as at Bau, others entered such occupations as market-gardening and coconut- and pepper-growing. Some Chinese colonists were specifically introduced into Borneo by Europeans to develop commercial agriculture or take up rice-

Plate 9   The Chinese Kampong in Kuching

farming. Today the Chinese are dominant in both Malaysian and Indonesian Borneo as well as in Brunei, in commerce, trade, the service sector and manufacturing. Although mainly an urban population, they are also found in rural areas as either merchants and shopkeepers, or as cash-crop farmers. Again it is difficult to estimate their population size, but in the former British territories of northern Borneo they probably now total about 700,000, and there is a substantial community in West Kalimantan of about 80,000, partly as a result of early Chinese goldmining there. Therefore, their numbers in Borneo as a whole must now be in the region of one million or more.

In this book, I shall not have much to say about these various immigrant groups. Instead I shall be concentrating on the Dayak populations of Borneo, including the Punan forest nomads, describing their history, cultures, economies and socio-political organizations, and the changes which have affected and are affecting them. However, as a result of the close relations between the tribal groups and the coastal peoples, especially the Muslim Malays, I shall also examine political relations, commercial links and cultural contacts between tribes and states, and, as a result of the process of Islamization of the native populations, devote some attention to the Muslim peoples, particularly in the context of the trading states of Borneo such as Brunei.

The Dayaks of Borneo are a very significant population numerically and probably now comprise over three million people. However, the broad cover term 'Dayak' disguises a great deal of cultural complexity, and it is necessary to document these internal variations before proceeding with our consideration of the Dayaks in more detail in subsequent chapters.

The main divisions of Dayak

The Dayaks are defined to some extent by what they are not. In other words, they are not Muslim Malays. Nevertheless, there are some similarities which unite at least some of the Dayak groups, although they do not mark out all Dayaks as a separate and positively defined category. Of course, all Dayaks are speakers of Austronesian languages and are of southern Mongoloid physical stock, but this does not serve to distinguish them from the coastal Muslim populations, who also share these characteristics. Some common themes, however, are relatively widely spread among the Dayaks and these are of some antiquity, certain of them going back to the culture of the early Austronesian settlers of the island. There are similarities in, for example, worldview, cosmology and symbolism, funeral practices and fertility cults such as headhunting (see chapter 8), in material culture (chapter 9) and in social organization (chapter 7). Many, but not all of the settled agriculturalists live in longhouses, large pile-houses on stilts accommodating many families (plate 10). Most Dayaks, but not all of them, are oriented to rivers and follow a riverine lifestyle. Again there are exceptions, but a dominant mode of subsistence is the shifting cultivation of hill rice, although this was probably a rather later development in Borneo following

Plate 10   An Iban longhouse in the Lemanak area of Sarawak

earlier horticultural and hunting-gathering modes of production (see below, and chapter 5). Finally, Dayaks, as the name
suggests, are people of the inland, interior or upstream areas of
Borneo, and their ways of life have been developed in close
association with the tropical rainforests.

What I am suggesting is that, despite the obvious variations
and divergences in culture, language, social forms, political
organizations and ecological adaptations among Borneo's
Dayaks, one should not lose sight of a number of elements
which cut across ethnic boundaries. These stem, in part, from
common cultural roots which we shall trace in the next
chapter. Over time there has been a process of cultural differentiation as communities have migrated and gradually populated much of this vast island. Groups have divided from each
other and been subject to internally generated adaptations and
change. These processes have been further complicated by
influences from outside – from other Indo-Malaysian regions,
India, China and Europe; there has also been cultural contact
and exchange between separate Dayak groups as well as the
assimilation or absorption of some by others, especially as

certain groups such as the Ibans began to migrate and expand across large areas of Borneo from the mid-second millennium AD.

Given that processes of both socio-cultural fission and fusion have taken place in Borneo, it would be a grave mistake to examine one Dayak group in isolation from others. What is more, we can only establish approximate ethnic categories and groupings in Borneo, because boundaries are invariably blurred, and social, political and economic relations do not correlate with particular ethnic identities (King 1982, 1989b). Just as it is misleading to consider Dayak groups as separate from each other, so it would be inadequate to examine coastal Muslim states and communities as distinct from interior tribal groups, and forest nomads in isolation from settled agriculturalists. These various populations have been interrelated and interconnected for a very long period of time. Although for ease of description and analysis I shall frequently use case-studies and examples from specific communities, and focus on a particular cultural trait or social form, one should always be aware of the larger complex context within which these units and elements are embedded.

This perspective on Borneo is not a new one. It can be seen in Edmund Leach's pioneering sociological and comparative work in Sarawak (1950). I have promoted this approach with regard to my own fieldwork in West Kalimantan (King 1985a); Bernard Sellato has recently undertaken a similar task with regard to nomadic groups (1989b), and perhaps most importantly of all Jérôme Rousseau has made sense of the ethnic complexities of central Borneo (1975, 1988, 1990) by examining the communities there as 'a number of related groups'. He explains:

It was very difficult to identify recognizable ethnic units, because groups with the same name might speak different languages, while groups with distinct ethnic names seemed to be identical. Central Borneo appeared as a checkerboard pattern of ethnic units distributed randomly through the vagaries of migration. It was not even possible to assume neat boundaries between hunters-gatherers and swiddeners, because they sometimes spoke the same languages and were in close contact with each other. (1990: 1)

Rousseau's remarks can be applied to Borneo as a whole. But to simplify this complex reality we can make some generalizations in order to sort Dayaks into broader categories (see map 4). Two categories based essentially on ecological criteria are hunters-gatherers and settled agriculturalists. Some of the settled agriculturalists can then be divided by sociological criteria into those which have stratified social orders comprising two or more named social classes or strata, and societies which are more egalitarian in organization, although they do acknowledge the importance of acquiring prestige or status. The settled agriculturalists can also be differentiated accord-

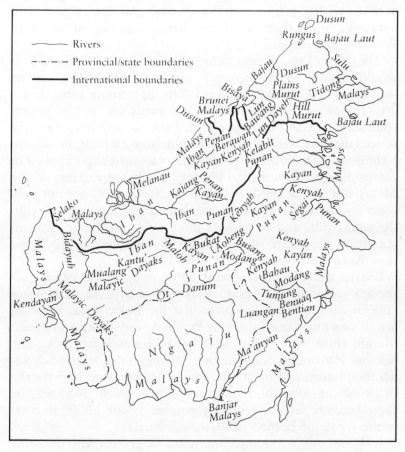

Map 4   The main ethnic groupings of Borneo

ing to language and various cultural traits into smaller sub-groupings. Let us begin with the forest nomads.

The nomads

Hunters-gatherers are found mainly in the distant interior regions of central Borneo, although some live near the coast in East Kalimantan. Although they are most commonly referred to as 'Punan', they are not a culturally or socially united population. Many of these groups are related linguistically and physically to the neighbouring settled agriculturalists such as the Kayans and Kenyahs, but some have affinities with various settled farmers of the Rejang and Baram rivers in Sarawak, and others with the Barito peoples of southern Borneo (see below).

The etymology of the term 'Punan' is uncertain, but it would appear to be a native word meaning 'to roam or wander in the forest' (Sellato 1989b: 25). Some other terms used by settled farmers to refer to nomads are 'Penan', which commonly covers those groups in Sarawak speaking Kenyah-related dialects; 'Basap' in East Kalimantan and 'Ot' in Central Kalimantan. However, there are also various names applied in central Borneo to nomadic groups, which are variants of the Malay term *bukit* (hill). In other words, nomads are not only conceived of as forest wanderers, but also as those people who live in the hills and uplands of the interior, in the headstream regions in the centre of the island. Common terms are 'Bukitan' (Ketan, Baketan), 'Bukat' and 'Ukit'.

Sellato differentiates several sub-groupings of Punan, although some of these may be closely related to each other (1989b: 25–6). These comprise first the Bukat-Ukit, Bukitan, Sru, Lisum and Lugat; then the Punan Aput-Busang and Punan Merah; thirdly the Basap and Punan Kelai-Segah; next, the Kereho, Hovongan, Seputan and Aoheng in the Müller-Schwaner mountains; and finally the Punan Murung and perhaps the Bukit of the Meratus mountains in the south. Nomads, or those recently settled, probably number about 12,000 in total in the whole of Borneo (Rousseau 1990: 21).

It should not be assumed that nomadic groups with the same name are related, or that those with different names are unrelated. Much depends on the nomenclature given them by the surrounding agriculturalists. Nor should it be assumed that nomads today merely represent an early evolutionary stage in the development of Bornean cultures and that those remaining constitute the remnants or survivals of this earlier mode of existence. I think we have to take Bellwood's proposition seriously when he casts doubt on the notion that Punan nomads represent an 'ancient stratum of Austronesian-speaking hunters and gatherers'. He suggests instead

a recent penetration of forested regions where a gathering lifestyle clearly became more economical for the very small groups involved. (1985: 134)

Hoffman (1983) too proposes an origin of forest nomads from already settled agriculturalists, to whom they are culturally related. But of course, it is difficult to test these suggestions positively because of the lack of archaeological evidence in the interior of the island. Certainly hunting and gathering comprised an early mode of subsistence in Borneo, but, as we shall see, present-day forest nomads are not direct descendants of these early hunting-gathering populations.

Central Borneo stratified agriculturalists

Most of these groups trace their origins from the mountainous Apau (Apo) Kayan or upper Kayan region of Central Borneo. In Sarawak they, along with the nomads, are now commonly called 'Orang ulu' (lit. 'the people of the upper reaches of rivers') (Rousseau 1988: 2). One of the most significant of these groups, demographically and politically, is the Kayans (Rousseau 1978, 1990) (plate 11). They number about 27,000 people. They are relatively homogeneous in language and culture and share a common origin, although they are now spread quite widely in the Kayan basin and near the Mahakam rivers in East Kalimantan, the Mendalam river in West Kalimantan, and in the Baram and Rejang basins of Sarawak. They are everywhere called 'Kayan', except in the Mahakam where some are known as 'Bahau' or 'Busang' (Rousseau 1990: 15ff.). Traditionally Kayan society comprised strata of aristocrats, from which village and regional chiefs were recruited,

Plate 11   Kayan family of the upper Rejang, Sarawak

commoners or ordinary villagers, and slaves. The Kayan live in massive, solidly built longhouses on stilts. The dominant political position of the Kayans in central Borneo is demonstrated by the fact that their language is used as a *lingua franca* there.

Next to the Kayans in importance are the Kenyahs (plate 12). They have close cultural and historical relations with the Kayans, and like them generally possess a similar social hierarchy, although they are, in the main, culturally and linguistically distinct. However, a few Kenyah groups may not be markedly stratified. The ancestors of the Kenyahs may well have been forest nomads who took up longhouse domicile and agriculture under the influence of the Kayans. Intermarriage between Kayans and Kenyahs has been quite common, and both sets of peoples have moved down some of the same routeways from the interior. The Kenyahs moved into territories in the upper Kayan basin, which had been previously occupied by Kayans, and from the nineteenth century they also migrated northwards into the Baluy and Baram areas of

Plate 12   Aristocratic Kenyah family of the upper Kayan, East
Kalimantan

Sarawak. Kenyahs are frequently found as close neighbours of the Kayans. However, while Kayans are culturally homogeneous, the Kenyahs are relatively diverse. There are over 40,000 Kenyahs comprising several differently named sub-units speaking different dialects (Whittier 1978). It is clear that a number of non-Kenyah groupings have over time been assimilated by or have identified with the Kenyah. Among the main sub-groupings are the Lepo' Time, Lepo' Tau, Badang and the Sebop.

There are other stratified ethnic groupings in central Borneo which are numerically much smaller in size than the Kayan and Kenyah. One such group has a common language and an origin from the Apau Kayan, but is known by different names in different regions. It is called variously 'Ga'ai' or 'Segai' in the lower Kayan, 'Segai' or 'Menggai' in the Berau, 'Modang' in the Telen and Klinjau and 'Long Glat' in the Mahakam (Guerreiro 1985) (plate 13). The Segai-Modangs, as Rousseau chooses to call them, number about 5,000, and, although originally a distinct group, their language is related to Kayan, and some communities have been subject to processes of Kayanization (Rousseau 1990: 16).

The Kajang peoples are another stratified minority in central Borneo, but they are found only in the Rejang and Baram areas of Sarawak. They are especially distinguished from the Kayans and Kenyahs by their language and distinctive funeral customs; they practise secondary treatment of the dead (see below p. 55 and chapters 3 and 8). In addition, the cultivation of the sago palm has played an important part in their economy until recently (Strickland 1986), while Kayans and Kenyahs are primarily rice farmers. The Kajangs are divided into named sub-groupings, in particular the Kejaman, Sekapan and La'anan, to which other smaller groups have attached themselves (Alexander 1989; Luhat 1989; Rousseau 1975). The Kajangs are also culturally and linguistically related to the Melanaus, who, it is claimed, moved to the coastal regions of Sarawak some time ago. The Melanaus are well known as sago-producers; originally pagans and longhouse dwellers, most of them have converted to Islam and now have much more in common with coastal Malays (Morris 1953, 1978). There are several other Kajang-type remnant populations in

Plate 13   A Saghai (Segai) Dayak, eastern Borneo

the lower Rejang basin, some of which have all but been assimilated by other groups; among these are the Kanowits and Tanjongs (plate 14). Another group historically related to the Kajangs are the Lepo' Pu'uns of the Baram river, but these people classify themselves as Kenyahs, who are dominant in that area. The Sepings of the Tinjar river are also culturally close to the Kajangs (Rousseau 1990: 17–18). These Kajang groups have been subject to pressures from the expansion of Kayans and Kenyahs into their homelands and have been culturally influenced by them. They also suffered from Iban aggression from the west. If one includes the Melanaus and other small associated groups, the Kajangs probably number about 100,000 people. Excluding the Melanaus their population size is probably about 5,000.

Another complex of peoples with a stratified social order, and which also practises secondary treatment of the dead, comprises various groups in the Baram area, including the Berawan and Long Tutoh, stretching southwards to the Punan Bah in the Rejang basin. The Punan Bahs are a culturally intermediate group between the Berawan and the Kajang. However, some of these Baram groups have a somewhat less rigid class structure than such peoples as the Kayan (Metcalf 1976). Metcalf proposes that these small scattered groups are 'a submerged complex' which constitutes the remnants of 'an ancient cultural substratum' (1975: 56–8). They have been reduced in number through subjugation and assimilation by

Plate 14   *Kanowits from the Rejang area, Sarawak*

more recent migrants such as the Kayans, Kenyahs and Ibans and through conversion to Islam in the coastal areas in the vicinity of Miri and western Brunei. With regard to funerary practices Metcalf draws parallels between these northern Borneo groups and the Ngaju peoples to the south in Kalimantan. Secondary treatment of the corpse is an ancient and widespread practice in Borneo, as we shall see in chapter 3.

Other minor central Borneo groupings include the Penihing of the upper Mahakam river, numbering about 3,000 people. This term, along with such variants as 'Peng', 'Ping' or 'Heng', is applied to these people by their neighbours. The Penihings call themselves 'Aoheng'. They comprise a heterogeneous category of former nomads, as well as agriculturalists. Some are related linguistically to the Barito populations of Central Kalimantan. Linguistically they also have affinities with the nomadic Kereho and Hovongan of the Kapuas area (Rousseau 1990: 18). Many of them, however, have been heavily influenced by the Kayans. Until recently a few lived as forest nomads in the upper Kapuas region.

Next come the Kelabits-Muruts, who are found in the Kelabit-Kerayan highlands, spread across interior East Kalimantan, certain western districts of Sabah in the Padas and Mengalong basins, and scattered through the easternmost regions of Sarawak (Crain 1978). They number about 40,000 people in total. These 'Murut', which is a term applied by lowland people to refer to the groups of the uplands, should not be confused with populations in north-eastern Borneo who are also referred to as 'Murut', but who are culturally and linguistically different. To differentiate them as a distinct linguistic group, Hudson refers to the Kelabits-Muruts as the 'Apo Duat' group (1977: 24ff.) The Kelabit-related Muruts refer to themselves as 'Lun Dayeh' (lit. 'people of the up-river') if they are interior upland communities, and it is a term commonly used in eastern Sabah and Kalimantan, while those in the coastal areas near Lawas in Sarawak prefer the term 'Lun Bawang' (lit. 'people of this place'); the latter is now a much more popular term in Sarawak (Jayl Langub 1987). Some of the communities, such as the Kelabit of the Bario plateau, are very different culturally from their Kayan, Kenyah and Kajang neighbours. Although they practise shifting cultivation, they are also well known for irrigated rice agriculture; they raise cattle as well, and they have a megalithic tradition which was flourishing until recently (T. Harrisson 1959c). The ritual and memorial use of stone monuments is also known elsewhere in Borneo, and especially among some of the groups in Sabah. It may well be a very long-established institution in Borneo, perhaps going back to early Austronesian times. But evidence suggests that it was not widely known in the recent historical period, and certainly not practised by some of the major Dayak groupings in Borneo. The Kelabit peoples are also much more oriented to the land than to the rivers, in contrast to most other Dayaks. But this must be a result of their adaptation to the high tablelands of interior Sarawak.

Finally, there is a population inhabiting the interior regions of the Kapuas basin of West Kalimantan which is very difficult to classify. They are called by the neighbouring Ibans 'Maloh' or 'Memaloh' (King 1985a), but they comprise three named sub-groupings – Embaloh, Taman and Kalis – and they have no commonly agreed internal name to refer to themselves as a whole. Linguists often refer to the overall language group as 'Tamanic' (e. g. Hudson 1977: 20). They number about 12,000 people. In terms of social organization they are similar to other central Borneo groups such as the Kayan. They are stratified; they live in large, impressive longhouses; and they are shifting cultivators. Certain elements of their material culture also indicate possible borrowings from Kayan. Some communities have also been influenced by the Ibans who have expanded into Maloh-Taman territory from the west. However, they are unique among Borneo Dayaks in that linguistically they have affinities with the languages of southern Sulawesi, especially Bugis (Adelaar 1990: 10ff.) (see chapter 3). They were also famed as itinerant silver-smiths and workers in brass and copper whose main markets were among the Ibans of Sarawak (see chapter 9).

Ibanic groups: an egalitarian society

One of the most important swidden-cultivating peoples of western and north-western Borneo are the Ibans or Sea

Dayaks who trace their descent from the Kapuas basin and the coastal regions of West Kalimantan. They had a reputation as inveterate headhunters and aggressive, migratory people, and it is clear that in their expansion across Borneo, and particularly into Sarawak, they submerged and assimilated other weaker groups including small bands of hunters-gatherers such as the Srus and Lugats (Freeman 1970; Pringle 1970) (plate 15). They are longhouse dwellers, culturally homogeneous and skilled weavers of tie-dyed textiles (see chapter 9). They build less substantial dwellings than many of the central Borneo groups. Now they are a major population in Sarawak, and they are also found in smaller numbers in Brunei, Sabah and West Kalimantan. They probably number between 500,000 and 550,000.

They are a markedly egalitarian people, highly competitive and prestige-conscious (Freeman 1981). They are also related culturally, linguistically and historically to a collection of separately named groups in the middle Kapuas basin of West Kalimantan, some of whom show more definitive signs of social ranking (King 1978b). The Kapuas Ibanic groups include the Kantu', Seberuang, Bugau, Mualang and Desa (Dove 1985a; Dunselman 1955), perhaps numbering another 100,000 people. Ibanic languages are relatively close to Malay, and are often designated by linguists as 'Malayic' (see below). These Ibanic people are quite different in culture, language and social order from the central Borneo stratified groups and they must have developed separately from them over a long period of time.

Bidayuh groups: an egalitarian society

Sometimes called Land Dayaks in Sarawak, the Bidayuhs are linguistically and culturally distinct from the Ibanic peoples (plate 16). Furthermore, the various constituent sub-groups exhibit quite marked linguistic and cultural diversity (Geddes 1954: 6). However, like the Iban they are generally egalitarian, they trace their origins from western Indonesian Borneo and they dwell in longhouses, although these are rather different in form from Iban houses. They are found in the Sambas, Sanggau, Sekadau, Tayan, Landak and Sekayam areas of West

Plate 15 'A Sea Dyak in extra fine War Costume'

Plate 16   Land Dayaks (Bidayuhs) from Sarawak

Kalimantan, and spread southwards to the Ketapang basin and
northwards to the Kuching and Samarahan divisions of Sarawak. They are culturally distinct with regard to the institution
of the headhouse; this is a circular building separate from the
longhouse where men meet, bachelors sleep, guests are accommodated, and traditionally where severed heads were hung.

In Sarawak the Bidayuhs number about 135,000, but the figures for Kalimantan are unavailable and may be up to about another 100,000 people.

Malayic Dayaks: an egalitarian society

There is a host of Dayak groups in western Borneo, generally socially egalitarian, speaking Malay-related languages. There are some linguistic and cultural distinctions between these groups and the Ibanic complex, but, in linguistic terms, they are all part of the same broad category of peoples. Hudson has coined the term 'Malayic Dayak' (1970) for those languages akin to Malay but spoken by non-Muslims. It is difficult to determine whether some of the peoples in this category have over time been influenced by Malays and their language, or whether their languages simply share common roots with Malay (Avé et al. 1983: 21ff.). I think some combination of the two explanations is likely in certain cases. But overall, as Adelaar argues, 'Malayic Dayak languages are indigenous', and it is probable that western Borneo is the homeland of Malayic languages (1990: 10). Malayic Dayaks are spread widely in western Borneo, southwards to Ketapang and Kotawaringin: some are close neighbours of the Bidayuhs and the Ibans, but in Kotawaringin and in the Melawi region of the Kapuas basin they shade into Barito communities. Indeed, some are markedly transitional or intermediate groupings. The Selako Dayaks, for example, who live in the Lundu region of western Sarawak and extend southwards into the Sambas areas of West Kalimantan are, on occasion, classified as Bidayuh (Sellato 1989a: 21). However, there are anthropologists who separate them from Bidayuh and group them with other Malayic Dayak languages such as Banana' (Schneider 1978: 59). Another well-known Malayic Dayak group comprises the Kendayan, inland of Pontianak (Dunselman 1949, 1950, 1952). Malayic Dayaks are also found in the regions upriver and downriver of the important market centre of Sintang, and there are groups in the Melawi basin such as the Kebahan, Lebang and Tebidah, which have been so classified, although the Kebahan are said to have traditionally practised secondary treatment of the dead, like various of the Barito peoples (Sellato 1987: 102ff.). They are therefore probably transitional between the upriver Barito groups and the Malayic Dayaks in the vicinity of Sintang. Malayic Dayaks must number several hundred thousands, and we shall consider them in more detail in chapter 4 when we examine the relations between Muslim state formations and Dayak communities in the Kapuas basin.

Barito groups

Another major category of peoples, linguistically distinct from the central Borneo Dayaks and the Bidayuhs and Malayic groups of western Borneo, covers much of the southern part of the island. Some years ago Hudson identified a set of interrelated languages there which he termed the 'Barito isolects' (1967a). He coined the neutral term 'isolect' so that he would not have to make difficult decisions about whether some of his linguistic categories were separate languages or merely dialects of the same language. The Barito groups, who mainly practise shifting cultivation, together probably number over 350,000 people.

By far the most well-known population within this category is the Ngaju, who were the subject of detailed ethnographic investigation by the missionary-anthropologist, Hans Schärer (1963). 'Ngaju' in the local language means 'upstream', and is used by the Ngajus to distinguish themselves from the 'Oloh Tumbang' ('the people from the river's mouth', such as the Malays), and from those of the deeper interior of Central Kalimantan, the 'Ot Danums' ('[people] of the headwaters') who are related to the Ngajus (Jay 1991; Miles 1970). On the Barito river the Ngajus are known as 'Biaju'. The Ngajus are the dominant Dayak population in the Indonesian province of Central Kalimantan, and they are found in the middle courses of a series of rivers which flow southwards into the Java Sea, from the Barito river in the east, through the Kapuas, Kahayan, Rungan, Katingan and the Mentaya or Sampit river in the west. As is usual in Borneo, they subdivide themselves according to the river along which they live. Thus, there are 'Olo (Oloh) Kahayan' (Kahayan people), 'Olo Katingan' (Katingan people) and so on. They are also generally called Olo Kahayan by their neighbours, since those Ngajus of the Kahayan river are considered to be the repositories of Ngaju culture, and their homeland to be the cultural heartland of the Ngajus. The Kahayan dialect of Ngaju is also a *lingua franca* used throughout Central Kalimantan and even parts of South and West Kalimantan (Avé 1972: 185). As far as we know the Ngajus never built longhouses, but instead multi-family great houses on stilts (*betang*) rather different from the longhouse dwellers to the north (Jay 1991: 50–6). Traditionally the Ngajus also had social ranks of aristocrats, commoners and slaves, although whether the system was as highly stratified as that of the Kayans is difficult to establish (Jay 1991; King 1980; Schärer 1963: 39–41).

Hudson has demonstrated linguistic affinities between the Ngajus and the Ot Danums further upstream, whose settlements stretch from the Murung area in the east to the Saruyan in the west, and over into the Melawi basin in West Kalimantan. In the upper Barito they are known as 'Siang'. They are longhouse dwellers and possibly influenced by the northern Dayak groups. The Ot Danums comprise various sub-groupings: the communities in the Melawi, for example, are mainly 'Dohoi'.

Other major Barito-speaking peoples are in the east the Ma'anyan (Maanyan) and Luangan (Lawangan) extending northwards to the Kayan-speaking areas of the Mahakam (Hudson 1967a, 1972; Weinstock 1983). These groups too had forms of social stratification in the past, but apparently not as marked as the central Borneo peoples, and more recently ranks have been significantly undermined. According to Weinstock (pp. 67ff.) the Luangan comprise a number of sub-groups, including various communities labelled 'Dusun', and the Benuaq, Bentian and Taboyan. A sub-group known as Tunjung in the Mahakam apparently had links with the Penihing, but has gradually been assimilated to Luangan. The Tunjung claim to be the founders of the early kingdom of Kutei (see chapter 4). There are also communities of coastal Muslims in south-eastern Borneo such as the Pasir Malays, who were originally Barito-speaking Dayaks, but have converted to Islam.

Another defining feature of Barito Dayaks is their religious beliefs and practices collectively known as Kaharingan. The religion has been officially recognized by the Indonesian government as a religion proper (*agama*) and not merely beliefs (*kepercayaan*) or customs (*adat*). In other words, it has the same official status as the great traditions of Islam, Christianity, Hinduism and Buddhism, although it is formally categorized as a sect of Hinduism. The Barito groups have a set of distinctive customary practices which are important in Kaharingan. The Ngajus, for example, are famous in the ethnographical literature for their elaborate funeral feasts (*tiwah*) and their impressive wooden religious sculptures (*hampatong*) (see chapters 8 and 9). Various of the peoples of southern Borneo perform secondary treatment of the dead: the corpse is temporarily laid to rest, and after a suitable period of time, but certainly not before the flesh has fully decomposed, the remains are ritually treated; sometimes they are cremated, or the bones cleaned and placed in a receptacle, a jar or a carved wooden ossuary. The Ma'anyan are well known for cremating the remains of the dead in the context of a great feast (*ijambe*) (Hudson 1966). The Luangan call their secondary mortuary rites *gombok* (Weinstock 1983: 54ff.).

The north-eastern groups

These are mainly located in Sabah, and adjacent border areas of East Kalimantan, and most have closer linguistic affinities with populations of the Philippines. They probably number about 400,000 altogether. Significant numbers are known under the cover term 'Dusun', although now those 'Dusun' in the Penampang and Papar areas close to the state capital, Kota Kinabalu, are officially and popularly called 'Kadazan'. 'Dusun' was apparently a Malay-derived term and was used by the coastal peoples to refer to farmers or 'orchard' people (Rutter 1929: 30). It clearly had pejorative connotations and carried the meaning of backward, coarse countryfolk. Originally longhouse dwellers, some 'Dusun' communities have abandoned this form of dwelling; in the western coastal and upland plains irrigated rice agriculture is practised and there is cattle-raising; in the hillier regions towards Mount Kinabalu shifting cultivation is common (Appell 1968a, 1968b). Those

groups originally classified as 'Dusun' comprise several named
sub-groups, including Kadazan, Rungus, Ranau and Tambu-
nan, with quite marked divergences in their social and cultural
characteristics (Appell 1978) (plate 17). Although generally
egalitarian, they place importance on social prestige. Among
the Kadazan of the coastal plains there was a tradition of
erecting stone uprights, perhaps as memorials or land boundary markers. Kadazan also had a set of customary practices
which are found among other Borneo peoples: jar burial,

Plate 17   A Dusun of Marudu

headhunting, headhouses and body tattoos. There are also Islamized 'Dusun' found especially along the east coasts of Sabah; these are usually referred to as 'Idahan' (Ida'an, Idaan), although in early literature the term 'Idahan' was often used synonomously with 'Dusun' (Lebar 1972: 148). Some linguists have also used the term 'Idahan' to refer to a broad linguistic category covering Dusun and Murut languages (see below) (Hudson 1977: 20–1).

Other related groups linguistically are the Bisaya, found further down the coast in Brunei and eastern Sarawak along the rivers which flow into Brunei Bay (Peranio 1972: 163). In Brunei, the Bisaya are commonly called by the dominant Brunei Malays 'Dusun'. The terms 'Orang Bukit' (lit. 'hill people') or 'Tutong' are alternatives.

There are other longhouse-dwelling peoples in western Sabah, distinguished from Dusun, but also speaking languages akin to those in the Philippines, who are commonly known as 'Murut'. These are not to be confused with the culturally distinct Sarawak 'Murut'. The Sabah Murut are found in the lowlands from Keningau through the uplands and southwards into East Kalimantan. The various lowland Muruts call themselves 'Timugon'. The upland peoples are often referred to as 'Tagal'. There are also groups in eastern Borneo from the Bulungan river northwards to Cowie Harbour, and concentrated in the Sembakung and Sebuku rivers who are called 'Tidong' (Tidung). Some of these have been identified as linguistically close to Sabah Murut, although the downriver Tidong have been generally Islamized (Sather 1972: 167). In East Kalimantan, there are longhouse dwelling people who speak Tidong-related languages and are called 'Bulusu'' (Appell 1986: 166ff.).

Unity and complexity

As we have seen, the peoples and cultures of Borneo do present considerable diversity and we have to recognize a long history of physical migrations, differentiation and ecological adaptation, as well as culture contact and the infusion of ideas and traits from outside to account for this cultural complexity. Yet the diversity is not as marked as one might first suppose. The large numbers of differently named ethnic groups can be reduced to a quite small number of broad ethnic categories. The origins of most of the indigenous peoples of Borneo, despite processes of differentiation, can reasonably reliably be traced back to common roots when Austronesian speakers began to settle Borneo from the Philippines some 4,500 years ago (Bellwood 1978: 88ff., 121ff.; 1985: 70–1, 76ff., 122ff.). It is the descendants of these settlers who will preoccupy me in subsequent chapters, and it is the archaeology and prehistory of Borneo which we now consider in order to examine some of the cultural foundations of the present-day inhabitants of the island.

3

Prehistory: Pre-Austronesians and Austronesians

Introduction

Although we have evidence of human habitation in Borneo going back at least 35,000 to 40,000 years, the Austronesian-speaking ancestors of today's native populations of the island only began to settle there quite recently, probably about 4,500 years ago. These later migrations link the natives of Borneo with those of the Philippines and of the rest of what is now called the Indo-Malaysian archipelago. Apart from Borneo, the main islands and regions in Indonesia and Malaysia inhabited by peoples of a common stock are the Malayan Peninsula, Sumatra, Java, Bali, Sulawesi and the islands of eastern Indonesia. The exceptions are the Austro-Asiatic-speaking Negritos of Malaya, and some eastern Indonesians who speak Papuan languages. Austronesian speakers are also found much further afield in Madagascar to the west, Micronesia, Melanesia and Polynesia to the east, and Vietnam and Cambodia to the north. The remnant indigenous populations of Taiwan are also of the Austronesian ethnolinguistic group (map 5). The South-East Asian Austronesians are of southern Mongoloid physical type, generally characterized by medium stature, yellowish-brown or brown skin, straight dark hair and wide, flat faces (Bellwood 1978: 30, 43).

It is now accepted by archaeologists, prehistorians and anthropologists that prior to the settlement of maritime

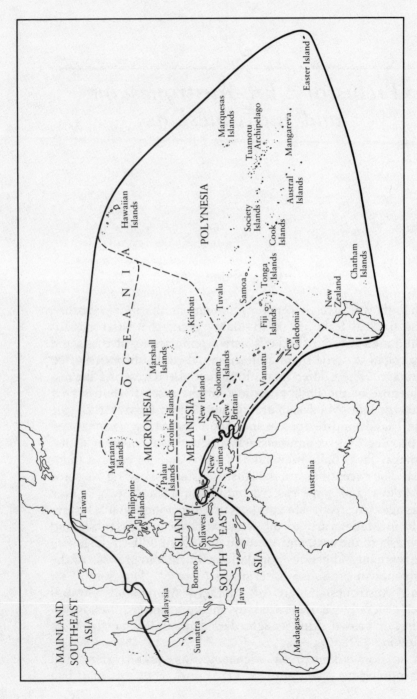

Map 5 *Limits of Austronesian language family*

MAINLAND
SOUTH-EAST
ASIA

Taiwan

Philippine
Islands

ISLAND

Sulawesi

Borneo

SOUTH-
EAST

Malaysia

Sumatra

Java

ASIA

Madagascar

Australia

Mariana
Islands

MICRONESIA

Palau
Islands

Caroline Islands

Marshall
Islands

MELANESIA

New Ireland

New Britain

New
Guinea

Solomon
Islands

Vanuatu

New
Caledonia

New
Zealand

O C E A N I A

Hawaiian
Islands

Kiribati

Tuvalu

Samoa

Fiji
Islands

Tonga
Islands

POLYNESIA

Marquesas
Islands

Tuamotu
Archipelago

Society
Islands

Cook
Islands

Austral
Islands

Mangareva

Easter Island

Chatham
Islands

South-East Asia by Austronesian-Mongoloid agriculturalists, the earlier inhabitants of the region were of Australoid or Australo-Melanesian stock; in other words, they were related to the ancestors of the present-day indigenous inhabitants of Australia and much of New Guinea, which was populated from South-East Asia by at least 40,000 years ago, as well as to the small remaining groups of Negritos in South-East Asia. The Australo-Melanesians are physically different from Mongoloid populations, being commonly of darker skin, larger-toothed, with tightly curled black hair (pp. 26ff.), and many in New Guinea and its vicinity are linguistically distinct as well.

As Bellwood and others have suggested, it is difficult to establish clear boundaries between these two broadly defined linguistic and physical types. In such places as eastern Indonesia one finds evidence of much intermixture, and even prior to Austronesian settlement the Australo-Melanesians were probably physically diversified and some were possibly evolving in physical terms in ways similar to the Mongoloids, so that there was a grading rather than a sharp disjuncture between the two racial types (Bellwood 1985: 95). Nevertheless, in Borneo there are now no obviously visible representatives of Australoid stock, and what has presumably happened is that the early inhabitants of the island were gradually displaced or assimilated or both, by Austronesian settlers moving in from the north (Bellwood 1991: 168). Thus, some gene stock probably does survive in present populations.

I shall be briefly examining the pre-Austronesian Australoid occupation of Borneo, but it must be said here that it has very little relevance for the understanding of more recent cultural developments on the island. What it does do is tell us something about early ecological adaptations to the Bornean environment, some of which have remained remarkably constant in Bornean economic and cultural life.

It is problematical at present to reconstruct the prehistoric development of human settlements and cultures in Borneo. The archaeological records are very patchy indeed, and, as Harrisson has remarked, 'Before 1945 no systematic excavation had been attempted anywhere in Borneo' (1984: 299). Even now Indonesian Borneo remains a *terra incognita* in

archaeological terms. Van Heekeren's two summary studies of
the 'stone age' and the 'bronze-iron age' in Indonesia, first
published in the late 1950s, serve to demonstrate how little
had been done in Kalimantan archaeology up till then (1957,
1958). In explanation van Heekeren says 'Borneo, so difficult
to travel, has attracted only a few explorers' (1957: 106).
Archaeological surveys undertaken in Kalimantan in the
1970s by the Indonesian Pusat Penelitian Purbakala dan Peninggalan Nasional within the Department of Education and
Culture continued to show how much needed to be done there
and how little had yet been achieved (e.g. 1976, 1977).

On the other hand, excavations have been undertaken in
Sarawak, Sabah and Brunei Darussalam, and much of our
knowledge of Bornean prehistory is heavily dependent on the
work organized and sponsored by the Sarawak, Sabah and
Brunei Museums. Even so, major post-war excavations have
been restricted to a few sites, mainly in easily identifiable
limestone cave formations. Because of the natural environment in Borneo with extensive swamplands and ever-wet
dense tropical vegetation, there are problems in finding suitable archaeological sites. What is more, some of the work that
has been accomplished has proved to be less than satisfactory
by the standards and requirements of modern archaeology.
Nevertheless, scientists have been able to piece together some
of the details of early human habitation in Borneo, and I have
relied especially on the work of Bellwood, Solheim and Zuraina Majid in this regard.

The pre-Austronesian period

Borneo is structurally part of what is known as Sundaland.
The Sunda continental shelf is largely submerged beneath the
South China and Java Seas and the Gulf of Siam; it is demarcated by the 100 fathom (183 m.) contour line beyond which
the gradient dips steeply away (map 6). Its highest areas are
exposed and comprise such major islands as Borneo, Java,
Sumatra and Palawan, as well as the long tongue of land
extending southwards from mainland South-East Asia. Its eastern edge is defined by Huxley's line, which is partly coincident

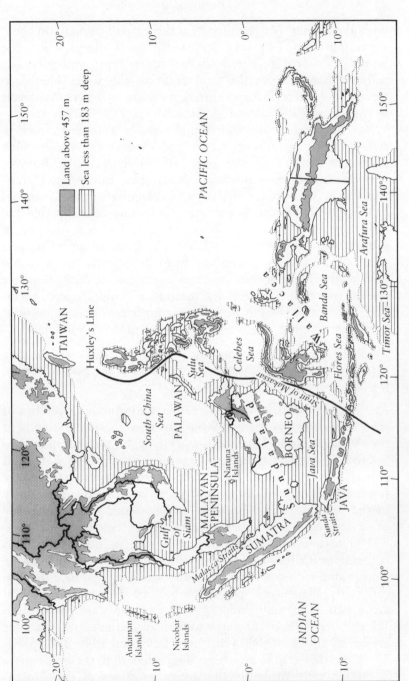

Map 6 Sundaland and the continental shelf

Land above 457 m

Sea less than 183 m deep

TAIWAN

Huxley's Line

South China
Sea

PALAWAN

Sulu
Sea

Celebes
Sea

Wallacea

Banda Sea

Timor Sea

Arafura Sea

PACIFIC OCEAN

MALAYAN
PENINSULA

Natuna
Islands

Gulf
of
Siam

Strait of Makassar

BORNEO

Sunda   Shelf

Java Sea

Flores Sea

SUMATRA

Malacca Straits

Sunda
Straits

JAVA

Andaman
Islands

Nicobar
Islands

INDIAN
OCEAN

with the earlier Wallace line. To the east of Sundaland then, separated from it by very deep seas, lies Wallacea where the fauna and flora are closer to Australian types and generally rather different from the land areas to the west. This deep water was never bridged during periods of lower sea-levels in the various Pleistocene glaciations.

Borneo's vegetation and faunal types are instead closer to Asian ones and are very rich and diverse in species. One dominant feature of the parts of Sundaland like Borneo, which straddles the equator, is the tropical rainforest. Harrisson (1984: 314) points to the great antiquity of the equatorial *dipterocarp* forests in Borneo, and Bellwood confirms that the rainforest 'has clearly maintained a stable composition in Borneo since the Miocene' (1985: 34), from about 20 million years ago. As one moves away from the equator there would have been different climatic and vegetational regions where one would expect longer dry seasons and more open vegetation, in contrast to the wet, dense rainforest of the equatorial belt. Furthermore, Bellwood notes that most of Sundaland

would have been exposed as dry land by low sea-levels for long periods during the Pleistocene, and especially at the peak of the last glaciation about 18,000 years ago. (p. 7)

At these times there would have been continuous stretches of land connecting Borneo to what are now the main islands of the Western Indo-Malaysian archipelago and to mainland South-East Asia. Changes in sea-level would also have had climatic effects; larger land masses would presumably have produced drier conditions, and parts of Borneo, particularly in the present coastal regions of the island, would probably have enjoyed a more open vegetation (see below).

The archaeological record for Borneo is quite late. This contrasts with fossil finds in neighbouring Java of a possibly stone-using *Homo erectus*, which made an appearance there in the Early Pleistocene period, sometime before one million years ago. The main *erectus* finds in Java date to between 1.1 and 0.5 million years ago and then, in the form of a later group, to about 100,000 years ago (Bellwood 1978: 38ff.; 1985: 29; 1991: 164–5). It has been suggested that these Javanese hominids were probably the direct ancestors of the Austra-

loids and Australo-Melanesians in South-East Asia, Australia
and Melanesia, although this is a subject of some dispute
(Bellwood 1985: 49ff., 318–19). Unfortunately there is a large
gap in the fossil record between the latest *Homo erectus* in
Java and the earliest finds of *Homo sapiens sapiens* post-
40,000 years BP (Before Present), which were made in Borneo
during excavations in the 1950s. What is certain is that for
Borneo we have evidence from the archaeological work at the
West Mouth of Niah great cave in northern Sarawak of a
sequence of pre-Austronesian, pre-Mongoloid human habitation dating from about 40,000 years ago (Zuraina Majid
1982: 1).

The Niah caves

The most well-known archaeological site in Borneo, and indeed one of the most significant in South-East Asia, is undoubtedly the West Mouth of the Niah great cave in the
Gunong Subis limestone massif some 16 kms. from the sea
(map 7). Excavations were conducted there by the Sarawak
Museum under the direction of its Curator, the late Tom
Harrisson. Preliminary work began in 1954, while the main
excavations commenced in earnest from 1957 (T. Harrisson,
1957, 1958b, 1959a, 1963). The sequence of habitation has
been said to span some 38,000 years, from 40,000 to 2,000
years ago, covering the most recent phases of the Late Pleistocene period, the Holocene (from about 10,000 BP) and into the
Neolithic.

Unfortunately certain of the substantial archaeological efforts of Harrisson and his colleagues are surrounded in con-
troversy, so much so that some of Harrisson's interpretations
and conclusions have been called into question (Bellwood
1985: 176; Solheim 1977a, 1977b, 1983). Solheim, in his evaluation of the excavation, says the following:

the many [carbon 14] dates reported by Harrisson in many different
articles present a reasonably reliable series and with them a reasonably reliable sequence. Other than for specifically dated burials,
however, no date can be reliably associated with a specific artifact
and conversely except for artifacts associated with burials, the recovered artifacts cannot be associated with specific dates. This makes

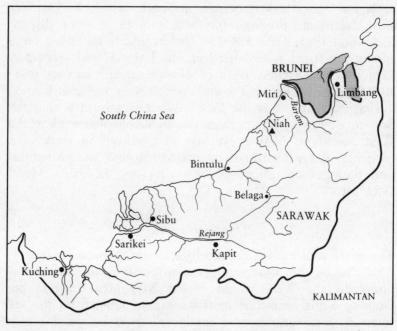

BRUNEI

Miri

Limbang

South China Sea

Niah ▲

Bintulu

Belaga

SARAWAK

Sibu

Rejang

Sarikei

Kapit

Kuching

KALIMANTAN

Map 7   Sarawak and Niah

it impossible to distinguish contemporaneous (within two to four generations even) artifacts or in any way to reconstruct the culture of the people living and/or using the cave at any one time. (1983: 43)

Nevertheless, a considerable amount of useful information was derived from the Museum investigations, particularly from the burials and animal remains, and we have been aided by the more recent salvage work of Zuraina Majid undertaken at Niah in 1977. She too remarks of Harrisson's excavations that

hard archaeological data derived from sound field techniques designed for the maximum recovery of artifacts and non-artifactual information were neglected. (1982: 35)

But she has attempted a re-evaluation of the cultural sequence at Niah.

The most important find at the West Mouth was a skull of a fully modern *Homo sapiens* dated originally at 40,000 BP, based on the depth at which it was found at the site, and on carbon-dates for materials above the skull of 41,500 ± 1,000

BP and 39,600 ± 1,000 BP (B. Harrisson 1967; T. Harrisson 1959b: 137; 1972: 396). Confirming the early occupation of Borneo by Australoid-related populations, the skull was identified as closest in form to Tasmanian physical types (Brothwell 1960: 339; Solheim 1983: 43). However, there is uncertainty over its date, and informed opinion now places it somewhat later than the first estimates given by Harrisson. Even Harrisson himself subsequently changed the date of the skull to 35,000 BP (Solheim 1977b). The problem is that one cannot be certain of the relations between the skull, the dated carbon samples and the depth at which it was found. Bellwood too suggests the possibility of a younger date for the skull 'on the grounds that . . . [it] . . . must have been buried from a higher level' (1985: 89). Perhaps some new dates will become available soon with the submission of a tooth from the Niah skull for dating to the Oxford Research Laboratory. One of the basic problems with Harrisson's work was his lack of attention to the stratigraphy of the site and proper sectional analysis. Instead he assumed a correlation between the age and the depth of materials (2″ per 1,000 years), and that this relationship was uniform across the site (Zuraina Majid 1982: 38).

Let us now turn to the cultural sequences at Niah prior to Austronesian settlement. All the evidence suggests that in Borneo and throughout the island region the pre-Austronesian economy was based on hunting and gathering. Small groups of hunters-gatherers established dwelling places in limestone caves such as at Niah, and, as Harrisson notes, given the difficulties of exploiting the rainforest with simple stone equipment, populations generally kept at or close to the coast and in the more open sites along the lower courses of rivers (1984: 315; see also Glover 1979: 172). However, some communities also penetrated to inland lake sites some distance from the sea (Bellwood 1985: 161; 1991: 166) and in some inland cave locations (Ipoi Datan and Bellwood 1991). But these areas may also have had more open vegetation at various times when the climate was somewhat drier than today; and there is no evidence as yet that human populations settled the more intractable forest regions of the remote interior. Bellwood too has stated that he is inclined to doubt that the densely forested interior was inhabited very much, if at all, prior to Austronesian settlement. (1985: 161)

Zuraina Majid has isolated five phases or sequences at Niah, four of which are pre-ceramic and pre-Austronesian, and the fifth an Austronesian ceramic stage. I have to say that I am not sure to what extent these sequences can be properly separated out, or whether her scheme has received general acceptance among archaeologists. Be that as it may, it does give us some idea of the economic and cultural changes experienced by the populations at Niah and I shall consider her first four phases in the discussion here. Zuraina's first phase extends roughly from 40,000 to 20,000 years BP. The Niah skull can be attributed to this early period. Clearly the cave dwellers hunted a range of animals. The remains of several species were discovered, most of which are still found in the region (Medway 1959). The only extinct species is the giant pangolin (*Manis palaeojavanica*), discovered in the lowest levels at Niah prior to about 30,000 years ago. Other early species present were wild cattle (*banteng; Bos javanicus*), which has now virtually disappeared from Borneo because of excessive hunting (Medway 1977: 150–1); the Malayan tapir (*Tapirus indicus*), which is thought to have been present in Borneo until about 8,000 years ago (p. 143); the bearded pig (*Sus barbatus*); various species of deer, including the large mouse-deer (*Tragulus napu*) and the samb-hur deer (*rusa; Cervus unicolor*); the white-toothed tree shrew (*Crocidura fuliginosa*) as well as species of monkey, porcupine, and the *orang utan*. Bellwood remarks that

What is clear, and of extreme importance, is that a modern fauna was fully established at Niah by 30,000 years ago. (1978: 59)

The inhabitants of the caves also ate freshwater shellfish (*Clea* sp. and *Neritina pulligera*). Animals, apart from serving as a source of food, were also presumably used for their skins, and for bone-implements (T. Harrisson 1984: 314; Zuraina Majid 1982: 134–5).

The lithic finds for this early period comprised pebble and flake artifacts, probably multifunctional, and produced by the simple technique of shattering or smashing quartzite pebbles and selecting appropriate pieces for use without further modification. Harrisson frequently remarks on the lack of supplies of good stone for working at Niah, and Zuraina suggests that sandstone was probably brought from the Tinjar river about 50 kms distant (1982: 75ff., 94). Even so the absence of good quality fine-grained sandstones in the region meant that a shattering method of making tools from coarse-grained pebbles, without the use of refining techniques, was the most convenient way of producing implements. Harrisson states that, given the limited supplies of stone, 'some tools have been used and reused over long periods of time' (1984: 313) and presumably equipment was also fashioned from wood, bamboo and other perishable materials, which have not survived.

In her study, Zuraina has distinguished between the pebble artifacts, used probably as choppers and axes for the heavy tasks of pounding and chopping, and flake items comprising pieces of stone taken from shattered pebbles, and employed in the lighter tasks of scraping and cutting. Clearly some implements served multiple purposes and are difficult to classify. Zuraina characterizes the Niah tradition as one of 'rather casual and simple artifact-making techniques' – 'a technology neither precise nor complex' (1982: 53, 54), but one which was 'efficient and adaptive in the environmental context' (p. 145). Bellwood concurs in his assessment of the general pebble and flake stone tradition of the Late Pleistocene and Early Holocene in Borneo and more widely in Indonesia. He notes that although

the tools appear to be simple, amorphous and undifferentiated to a modern observer with a fairly Eurocentric (or Afrocentric) bias . . . they do have durable and useable edges [and he sees no reason] why they should not have served their intended purposes with a quite acceptable level of efficiency. (1985: 68)

During this early phase the climate in and around Niah was probably on average some 5°C cooler than the present day, and rainfall was lower. These early inhabitants of Niah then exploited a nearly open forest environment, drier and cooler than today. They hunted larger forest mammals, such as cattle, which would have moved in herds for grazing. The riverine ecosystem also provided freshwater fish and shellfish in lowland swamp areas. Fruits such as *kepayang* (*Pangium edule*) and *kusap* (*Elaeocarpus*) were gathered, as well as *Cyrena* shellfish from estuarine areas, although given the lower sea-levels during this glacial period, Niah was some distance from the coast. The cooler climate at that time is also demonstrated by the remains of such animals as the lesser gymnure (*Hylomys suillus*), ferret-badger (*Melogale orientalis*) and smooth-tailed treeshrew (*Dendrogale melanura*), which are submontane creatures, still found in some of the upland areas of Borneo.

Zuraina's second phase of cultural development at Niah spans some 5,000 years from 20,000 to 15,000 years BP (1982: 136), but this would appear to shade into her third phase commencing some 15,000 years ago up to about 6,000 BC. The second phase is marked by the emergence of axe-adze pebble tools and techniques of secondary trimming, along with the continuation of the earlier method of shattering. Based on the Niah finds, Bellwood also points to the existence of edge-grinding of pebble axes between 20,000 to 10,000 years BP. He suggests that grinding was probably adopted because of the difficulty of finding good stone for flaking, but despite the problems of dating these finds, Bellwood does accept that the technique of edge-grinding occurs at Niah much earlier than the general establishment of polished Neolithic tools in the region after 3,000 BC (1985: 177ff.). For that reason he remarks, with regard to Niah, that it has 'a fairly innovative prehistory somewhat unique to itself' (p. 179).

From about 15,000 BP, Zuraina indicates an increase in the variety and quantity of animal remains at Niah and signs of more food being cooked. The most common are still pigs, monkeys and *orang utans*, but also bear, rhinoceros, deer, badger, otter, weasel and bearcat, and freshwater and estuarine shellfish. At this time sea-levels were still lower than they are today, with Niah some distance from the coast. Zuraina suggests that there may have been an increase in the intensity of hunting in lowland forests then, perhaps associated with an expansion in the size of communities (1982: 137).

The final pre-Austronesian phase is marked by a change in climate and a rise in sea-level approaching current levels, as a result of post-glacial warming. The climate then becomes slightly hotter and wetter, and the vegetation more lush and dense at Niah (p. 138; Bellwood 1985: 161). The Holocene period commences at this time, roughly 10,000 years BP. Indeed, the rise in sea-level would have begun about 15,000 years ago, reaching present levels by about 8,000 years BP. These changes resulted in the larger animals such as cattle disappearing from the Niah area in favour of smaller arboreal rainforest animals such as the mongoose, palm civet, otter and squirrel. These are generally more difficult to hunt and kill; there is still evidence of pigs, monkeys and *orang utans*, large quantities of freshwater shellfish, and, with the advance of the coastline, a greater amount of estuarine species. There is apparently little change in implement types, other than that earlier semi-lunar and pointed flakes have disappeared, and there are now more pebble axe-adzes, pounders, hammers and sharpeners.

Thus, in this later phase, Australo-Melanesian populations were beginning to exploit the same kind of rainforest environment as later Austronesian hunters-gatherers, in terms of the kinds of animals and water-life caught, gathered and eaten. Nevertheless, Austronesians brought with them several significant innovations, and we do see certain cultural and economic disjunctures between the early occupation of Niah and later Austronesian settlement.

Some of the most important finds at Niah comprised the large number of burial remains. It was Barbara Harrisson who was mainly responsible for the analysis of these (1967). They were dated from sometime after 20,000 years to about 2,000 years ago. One set consists of flexed, seated and 'mutilated' or fragmentary burials associated with stone, bone tools and ritual shell, but not with ceramics. One has been dated at about 13,600 BP, but they probably spanned the period from 15,000 BC to 4,000 BC. They have been identified as Australoid-Melanesoid on the basis of dentition (von Koenigswald 1958). The seated burials have been dated at between 12,000 BC and 6,000 BC, and the flexed types from 9,000 BC onwards (Bellwood 1985: 179). Zuraina has indicated that towards the end of this last pre-ceramic period, there was also a marked increase in haematite-producing stones 'suggesting their use in burial rites' (1982: 139; see also Solheim 1983: 44). Indeed, some of the burials were sprinkled with haematite powder or partially burnt prior to burial, although there are no full cremations, and most skeletons remain articulated. (Bellwood 1978: 60)

The second set of burials brings us into the culturally different Neolithic period and has been dated mainly between about 1,200 BC and 0, associated with pottery, and comprising extended burials, cremations and 'burnt burials'. But before examining this later period, we shall first spend a little more time considering two other important pre-Austronesian sites.

Gua Sireh

This limestone cave was first excavated by Harrisson and Solheim in 1959, and was recently examined in 1989 by Ipoi Datan and Bellwood with a Sarawak Museum team (Ipoi Datan and Bellwood 1991: 1). The site is some 55 kilometres south-east of Kuching in the Serian District. Initial investigations suggest that it was perhaps occupied from about 20,000 BP, and, if so, provides evidence of early human settlement at some distance from the coast. Ipoi and Bellwood suggest that at the last glacial maximum the coast would have been some 500 kilometres distant from Gua Sireh.

The diet of the inhabitants of the cave conforms very much to that of Niah. Ipoi and Bellwood state that 'Freshwater shellfish appeared to have formed a substantial part of the diet of the occupants of Gua Sireh' (p. 4). The species *Brotia* was dominant in the lower layers of the site. Aside from shellfish, animal remains were found including pigs, monkeys, barking deer, mousedeer and porcupines; and reptiles such as the soft-shell turtles, monitor lizards and snakes.

The importance of Gua Sireh is based principally on the recent finds of rice-husk temper in some of the pottery sherds in the upper levels of the site. I shall refer briefly to this matter below.

Madai-Baturong

Cave sites in the Madai and Baturong limestone massifs of eastern Sabah have been excavated and reported on by Bellwood (1988, 1990) under the auspices of the Sabah Museum (map 8; plate 18). It appears that the Baturong caves were once

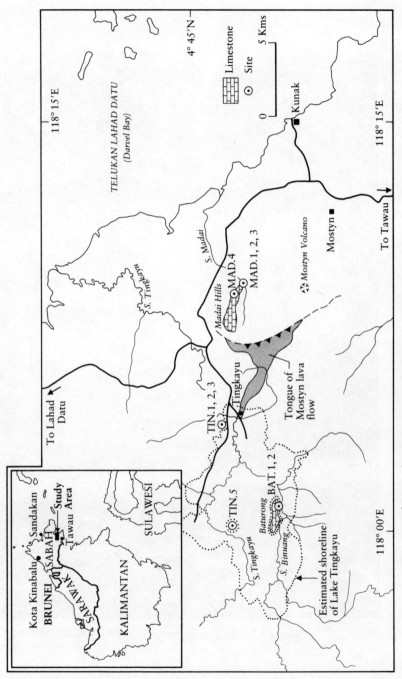

Map 8 The Madai (MAD.) and Baturong (BAT., TIN.) sites of eastern Sabah

Plate 18   The Madai caves, eastern Sabah

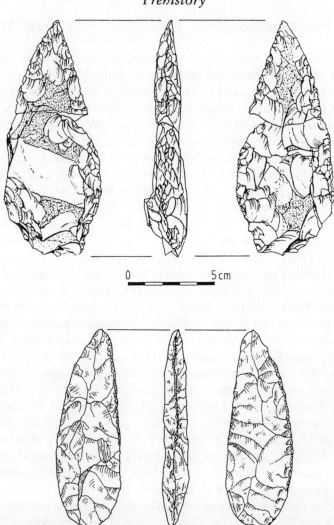

Figure 1   Tingkayu pointed bifaces, eastern Sabah

enclosed by a large inland lake some 100 km² in extent, formed
about 28,000 years ago, when the nearby Tingkayu river was
blocked by a lava flow. It drained away some 17,000 years ago.
There is also evidence of human settlement around the shores
of the lake at that time. As with Niah these sites would have
been some distance from the coast (probably about 100 to 150

kms) before the post-glacial phase began some 10,000 years
ago.

The Tingkayu stone industry, based on local tabular chert,
differs markedly from the more usual Indo-Malaysian pebble
and flake traditions, and Bellwood notes 'a unique level of skill
for its time period in South-East Asia' (1985: 182). Aside from
the usual examples of basic implements, there are large tabular
bifaces and more particularly bifacial lanceolate knives, an
example of which shows 'very fine surface flaking' (p. 182;
figure 1). Bellwood surmises that this was a locally developed
skill perhaps to serve a local lacustrine-derived need.

Evidence of human habitation in the Baturong massif itself,
especially in the shelter of Hagop Bilo, dates from about
15,000 BP to 10,000 BP, when the site was then abandoned.
As with Niah, there were remains of familiar Bornean mammals: bearded pig, monkey, porcupine, snake and lizard, with
the usual pebble-and-flake equipment, although with some
long blade-like knives. There was also evidence of riverine
gastropod remains in the middens, but not marine shellfish.

As sea-levels rose the distance from the coast decreased, but,
in any case, Bellwood indicates that the inland dwellers of
Hagop Bilo apparently moved eastwards to Madai around
9,000 BC, and Baturong was abandoned. Two of the Madai
caves, Agop Atas and Agop Sarapad, show signs of habitation
by hunters-gatherers in the Holocene period from 9,000 BC to
5,000 BC (T. and B. Harrisson 1969–70: 7, 157ff.; T. Harrisson
1984: 302). Again the stone industry based on local river
pebble chert is similar to Hagop Bilo, but without the blade-
like knives. Being closer to the coast, there is also an orientation to collecting estuarine shellfish, although riverine species,
as with the Baturong cave sites, continued to be exploited. The
same range of animals was hunted – pig, monkey, deer – along
with larger creatures, such as cattle and rhinoceros (Bellwood
1985: 186; T. and B. Harrisson 1969–70: 157ff.). Javan rhinoceros and Asian wild dog (*Cuon*), both found in Agop Sarapad, are now extinct in Borneo.

Apart from these archaeological finds the pre-Austronesians
have left virtually no legacy of their occupation. Clearly the
more accessible and open sites on the fringes of the equatorial
rainforest were exploited, and in the Holocene period cave-

dwellers were hunting arboreal animals, as later Austronesian forest nomads and to some extent settled agriculturalists were subsequently to do. The lessons of the pre-Austronesian period are clear. With such a range of fauna and flora to exploit, there was no need for specialization. As Bellwood says,

The indication is that these early hunters caught and ate everything that they could lay their hands on . . . Why should man specialise amidst such variety? (1978: 59)

Nevertheless, there is no evidence that they penetrated the deep rainforest, and it was left to the Austronesian-speaking Mongoloids to begin to open up the interior on an increasing scale – that mysterious, remote world which European travellers were later to create in their vivid images of exotic places.

The Austronesians

Peter Bellwood has been one of the most eloquent exponents of the view that the Indo-Malaysian region was settled by Austronesians from 3,000 BC onwards (1985: map 9). Elements of this view, although often with different emphases, have also been forwarded by Barth (1952), Coon (1962, 1966), Howells (1973) and Brace and Hinton (1981). The origins of the Austronesians lay somewhere in southern mainland China, but they were in Taiwan by about 4,000 BC, settled the Philippines from 3,000 BC, and had probably moved into northern Borneo by about 2,500 BC. The colonization of the Pacific Islands had begun by about 1,500 BC, and it is suggested that western Indonesia, including Java and Sumatra, were not settled by Austronesians until perhaps 1,000 BC or later. Based on linguistic, archaeological and anthropological evidence, Bellwood's scheme appears the most sound, and comprehensively makes sense of the data available. It certainly does so for what little material we have on Borneo. There are other theories, such as Dyen's (1965), which proposed western Melanesia as the homeland of the Proto-Austronesian language, but Dyen's linguistic analysis does not square with other data.

Nevertheless, it is worth emphasizing again, as Bellwood does, that the proposed Austronesian southward migration

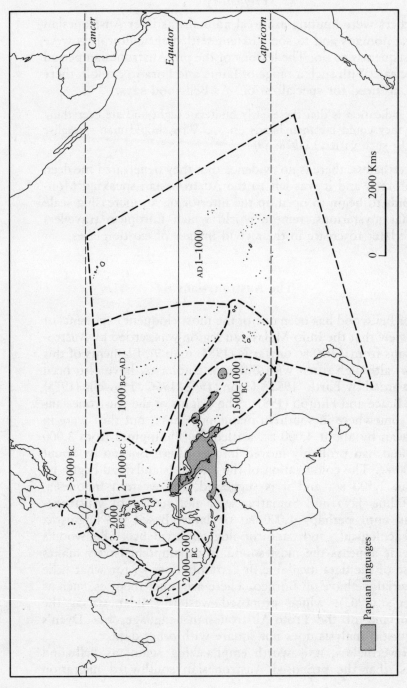

Map 9   The expansion of Austronesian settlement

Cancer

Equator

Capricorn

2000 Kms

0

AD 1–1000

1000 BC–AD 1

1500–1000 BC

>3000 BC

2–1000 BC

3–2000 BC

2000–500 BC

?

Papuan languages

does not entail the view that there was a simple displacement of one physical and linguistic type by another. Boundaries were not clear-cut; local transformations and differentiation without external inputs did occur; cultural contacts were variable with different results – there were complex processes of exchange, intermixture, assimilation and subjugation; physical movements were incremental, sporadic and irregular.

In the course of the expansion from Taiwan, languages began to differentiate. The languages of Borneo are generally classified as Western Malayo-Polynesian, originating from Proto-Malayo-Polynesian, which developed in the Philippines and divided from Formosan, both of which, in turn, had emerged from an original Proto-Austronesian language in Taiwan (Bellwood 1978: 117ff., 1985: 107ff.; Blust 1976, 1977, 1980, 1982, 1988; Nothofer 1991). Other Western Malayo-Polynesian languages in South-East Asia are to be found in central and southern Vietnam and Cambodia (Cham), Malaya, Sumatra, Java, Sulawesi, Bali, Lombok and western Sumbawa. Madagascan Austronesian languages are also part of this sub-group. In this scheme Borneo and Sulawesi were settled before Java, Sumatra, Bali, Malaya and southern Vietnam, and Austronesian peoples divided into western and eastern branches in the vicinity of Borneo and Sulawesi. The eastern movements gave rise to other linguistic sub-groupings of Central Malayo-Polynesian in the Moluccas and Lesser Sunda Islands, and Eastern Malayo-Polynesian in southern Halmahera and the Pacific Islands.

With specific reference to Borneo, it might be useful to quote Blust's formulation at length. This seems, to my mind, the most plausible proposal for the spread and differentiation of languages there. Blust says

By perhaps 2000 BC a language . . . called 'Proto-Northwest Borneo' apparently was spoken in coastal areas of western Sabah. Several centuries later this language split into two groups. One remained in northern Borneo, giving rise to the modern indigenous languages of Sabah, while speakers of the other migrated to the area about the mouth of the Baram River, eventually giving rise to the modern Bintulu, Lower Baram, Kenyah, and Kelabit languages, perhaps among others.

At a considerably later date – probably in the third or fourth century BC – an extensive population movement from Southwest Borneo led to the settlement of eastern Sumatra, the Malay Peninsula, and large parts of the coast of Mainland Southeast Asia. . . . (1988: 56)

As Blust indicates, this latter complex ultimately gave rise to a northern linguistic grouping, which includes Cham and Acehnese, and a southern 'Malayic' grouping, comprising Malay and the 'Malayic Dayak' languages of Borneo. These Malayo-Chamic languages are, in turn, related to the Java-Bali-Sasak group, and then with the Barito language family in south and central Borneo, and with Malagasy.

Blust therefore proposes

. . . an earlier protolanguage spoken in Southeast Kalimantan perhaps in the period 1000-1500 BC, which first split into the ancestor of the Barito group and a language ancestral to Malayo-Chamic and Java-Bali-Sasak. (p. 57)

It is certainly clear from linguistic evidence and also from cultural artifacts that the peoples of north-eastern Borneo such as the Kadazan do have relatively close affinities with the populations of the Philippines. On the other hand, the languages of the western parts of the island, including Ibanic and other Malayic Dayak groups, are close to the Malay-type languages of Malaya and Sumatra and of the Chams of Indochina. We must also note that such groups as the Ibans claim ancestral links with Sumatra, and many of the accessible Dayak communities in Borneo, especially in the coastal districts and the western regions, have been strongly influenced during the past 600 to 700 years by Malay culture. As a consequence of the expansion of the Malay language in trade and the conversion to Islam, many Dayaks have 'become Malay'. Therefore, earlier movements of peoples and traits westwards and southwards from Borneo have been subsequently overlaid by counter-movements, or at least the passage of traits and ideas eastwards and northwards from Malaya, Sumatra and Java. This later west–east contact has been clearly a product of the increasing influence of Malay trading states along the coasts of Borneo, an influence which may well have already been under way during the period of the Sumatran empire of Srivijaya from the seventh century AD. Links with Java were also certainly significant during the period of Majapahit from the fourteenth century. Furthermore, Hudson has noted that Banjar Malay in south Borneo has elements borrowed from Javanese, probably dating from the seventeenth century when traders from Java fled from the depredations of the Javanese Muslim kingdom of Mataram (1967b: 52–3, 65–6) (see chapter 4).

Other interesting external relations between Borneo and places beyond concern Madagascar and Sulawesi. Madagascan languages are most closely related to the south-east Barito language family, including Ma'anyan (Dyen 1971). It has been suggested that Austronesians from southern Borneo may well have settled in east Africa relatively recently, from the mid- or late-first millennium AD (see Bellwood 1978: 124) and may have been members of boat-crews organized under Malay or Javanese control (Adelaar 1990: 7). But Glover draws attention to regular trading contacts across the Indian Ocean even during the first millennium BC (1979: 179, 184).

On the other hand, the central Borneo language of Maloh (Embaloh/Taman) Dayak has very close affinities with southern Sulawesi languages, especially Bugis (Hudson 1977; King 1988a). It is difficult to account for this linguistic affiliation. The Malohs are a small population located in the distant interior of the island and surrounded on all sides by different Dayak groups, speaking rather different languages. It was originally suggested by Hudson that Maloh should be classified as 'Malayic Dayak' (1970). He then altered his view and maintained that Maloh is 'unique on the Bornean scene', and the 'closest match' is Bugis (1977: 20). I have argued elsewhere (King 1985a) that many Malay elements in Maloh are the result of contacts with Malay speakers and speakers of Malay-related languages such as Iban during the last 200 years or so (cf. Nothofer 1991: 394). But it appears that the earlier Maloh language is an outlier of south Sulawesi languages, and presumably, given the close relationship, cultural and perhaps physical contacts between the Bugis region and central Borneo have taken place during the last 1,000 to 1,500 years, possibly as recently as 400 to 500 years ago (King 1988a: 29–56; cf. Adelaar 1990: 12).

These few examples illustrate the complexity of the cultural history of Borneo. But as a result of the very substantial gaps in our knowledge of Austronesian societies prior to European contact from the sixteenth century, we shall have to content ourselves in the remainder of this chapter with sketching the broad outlines of these societies before Indian and Chinese mercantile relations became significant from the first millennium AD. Then in chapter 4 we shall examine some of the consequences of the spread of religions and traits from India and China.

Austronesian culture

What were the main cultural elements which the Austronesians carried with them southwards into Borneo from the Philippines, bearing in mind that there was subsequent innovation and adaptation as Austronesians settled in the islands? Some groups have obviously lost certain early cultural items over time; others have acquired new traits from Indian-derived Hindu-Buddhist polities, Chinese commercial contacts and Muslim trading states.

The reconstruction of early cultural forms has been undertaken by such scholars as Blust (1976, 1980) on the basis of linguistic evidence, as well as by archaeologists and comparative ethnologists. Bellwood has brought much of this material together (1985: 143–58), although it is well to remember that the Austrian ethnologist, Robert von Heine Geldern had set down the main features of early Austronesian culture in seminal publications produced over 50 years ago (1932, 1937). Similarly, van Heekeren, in his surveys of the 1950s, points to an Indonesian Neolithic culture with quadrangular adzes, pottery, agriculture, bark-cloth, headhunting, and domesticated dogs and pigs (1957). Many of these traits show a remarkable persistence among the tribal peoples of maritime South-East Asia, including the Dayaks, the Bataks of Sumatra, and the Kalingas and Ifugaos of the northern Philippines. Some have survived even to the present time or at least to the recent historical past when European intervention led to the demise of such institutions as headhunting.

As Bellwood notes, Austronesian dwellings 'are almost universally rectangular, with the great longhouses of Borneo at the upper end of the size range . . .' (1985: 150–1). Borneo peoples either live in large multi-family longhouses or, as in

southern Borneo, 'great houses' (Avé and King 1986: 52ff.).
Waterson (1990), following Blust, also suggests that early
Austronesian houses were pile-dwellings, raised off the ground
on stilts and reached by notched ladders; they had ridge-poles
and gabled roofs; cooking hearths were located inside the
house (plate 19). Certainly in the Bornean context, aside from
the social and community reasons for living in close proximity
to kin and neighbours, considerations of defence and security
also played a part. Even in nineteenth-century Borneo, when
raiding and feuding were still rife, many longhouses were
heavily fortified structures, high off the ground, surrounded
by palisades, ditches and man-traps, with ladders which could
be raised and stored in the house at night and hinged trap-
doors which were closed over the main entrances to the gallery
(Enthoven 1903: 58–9) (plate 20). Aside from the main dwellings, many Austronesian groups also constructed special structures for ritual purposes, for example as foci for male cult
activities, and for the storage of severed heads or sacred ritual
paraphernalia, which ensured the well-being and prosperity of
the community. These are not so common in Borneo today,

Plate 19   *A cooking-hearth in a Kenyah longhouse compartment*

Plate 20   Kanowit longhouses in the Rejang

but headhouses are still found among the Bidayuhs.

Austronesians were also pottery makers, a skill which, from the archaeological record, was not present in Borneo prior to the third millennium BC. Up until recently in Borneo many communities made basic pots and other containers for everyday use (plate 21). Then increasingly during the European period the availability of imported metal containers and finally plastic goods led to the rapid decline in pot-making. Special jars and urns were also traditionally manufactured for use in rituals, especially for funeral ceremonies, but these too began to be replaced in the second millennium AD when decorative jars were increasingly imported from China and mainland South-East Asia; many such imported jars are still found in Borneo, kept as precious heirlooms and for storage and brewing rice wine (B. Harrisson 1986) (see chapter 4).

Early Austronesian communities made clothing of barkcloth. This was beaten out from the inner bark of certain trees such as the Chinese paper-mulberry (*Broussonetia papyrifera*), which was probably the main bark-cloth supply for these early populations (plate 22). Again up until recently bark-costume was still quite widely used in Borneo. Sometimes jackets, skirts and loincloths were left plain, though perhaps with coloured cloth sewn on in decorative patterns and borders, or with ornate embroidery. Plain bark-cloth was also frequently used

Plate 21   Kenyah pottery manufacture

Plate 22   Beating bark to make cloth

as mourning costume by widows and widowers. Again with the availability of cheap imported textiles, especially from the nineteenth century, bark-cloth has fallen into disuse.

Aside from bark-cloth manufacture, textile weaving, using a backstrap loom, has been widespread in Borneo. However, Bellwood suggests this as an early Western Malayo-Polynesian innovation rather than as Proto-Austronesian (1985: 114). Again, more recently weaving has declined in importance in Borneo because of competition from imported items. The Kenyahs and Malohs, for example, did weave plain cotton garments, dyed in black or blue; they no longer do so (plate 23). It is really only the Ibanic groups, famous for their intricately woven and patterned *ikat* or tie-dyed blankets, skirts, jackets and loincloths, which continue to weave. Early Austronesians also practised the plaiting and weaving of mats and baskets from such natural forest fibres as rattan and pandanus.

A very common and early form of Austronesian bodily decoration for both males and females was tattooing. The motifs and patterns and their positioning on the body are very varied indeed, but many of the tribal groups in Borneo practise it, including the Iban, Kayan, Kenyah, Ngaju and Ot Danum. It usually denotes social rank, prestige or success in particularly valued activities (plate 24). In many cases male tattooing was closely associated with achievements in headhunting, and this practice, in the context of a male-oriented fertility cult, was again very common in South-East Asia. The Ibans were especially renowned head-takers and heavily tattooed. It has been suggested that headhunting may have been undertaken in the region as early as 2,000 BC (Blust 1976) (plate 25).

Another practice, which is clearly of some antiquity in Borneo, and has been claimed as an early Austronesian cultural form, is secondary treatment of the dead. It has been commonly associated with jar burials, although there were a number of ways of storing the remains (see below). Secondary funeral rituals are found among some of the north-eastern Dayaks such as the Kadazan, the minority populations of northern Sarawak like the Berawan, and the Barito groups, including the Ngaju. Beliefs concerning the Afterlife or Other-world are particularly important in these rituals and focus on such features as a spirit or soul journey after death, and on

Plate 23   Kenyah loom

Plate 24   Kenyah arm tattoos

Plate 25 '*Iban women dancing with human heads*'

ancestor spirits to which ritual activity is directed; these are designed to maintain appropriate relations between the human and the spirit worlds to ensure protection and well-being. Beliefs in ancestor spirits are quite common in Austronesian cultures, and along with headhunting cults, are part of a wider complex of beliefs in a supernatural world inhabited by a host

of spirits and deities with which humans have to engage and
come to terms. Again a very widespread religious orientation,
and one which is likely to be an ancient one in Austronesian
cultures, is a dual conception of the cosmos: there is a division
between an Upperworld and an Underworld, and between the
cult of heads and the male sphere on the one hand, and
agricultural fertility cults and the domain of females on the
other hand. This supernatural realm is also mediated by religious specialists such as shamans, who can control spirits,
mediums whose responsibility it is to deal with spiritually
induced illness, and augurs who interpret omens given by the
gods and spirits. Humans attempt to harness spiritual power
for their own purposes through various agencies, activities and
observations and by the use of charms, amulets and taboos
(see chapter 8).

Bellwood proposes that with regard to early Austronesian
weaponry, 'Bows and arrows and spears are of at least Proto-
Austronesian antiquity, but the blowpipe is probably more
recent' (1985: 152). In Borneo the spear has been very widely
used in hunting and in warfare. Usually Dayaks hunt with
spear and dog, and from the archaeological record, it appears
that dogs were completely absent from Borneo until after 2,500
BC. The bow and arrow does not seem to have been particularly important in Borneo in contemporary times, but it was
known to be used for catching fish as in most equatorial-
tropical communities (Avé and King 1986: 49, 127). It may
have been more popular in the distant past. On the other
hand, the blowpipe is very commonly used in Borneo, usually
with an attached spearpoint, and especially employed by the
forest nomads for hunting tree-dwelling animals and birds. It
seems to be an adaptation to tropical wet forest life, appearing
not only in South-East Asia but also independently in Africa
and the Americas.

In addition to hunting and fishing, early Austronesians had
domesticated pigs and fowl. They were also clearly knowled-
geable in the trapping of animals, fish and birds. They used a
variety of equipment for fishing, including basket-traps, nets,
drives, hook-and-line, and poisoned roots or *tuba* (*Derris*
spp.). It is clear too from the linguistic and archaeological
record, and in contrast to the pre-Austronesians, that they

were agriculturalists and were already cultivating rice and millet, along with a range of tubers, vegetables and fruits – coconut (*Cocos nucifera*), banana (*Musa* sp.), Yam (*Dioscorea* sp.), sago (*Metroxylon* sp.), breadfruit (*Artocarpas altilis*), citrus, ginger (*Zingiber*) and sugarcane (*Saccharum*) (Bellwood 1978: 135ff.; Blust 1988: 49ff.). Furthermore, they knew betelnut (*Areca catechu*) and chewed betel quids with the leaf of the *Piper betle*, mixed with lime, and they made alcoholic drinks. Above all they had a developed vocabulary for boats and sailing, and were clearly accomplished in travelling by water. We shall consider agriculture in more detail shortly, but the ecological adaptations of the Dayaks in Borneo are examined fully in chapter 6.

Finally, there have been some suggestions, particularly forwarded by Blust (1980), concerning early Austronesian social organization. Although it is difficult, given our patchy data, to confirm positively whether some of the cultural elements referred to above are indeed representative of societies which established themselves in Borneo some 4,500 years ago, it is even more problematical to determine early social forms. Austronesian peoples exhibit the whole range of kinship types: there are patrilineal societies in Sumatra and eastern Indonesia; the Minangkabau of Sumatra are one of the most famous examples of matriliny, and non-unilineal or cognatic social organization is found very widely among such lowland peoples as the Malays and Javanese and among the tribal populations of the Philippines and Borneo (Hüsken and Kemp 1991; Murdock 1960). I shall explore the nature of Bornean kinship systems in chapter 7, but suffice it to say here that social arrangements must have changed in response to local ecological adaptations, the relationship between land and demographic circumstances, the degree of physical mobility and the nature of contacts between different communities. In any case, the various categories of kinship organization are not mutually exclusive. All societies recognize relationships traced through both maternal and paternal lines, in other words cognation (Needham 1966). It is simply that some societies also develop additional ways of forming social groups, arranging inter-group relations, administering and passing on property and managing succession to office. They may therefore give special emphasis in group formation to links through either male lines (patriliny) or female ones (matriliny), or form two different sets of groups, one based on lines of descent through males and the other through females (double-descent or double unilineal descent).

Blust has proposed a double unilineal form of organization for early Austronesian societies; Dutch ethnologists too, in their reconstructions of early Indonesian social organization, argued for a social system with both patrilineages and matrilineages having discrete spheres of competence (de Josselin de Jong 1977). Following Goodenough (1955), it is my supposition, however, that rather than unilineal or double unilineal descent, an early, if not the earliest form of Austronesian social organization was based on cognation. With regard to Borneo societies there is no evidence that they were ever unilineal. Philippine tribal populations, to whom many northern Bornean societies are very closely related linguistically and culturally, are also cognatic. Early Borneo economies and patterns of livelihood such as shifting cultivation and hunting-gathering do not suggest a basis for unilineal descent groups. Where more permanent relations have been developed with regard to land, it has not been unilineal descent groups which have formed around property, but instead cognatic descent groups, which still do not give emphasis to one particular line of descent in recruiting individuals to a specific social group. Cognatic descent is based on utilizing ancestral lines through both males and females, or, in any given generation, a choice can be made between affiliation through either the paternal or maternal line.

In terms of social stratification, Blust has also suggested that Proto-Austronesian society had ranking and slavery (1980). Yet, as we have already seen, Borneo provides us today with the full range of social types. Some are radically egalitarian, while others are strongly hierarchical, all within relatively small-scale political systems based on one village community or a collection of them. What the early Austronesian social forms were like in this regard is again difficult to establish. Egalitarianism and hierarchy are responses to different ecological, demographic and inter-societal circumstances, and such external factors as access to and control over trade goods.

Presumably early village communities were organized around local leaders, but whether leadership was informal, non-hereditary and based on competition for prestige and influence, or whether it was in effect a chiefly office – institutionalized into permanent relations of superordination and subordination, hereditary and supported by sanctions and by religious and other ideologies – would have depended on the environmental, economic and political context in which these communities found themselves. We will examine some of these social variations in Borneo and the possible factors underlying them in chapter 7.

The archaeological evidence

How do these reconstructions square with such evidence as we have from the limited archaeological material at such sites as Niah? Following Zuraina's scheme of cultural phases for Niah, the most recent period is marked by ceramic manufacture – although she tentatively argues for the local evolution of this – and a decreasing use of pebble and flake artifacts (1982: 139ff.). We must note, however, that flaked stone technologies continued to function into the late first millennium BC onwards, and the Kelabits of Sarawak were still fashioning stone tools up until quite recently. Quadrangular adzes occur from about 2,500 BC, possibly a little later (Glover 1979: 173, 176).

Harrisson, in his overview of Bornean archaeology and prehistory, notes a transition between the Palaeolithic and Neolithic periods marked by technological innovation, population increase and physical mobility, the gradual vacating of caves, associated with the settlement of forest habitats, and the sporadic occupation of rock shelters, which are then used primarily for burials. Burials are accompanied by grave goods comprising such items as non-glass beads and ceramics (1984: 301, 316–17). Harrisson reported the first occurrence of pottery at Niah somewhere between 2,500 BC and 2,000 BC (1957, 1958b, 1959a; Glover 1979: 178). More generally, Bellwood indicates for northern Borneo, along with the Philippines, evidence of simple pottery forms dating between 3,000 BC to 500 BC (1985: 223).

According to Zuraina most of the pottery is plain with a globular body, rounded base and wide mouth. It is 'coarse-tempered earthenware, low-fired and generally thick-bodied' (1982: 115). The pots were hand-moulded with the use of a paddle and anvil. The same techniques could still be seen among the Kenyahs of East Kalimantan in the 1930s and the Ibans of Sarawak in the 1950s. On occasion designs were impressed on the surface of the pot using the carved face of the paddle; these comprised lozenges, checks, ribs, or simple incisions with lines, crosses, diagonals, lattice-work, triangles and squares. Zuraina notes the preponderance of plainware in the early Neolithic phases, with more evidence of resin-glazed, burnished- and slipped-ware in the upper levels at Niah, along with surface work produced with a cord-bound or carved paddle on the sherds (pp. 124–5). The Niah excavations also produced some unusual ceramics, possibly from the second millennium BC. The less common forms are double-spouted water vessels, and pots with painted geometric designs such as keys and hooks enclosed within incised lines. This latter so-called 'three-colour ware' is painted in greenish-yellow, with black incisions and a red-slipped body (Bellwood 1978: 216–17; 1985: 254ff.; T. Harrisson 1971; Solheim et al. 1958). These vessels were associated with burials (Chin 1980: 11; Solheim et al. 1961); double-spouted vessels and some painted in red with charcoal-filled incisions on an unslipped background have also recently been discovered at Lubang Angin (Wind Cave) in the Gunung Mulu region, some 160 kms north-east of Niah (Ipoi Datan and Bellwood 1991: 13ff.). These vessels, along with cord-marked pottery, iron knives, monochrome glass beads and marine bivalve shells, were found in association with extended and flexed burials, probably occurring between 500 BC and AD 500 and resembling those at Niah.

In the Madai site of Agop Atas rather different pottery styles were found, resembling those of the Philippines, northern Sulawesi and Halmahera, rather than Niah. The oldest pottery at Madai, dated between 2,000 BC and 500 BC, comprised simple globular vessels with red slip as the main form of surface finish, plus some rare paddle impression and incision (Bellwood 1985: 227). These are accompanied by the continuation of a stone-flake industry, and the expansion of stone use. But then from the late first millennium BC to AD 1,000, copper, bronze and iron tools occur, with glass beads, carnelian, jar burials and ornate pottery (Bellwood 1988: 245ff.; T. and B. Harrisson 1969–70: 192ff.).

In a site to the south-east of the Madai-Baturong excavations, the Sabah Museum also undertook a brief archaeological investigation in 1987. The rock-shelter complex of Bukit Tengkorak revealed examples of plain or red slipped pottery; these comprise thin-bodied, rather short-rimmed vessels, with some occasional incision or punctuation. They date from the early first millennium BC, and 'are paralleled quite precisely in the Early Atas assemblage from Madai Cave . . .' (Bellwood and Koon 1989: 618). In addition, a distinctive vessel was discovered, incised with 'a repetitive geometric "fence" or "cricket-stump" motif superimposed by patterns apparently stamped with an unusual wavy die, and the rim . . . slipped bright red' (p. 617). The accompanying lid is decorated with joined circles of two different diameters. Bellwood and Koon suggest similarities with Lapita pottery from the western Pacific, and that the vessel might be an import, along with supplies of obsidian, probably worked into spear barbs or knife blades, whose origin might be the Lapita regions of the Bismarck and Solomon archipelagoes (pp. 619–20).

After about 300 BC, pottery styles at Bukit Tengkorak become 'more florid' with several examples of cord marking, carved paddle decorations, perforations and indentations, which demonstrate similarities with pottery assemblages in Sarawak, western Sulawesi, the Philippines and western Micronesia.

Bellwood suggests, on the basis of this evidence of widespread contacts across the seas, that these early populations of the Semporna Peninsula, oriented to the exploitation of marine resources, were very different from those at the Madai site of Agop Atas. The Semporna communities demonstrate a maritime adaptation 'with impressive mobility and long distance trade links' (1989: 155), while the Madai populations further inland were much more 'land-based', probably dependent 'primarily on agriculture'. Bellwood therefore proposes that the important distinction in Borneo between coastal and inland groups might have already been established at least 3,000 years ago or more.

Returning to our discussion of pottery finds, other later examples of paddle and anvil pottery manufacture with geometric decorations executed by the carved surfaces of the paddles can be seen from the Bau finds not far from Kuching (Solheim 1981). Solheim refers to these as the 'Malay' or 'Bau Pottery Complex'. Carved stamps were also used. The pots have ovate or globular bodies, narrowing at the top, with simple, slightly flaring rims. Apparently other influences subsequently led to the addition of such elements as flat bottoms and handles. In the Santubong area of western Sarawak the same kinds of pots have been dated to between the seventh and tenth centuries AD, and from Brunei in the eighth century. Similar styles are also found in southern China and Taiwan, and Solheim proposes that the Niah paddle-impressed vessels of 1,000 BC are also part of this 'Malay' tradition (1959: 1–5). Bellwood too suggests that

With its high proportion of paddle-impressed decoration, the Niah Neolithic pottery may also be directly ancestral to the 'Bau-Malay' impressed cooking pots which are so common in Borneo and Palawan today. (1978: 217)

Nevertheless, the main evidence for the Austronesian transition at Niah can be discerned from an examination of about 130 burials there, dated mainly between 3,000 BC and AD 100, a relatively detailed report of which was supplied by Barbara Harrisson (1967; Brooks et al. 1977; T. Harrisson 1984). Over half the burials were extended and not as in the earlier Australo-Melanesian ones flexed or contorted; the skeletons were coated with haematite or partially burned, and placed in log coffins or cigar-shaped caskets made of sewn bamboo; sometimes they were wrapped in pandanus mats before being placed in containers (T. Harrisson 1984: 316–17). Some were accompanied by grave goods, two later ones with remnants of textiles: three-colour ware, bone rings and a wooden earplug were found. There were also 59 cremations and burnt secondary burials in pottery jars, baskets or small wooden coffins. Grave goods included a quadrangular adze, shell rings, perforated discs for necklaces and double-spouted jars. Jar burials appear to have come in somewhere from the late second millennium BC; but many occurred after 200 BC, and continued into ethnographic times. Bellwood states that

Burial in pottery jars seems to be an indigenous development in Indonesia and the Philippines, with an offshoot represented by the Sa-Huynh Culture in South Vietnam. (1978: 213)

Bellwood further indicates that, given the problematical excavations at Niah, certain of the dates for burials are unreliable, and it is difficult to associate firmly some objects with others, particularly artifacts with dated bones (1985: 256). One of Bellwood's students, Aubrey Parke, has provided a plausible sequence of burials as follows:

First, there are pre-ceramic extended burials in coffins or bamboo caskets; flexed burials continue in a period unreliably dated between 4,000 BC and 2,000 BC. Then there is a phase marked by a new complex of cremations, jar burials and pottery, including double-spouted ware; the dates may run from, at the earliest, 2,000 BC to possibly the late first millennium AD. Finally, there are the same burial forms but with copper and perhaps textiles in the Early Metal phase after AD 1.

Furthermore, in the famous 'Painted Cave' at Niah in which wooden boat coffins have been dated variously at 460 BC, AD 825 and AD 1,000 there are drawings on the cave-walls in haematite, obviously associated with the cult of the dead (T. Harrisson 1958a). Boats and a variety of figures, many of them human-like, are represented. The belief in 'boats of the dead' or 'soul boats', with their accompanying entourage of spirits, to carry the soul of a newly dead person on a river journey to the Land of the Dead, is a very widespread one in Borneo. Associated with these coffins were glass and metal remains and porcelain, suggesting the Metal Age period, sometime in the first millennium AD.

Agriculture

Now let us turn to a few speculations about early agriculture in Borneo. The question of whether rice cultivation was an early form of agriculture in the island is still unresolved.

Harrisson has suggested that the Niah caves were probably only used in the Neolithic period for burials and occasional visits (1984) and therefore not as a base for agriculture. But we have already seen that rice and millet cultivation, along with tubers, was known by the early Austronesians prior to their arrival in Borneo. Indeed, Bellwood has previously suggested that a major reason for Austronesian expansion

involved the development of shifting cultivation of rice, as well as the continuation of the original and less extensive swamp and alluvial bottomlands type of cultivation. (p. 223)

This is for the main reason that shifting cultivation demands an extensive form of land use. We shall examine the properties of this kind of agriculture in chapter 6. Agricultural exploitation has clearly often been an ingredient in expansion, but we must not forget that Austronesians were also traders and involved in contacts by sea, and, it has also been proposed that the development of trade and exchange could have been motives for expansion (Waterson 1990: 23). Indeed, more recently Bellwood has come to the view that shifting cultivation was not very important in Austronesian expansion; it was a 'secondary form of cultivation, following an earlier focus on wetlands for rice and taro' (Bellwood, pers. comm. 1992).

Be that as it may, Avé and King (1986: 14–15) have argued that early agriculture in Borneo was probably not based on rice but on sago. In the period of early Austronesian settlement in Borneo there must have been large expanses of wild sago-palms (*Metroxylon* sp.) in coastal districts. These can be exploited in naturally growing stands, or, as with the present-day Melanau, easily propagated and cultivated to increase yield and production. The coastal dwellers today manufacture sago flour from the edible pith of the palm, using again a very simple process (see chapter 6). Other activities would include gathering, hunting and fishing in the coastal swamp forests, and the cultivation of other tubers and fruits.

Without iron tools the wet interior forests still presented formidable obstacles to early Neolithic agriculturalists, and it is likely that inland horticulture and hunting and gathering comprised the main elements in early Austronesian economy as it very gradually expanded inland. The inland sago palm,

however, is not the *Metroxylon* but the species *Eugeissona*.
Bellwood too has suggested that

the activities of cereal cultivation, forest clearance and weaving
received temporary setbacks during and after the period of Proto-
Malayo-Polynesian, when settlement was expanding into the more
forested regions towards the equator. (1985: 232)

Evidence of rice cultivation in the two major Bornean Neolithic sites of Madai and Niah is lacking. However, Ipoi Datan
and Bellwood have reported the existence of rice at Gua Sireh
in their recent excavations there. Rice-husk temper and 'some
whole carbonised grains' have been found in the pottery sherds
and these have been dated at about 2,300 BC (1991: 391, 393).
However, on the basis of this one find we cannot make any
firm claims as to the extent or importance of rice agriculture at
this time. I am of the view that horticulture was still the
dominant form of agriculture in Borneo until the increasing
use and availability of iron made rainforest clearance less
arduous. But, of course, growing rice in a mixed economy
with tubers, and hunting and gathering could well have occurred in certain more favourable, open and accessible locations.

Metal

As van Heekeren has argued, there is no clearly demarcated
copper or bronze age in Indonesia. Iron materials occur together with copper-bronze in various sites, and van Heekeren
therefore proposes the term 'Bronze-Iron Age' (1958: 1). We
now usually refer to a 'Metal Age' in South-East Asia. Even so
it is difficult to determine how and when metal manufacture
was introduced into Borneo among the Neolithic stone-users.
Bellwood has dated fragments of iron, and copper-bronze tools
at Madai in Sabah from about 200 BC, including a forged iron
tanged spearhead and a small iron knife (1985: 309–11, 1988:
130ff., 245ff.). But he had no evidence that metal was worked
at this time. In Tapadong on the Segama river in Sabah, local
casting of metals probably began somewhere between AD 500
and 1,000 (T. Harrisson 1965). Bellwood suggests an early first

millennium AD date for metal-working in Borneo (1985: 310–11). But it is well to note that there is no agreement on this. Harrisson previously proposed a later date for iron tool manufacture in Borneo, perhaps about AD 700. He argues that

the general impact of metal and its technology cannot now be placed much earlier than the seventh century at any point. (1984: 321)

Certainly the fashioning of metals in Borneo followed several centuries behind the famous Dong Son culture and its predecessors in Vietnam, which where manufacturing bronze axes, spearheads, sickles, arrowheads, knives and fishhooks from about 1,500 BC. Dong Son also provides evidence of a relatively large-scale society, stratified, with high-status burials associated with prestige objects such as bronze drums and the first evidence of iron, from between 600 BC and 400 BC (Bellwood 1978: 182ff.). It is likely that metal goods were imported into Borneo from mainland South-East Asia well before manufacture commenced on the island, but it was probably not until various Bornean communities became increasingly integrated into extensive networks of trade within South-East Asia and with India and China that metal was adopted more generally and then made on any scale.

No firm published evidence of Dong Son drums in Borneo is yet available, although D. D. Bintarti of the Indonesian National Research Centre for Archaeology has recently reported the discovery of two bronze drums in Central Kalimantan (Glover, pers. comm. 1992). Furthermore, the decorations and symbols used on the drums do demonstrate some remarkable similarities with motifs used by various of the central Borneo groups such as the Kayans (Bellwood 1978: 228). Therefore, it cannot be discounted that cultural influences, along with the small-scale import of metal objects from mainland South-East Asia, did involve Bornean communities from the last few centuries BC and into the first centuries of the Christian era.

There is also good reason to suppose that the early period of the Metal Age in Borneo, probably in the first millennium AD, was associated with the so-called 'megalithic cultures' but these may go back to the first millennium BC (Harrisson and O'Connor 1970: 193ff.). Stone monuments, dolmens, avenues and menhirs are quite widely spread in interior Borneo and in

Plate 26   Carved stone figure at Pa' Bangar, Kelabit highlands

the western coastal districts of Sabah, although these are almost impossible to date, and many have been erected by such groups as the inland Kelabits in fairly recent times (T. Harrisson 1959c). They have been found in the Apau Kayan area of East Kalimantan too in such forms as stone graves (van Heekeren 1958: 63; Tillema 1989: 239), but they may well not be of great antiquity there either. Some rock-carvings have also been found in such places as Santubong in western Sarawak as well as in the Kelabit highlands (plate 26).

These stone monuments have served a variety of purposes. Many of the single stone menhirs in the Kadazan area appear to mark land boundaries and are used to assist in the distribution of riceland property and act as a symbol of status (T. and B. Harrisson 1969–70: 130ff.; Harrisson and O'Connor 1970: 86ff.). Others, among the Kelabits for example, are very clearly related to status feasting, marking a funeral ritual in association with jar burials, or the commemoration of an illustrious individual or an act of bravery.

Thus, by about 2,000 years ago, and certainly by the time that Indian and Chinese contacts increased in intensity from the first part of the first millennium AD, the main outlines of Dayak tribal culture were in place, although it seems that there were three important developments which were yet to occur: first, the growth of port centres around the coasts of Borneo, which led to a progressive differentiation between state formations and tribal societies on the island; secondly, the widespread adoption of shifting cultivation of rice, which had to await the more general use and manufacture of iron tools in Borneo; finally, and associated with agricultural development, the decisive penetration of the interior and the subsequent large-scale migrations across major parts of the interior of the island. We shall examine in particular the emergence of trading states in Borneo in the next chapter.

4

India, China and Islam

Introduction

Unfortunately we know little about the early development of the societies and cultures of interior Borneo until we begin to obtain evidence about them from ethnological investigations in the later colonial period. However, we do know rather more about the early coastal states, which we shall consider in this chapter. We can assume that shifting cultivation continued to expand in extent following the adoption and manufacture of iron sometime during the first millennium AD, although there were communities which continued to depend on horticulture, specifically sago cultivation, and hunting and gathering. We must also remember that stone tools continued to be manufactured and used for much of the first millennium AD, and were still to be found in isolated pockets of the interior until quite recently.

What is more, inland peoples were also progressively linked into networks of trade during the first millennium AD, as India first, and then China, became more and more economically involved in the South-East Asian region. The interior peoples, both settled agriculturalists and forest nomads, but especially the latter, supplied downriver trading centres with various forest products sought-after in Asian trade. Usually hunters-gatherers were the main suppliers, the settled longhouse people acting as intermediaries between them and the coastal traders. Indeed, some native communities may well have deliberately decided to specialize in forest hunting and gathering for purposes of trade, as well as continuing to meet their own subsistence needs. But commercial considerations cannot be the main reason for the emergence of forest nomad society, which early on had presumably been based on subsistence activities.

Obviously the colonization of the interior occurred in a gradual, piecemeal way, confined initially to the main rivers and more accessible regions of the island. Only subsequently when forest clearance was facilitated by iron tools, and Islam began to make its presence felt around the coasts of Borneo, spreading from the main trading centres, do we begin to get evidence of significant physical migrations in the interior. Presumably small indigenous groups initially settled scattered parts of the hinterland, quite distant from each other, and developed rather different cultural and social forms. But it is not until the seventeenth century that we have references in indigenous oral traditions of movements into the deep interior by Ibanic peoples (Sandin 1967), and it was probably the late seventeenth century into the eighteenth century when such peoples as the Kayans began to move out of central Borneo down the major rivers of the region (Rousseau 1990). However, these migrations indicate that vast areas of Borneo, even up to 200 years ago, were only inhabited by very small groups of forest nomads and horticulturalists. The whole interior of the island was still very sparsely populated indeed at the beginning of European contact in the sixteenth century.

Early Indian and Chinese trade

Information on early Indian and Chinese contacts and influence in Borneo is also very limited. We know, however, that some of the Muslim-Malay states of Borneo, which Europeans began to visit in the sixteenth century, had Hindu-Buddhist roots; for example, the sultanates of Brunei, Kutei and Banjarmasin (Leake 1990: 1ff.; Ras 1968; Rousseau 1990: 283). There is also evidence of certain Indian- and Chinese-derived elements in Borneo cultures, although it is often difficult to differentiate definitively what is indigenous from what is imported. A similarity in traits between Bornean and other cul-

tures should not lead us automatically to assume that these
have been brought in from outside. It was an unfortunate
tendency in diffusionist theories, such as those of von Heine
Geldern (1966) and Vroklage (1936), to propose the spread of
ideas from what were perceived as the more culturally sophisticated areas of India and China. Taking an obvious
example, Bornean practices of cremation were usually presumed to indicate Hindu-Indian influence, while we now
know that cremation was a very early Austronesian cultural
form in Borneo, and a fairly recent one in India.

During the first millennium AD it was commercial contacts
with India which attracted most South-East Asian interest, and
small trading states, showing evidence of Indian influence,
began to emerge in the region between the first and fifth centuries
AD. However, it is certain that trade goods from India, such as
glass beads, and from as far away as the Mediterranean world,
were reaching South-East Asia during the last few centuries BC
(Glover 1989). Evidence suggests that substantial trade between the Indo-Malaysian area and China did not take place
to any extent until the period of the Southern Sung dynasty
from the mid-tenth century AD, although there were clearly
Chinese commercial contacts southwards well before then.

Although Borneo did not produce agricultural surpluses
because of its environmental constraints, it did provide important luxury goods for Asian-wide trade. For India in particular,
precious items such as gold and gemstones, including diamonds, were sought, as well as camphor (Meilink-Roelofsz
1962: 101). Crystalline scales of pure camphor, which formed
in crevices and the decayed heart of old trees of the species
Dryobanalops aromatica, were used in medicines and incense,
and were also subsequently much desired by the Chinese.
Borneo was known early on as an important source of high-
quality camphor. It continued to be in demand when Europeans came to the region, and Ralf Fitch, an Englishman,
who travelled in India in the 1580s and went as far as Malacca, remarked that

Camphora is a precious thing amongst the Indians, and is solde
dearer than golde. I think that none of it cometh from Christen-
dom. That which is compounded cometh from China; but that

which groweth in canes, and is the best, cometh from the great isle of Borneo. (in Nicholl 1975: 60)

A whole range of other products came from the rainforest, and became increasingly important in the China-trade towards the end of the first millennium AD. Beeswax was collected and used locally by shifting cultivators for tapers and caulking, but it was also an export item often used in ointment and medicines. Aromatic woods were used for incense, *gaharu* bark (*Aquilaria microcarpa*) for medicines, and *ketapang* fruit (*Terminalia catappa*) for dyeing and tanning. Other forest products included *gutta percha* from trees such as *jelutong* (*Dyera costulata*), used for medicines, adhesive and waterproofing, along with wild rubber from species of creeper. Resin (*damar*: *Agathis dammara*) was employed for sealing, and rattans for plaiting and binding. Vegetable tallow was derived from the seeds of the *engkabong tree* or illipe (*Shorea*).

Of the fauna of importance, species of swift (*Collocalia fuciphaga*, *C. Lowii*, *C. Linchaii*) made nests from their saliva, which was a food delicacy of the Chinese; the swifts made their nests in caves. Bezoar stones used for medicinal purposes were found in the gall-bladders and intestines of the long-tailed monkey (*Semnopithecus Hosei*, and *S. rubicundus*), and the wounds of porcupines. The Chinese wanted rhinoceros horn for its curative properties and as an aphrodisiac; anteater scales for magical charms; decorative feathers of tropical birds such as the rhinoceros hornbill and the argus pheasant. Hornbill 'ivory' from the hardened casque of the helmeted hornbill was beautifully carved by Chinese artists into cups and jewelry; deer antlers were also decoratively carved.

What is more, the settled agriculturalists, with whom forest nomads traded, also used some of these products locally such as rattans and resins, hornbill 'ivory' and feathers, as well as animal-skins of the bear, tiger-cat, monkey, gibbon and *orang utan* for war-cloaks and head-dresses.

The main evidence for early 'Indianized' states in South-East Asia, emerging as a direct result of trading contacts, comes from the mainland, in Vietnam, and the Gulf of Siam area southwards to the Kra Isthmus (Coedès 1968). What seems to have happened is that native rulers or chiefs of the coastal states trading with India began to adopt Indian religious and political models. Initially the Pallava rulers of Tamil Nadu in southern India appear to have been the main source of inspiration, given evidence from Sanskrit and Pallava inscriptions found in South-East Asia. The medium for this process of Indianization was not colonization by Indian merchants as was once thought, although trade provided the channels of contact. It was rather instruction from and reliance on Hindu Brahmin priests and Buddhist scholars, probably brought over by native rulers to enhance and legitimize their authority (Leake 1990: 5). Sanskrit loan words were increasingly incorporated into Austronesian languages at the court or higher administrative levels.

In maritime South-East Asia, Borneo must have been somewhat marginal in political and economic terms. Large empires were focused on Sumatra and Java in the first millennium AD, and Borneo's political systems were, in comparison, small-scale. There is however, quite early evidence of south Indian influence in south-eastern Borneo in the kingdom of Kutei (see map 10). *Yupa* inscriptions referring to a King Mulavarman were discovered there, dating from about the beginning of the fifth century AD (Chhabra 1965). In western Borneo at Batu Pahat, a site near the Tekarek river, a tributary of the Kapuas, a 'pyramidal' boulder was discovered, inscribed with eight Buddhist texts in Sanskrit (Christie 1990; Harrisson and O'Connor 1970: 259). Associated with the texts are relief figures of stupas, 'each of which is surmounted by a series of superimposed parasols' (Christie, p. 49). A similar stone text has also been found in Brunei, and these, in turn, are related to other stone inscriptions found in the Muda and Merbok valley region of Kedah on the Malayan Peninsula, dated to the late fourth or early fifth century AD. Christie suggests that they provide evidence of a Buddhist traders' cult directed to ensuring successful sea voyages, and presumably associated with small 'Malay-type' coastal trading states in Kedah, West Borneo and Brunei. These were linked together into commercial networks which extended both to China and across the Bay of Bengal to India.

Aside from these inscriptions, there have been several finds in scattered locations in Borneo of stone statues of Indian

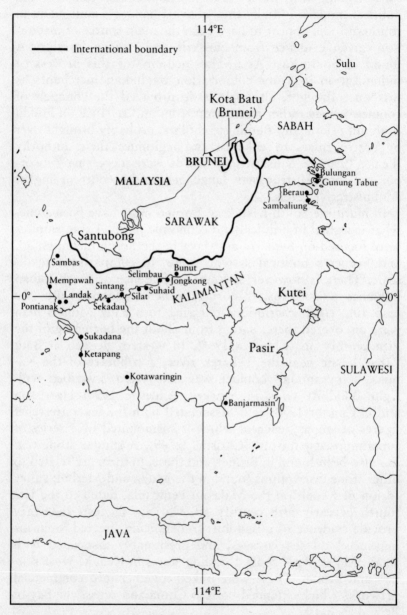

Map 10   Early kingdoms, port centres and sultanates in Borneo

gods, Nandi bulls as guardians of Sivaite temples, and *lingga* and *yoni* forms (Chin 1980: 15). Items have been dated from the eighth and ninth centuries AD through to the fourteenth and fifteenth centuries just prior to the advent of Islam in Borneo. One of the most important discoveries was the Tantric shrine in the Santubong area, located at the site of a former coastal trading and manufacturing centre, which we will consider in detail below.

Many of the examples of Indian influence in Borneo, especially during the later centuries, may well have derived not directly from India but from such South-East Asian Indianized states as Srivijaya in southern Sumatra and the series of Hindu-Buddhist states in eastern and central Java. Srivijaya was founded towards the end of the seventh century AD at a time when Indian influences were reaching South-East Asia from northern India, particularly Bengal (Wolters 1967). Apparently parts of Borneo were nominally subject to Srivijaya, which was trading in Bornean camphor and luxury woods as well as turtles and pearls in the latter second half of the first millennium AD (Meilink-Roelofsz 1962: 101).

The influence of Majapahit on Borneo in the fourteenth and fifteenth centuries seems to have been more significant. This Javanese state clearly had some economic and political prominence in various coastal regions of Borneo. For example, the chronicles of the kingdom of the Banjarese Malays at Banjarmasin in southern Borneo record just such a contact. Prior to Islamic conversion, Banjarmasin's historical traditions indicate Javanese influence. The origins of the state are given in the 'Story of Lambu Mangkurat and the Dynasty of the Kings of Ban(d)jar and Kota Waringin' (Ras 1968). The early court and capital was apparently modelled on Majapahit and based on the Javanese style of palace (*kraton*), and on Javanese origin myths (pp. 182ff.). Hudson indicates that an 'Indianized' kingdom was established in the hinterland region of the present-day Banjarmasin in the mid-fourteenth century and called Negaradipa (1967a: 55–8). Subsequently the capital was moved to the coast and came under the influence of the Muslim Javanese state of Demak in the early sixteenth century (p. 60). In the south-western regions of Borneo other pre-Islamic states mentioned as coming under Majapahit patronage were Lawe and Tanjungpura, which were important sources of gold and diamonds (Meilink-Roelofsz 1962: 101).

In northern Borneo, at Limbang, close to present-day Brunei, a stone figure of the elephant-headed Hindu deity Ganesa, along with Indian-style gold ornaments, have been discovered, and dated from the Majapahit period (plate 27). A fourteenth-century dependency of Majapahit, referred to in a Javanese document as Buruneng, presumably Brunei, again indicates some Javanese influence there.

Various Dayak populations are also reputed to have links with Java, although the precise nature of these connections and when they occurred are difficult to determine. The Kedayans of Brunei are said, in some popular reports, to have originated from Javanese immigration (Lebar 1972), as have the Desa Dayaks of the Tayan area of western Borneo (Enthoven 1903). Certain elements of Dayak cultures can more definitely be connected to Indian influence, probably via Javanese Majapahit. For example, the Ngaju Dayaks of southern Borneo distinguish two supreme deities, or two major aspects of one united god-head, which represent the Upperworld and the Underworld respectively. That of the Upperworld is often symbolized by the hornbill, and, in addition to its local name, is referred to as *Mahatara* or *Bahatara Guru*. As Schärer notes, following Wilken, *Batara-Guru* originally designated the Indian deity Siva, and *Mahatara* is 'a contraction of Mahabatara i.e. the great lord' (1963: 13). The deity of the Underworld and the primeval waters, represented in local symbolism by the watersnake, is referred to as *Jata*, from the Sanskrit *deva* and *devata* (p. 15).

This evidence of Indian-derived terminology can also be found in Iban religion. The honorific term for important spirits is *petara*, presumed to be related to the Hindu *batara* ('lord') (Jensen 1974: 100–1). Jensen further suggests possible Hindu influences in the Iban deity of the earth, *Pulang Gana*, and the bird-god, *Sengalang Burong* (pp. 78, 83). Symbolic representations of supernatural beings were also adopted by some Borneo peoples from Indianized South-East Asian sources, but these appear to have been merged with or superimposed on earlier pagan motifs. For example, the ancient Bornean image of the serpent or watersnake as a symbol of

Plate 27 The elephant-headed god, Ganesa, found at Limbang, Sarawak

the Underworld seems to have incorporated the Hindu-Javanese dragon-serpent motif; it is often referred to as *naga* (King 1985b).

Nevertheless, overall Indian, and indeed Chinese influence in indigenous Bornean cultures seems to have been slight. It must have been the coastal centres of commerce which experienced the main effects of Indian civilization, but even here Hindu-Buddhist traits seem to have been used selectively by local rulers. For example, both in Borneo and more widely in South-East Asia there is no evidence of the adoption of the Hindu caste system. Indeed, Borneo was never incorporated into an Indian-dominated civilization as such. As Harrisson and O'Connor state

When added altogether, the number of Hindu-Buddhist objects found in western and southwestern Borneo would indicate that this section of Borneo was in minor contact with India or with 'Indianized' peoples in Southeast Asia. (1970: 260)

Contact with the large Indianized polities elsewhere in South-East Asia and involvement in wider networks of maritime trade were part of the process of social, economic and political differentiation whereby coastal states became established in Borneo and developed into larger-scale stratified social systems, linked to the great religious traditions of the East. Increasing economic and cultural specialization led to the emergence of different socio-economic groups: rulers and administrators, traders, skilled artisans and small-scale producers, soldiers, labourers, servants and slaves. Let us now look in more detail at one example of these emerging coastal polities, data on which have been made available from the archaeological work of the Sarawak Museum.

Santubong and P'o-ni

The excavations at Santubong in the Sarawak river delta downstream of Kuching, the present capital of the state of Sarawak, revealed a series of locally manufactured and imported items, which indicated a settlement of some size and importance. There were substantial finds of Chinese-made trade objects such as porcelain and stoneware dating from the Sung dynasty (AD 906 to AD 1279), especially the latter part of that period, and coins from the tenth century. It was originally claimed that some of the ceramics point to earlier dates of occupation and activity (O'Connor and Harrisson 1964). However, more recent opinion holds that some of the so-called 'Yueh' wares (thin-glazed celadonic stoneware) and 'Dusun' wares (large green- or brown-glazed jars) cannot be reliably dated to a period earlier than the tenth century (Christie 1985: 80–1). Along with Chinese imported goods there was evidence of what Harrisson and O'Connor call a Tantric shrine at nearby Bongkissam, probably of the twelfth century or thirteenth century at the latest (1967: 155; Solheim, 1983: 38), containing a silver deposit box, gold ornaments in the shape of the Buddha, a crescent moon, an elephant, a turtle and a snake, stone and glass beads, glass bracelets, carved stones and semi-precious stones. A stone Buddha in the Gupta tradition was also discovered. Of greatest significance, however, were the remains of a relatively extensive iron-working site, with residences, burial grounds and, of course, shrines.

Christie has suggested that the state of P'o-ni, referred to in Chinese chronicles, and the ancestor of Burni and the Sultanate of Brunei, might have been located at Santubong, given the evidence of considerable economic activity and population there, rather than at Brunei Bay (1985). Nevertheless, there was obviously a complex of interconnected collecting points along the north-west coasts of the island; levels of activity would have fluctuated in different centres over time, so that the foci of P'o-ni or Burni probably shifted. Ultimately, Brunei Bay did emerge as the focus of this increasingly powerful state. Following its emergence to prominence from the tenth century, Santubong then declined in significance from the thirteenth century onwards; its growth coincided with a period of increasing trade with China. Indeed, the first few centuries of the second millennium AD saw an enormous expansion in trade between China and the Indo-Malaysian archipelago in spices and forest products.

Given what were thought to be the large amounts of slag from iron-smelting in Santubong, as well as the fragments of earthenware assumed to be the remains of 'crucibles' used in refining iron, Harrisson and O'Connor concluded that these were the remains of a large-scale iron-working industry, relying on imported technology (1969). Subsequently Harrisson talked of 'a massive iron smelting industry' (1984: 304). In addition, it was suggested by Cheng, another of Harrisson's collaborators, that the substantial finds of Chinese glazed stonewares indicated the settlement of Chinese at Santubong, presumably as iron-smelters and forgers (1969: 18). This supposition tied in with Cheng's proposal that China at that time was in search of new, external sources of iron. Thus, Cheng's overall view, which has since been discredited, was that Chinese settlers, using imported technology from China, located themselves at Santubong and produced large amounts of cast-ironware for export to service the mainland Chinese market.

This is yet another example of the tendency in earlier writings on Borneo to assume that significant economic and other developments must have come from the great civilizations outside the island. This is not to say that Chinese did not settle in Borneo. Some Chinese traders and artisans did move to port centres on a semi-permanent or permanent basis; later in the fourteenth century, for example, it has been suggested that a Ming colony was established in Kinabatangan in northeast Borneo (Sellato 1989a: 15), and Chinese merchants were certainly resident in Brunei Bay by the sixteenth century (Groeneveldt 1880: 102). But for Cheng's proposals to square with the size of the industry claimed by Harrisson and O'Connor, it would require the technology to have been iron-casting using the blast furnace method. Yet, no remains of blast furnaces were found, only earthenwares, which Harrisson claimed to be remains of 'crucibles', and which would point to a smaller scale 'crucible' process. Cheng indeed argued for a peasant-based 'crucible' process, which was used in southern China at the time (1969: 21). Unfortunately this suggestion sits uneasily with the other evidence provided by Harrisson and O'Connor; and, in fact, the southern Chinese process used larger 'crucibles' than those identified as such at Santubong.

Harrisson and O'Connor were themselves unhappy with some of Cheng's suggestions, and his hypothesis of a Chinese technological connection. Instead they argued for a possible adoption in Santubong of a south Indian and Sri Lankan 'wootz' steel method, in which wrought iron is produced by simple 'bowl' bloomery furnaces and then converted in 'crucibles'. This proposal, in contrast to Cheng's, does not require the presence of large numbers of Chinese iron-workers, or close market links with China. It also appears to fit the other claims concerning the 'crucible' process employed and the size of the industry. Where it is somewhat problematical is that, like Cheng's view, it assumes an imported technology. Unfortunately, there is no evidence of these Indian methods anywhere else on the island, and the 'wootz' method does not square with any indigenous iron-smithing techniques. A greater problem for the Harrisson and O'Connor view is that the quantities of iron ore needed to account for the large amount of slag and the size of the industry suggest that the raw material had to be imported, and this is precisely what was suggested. Harrisson and O'Connor proposed that iron ore was brought to Santubong from other coastal locations and from interior Borneo. This, in turn, raises the question why a smelting industry was located at a distance from suitable sources of ore.

Christie has recently re-evaluated the Harrisson and O'Connor thesis (1985, 1988). She points out that the distribution of the iron slag and the local earthenwares in the Santubong sites presents particular difficulties for their explanations. Material identified as slag was widely distributed; it was found in some areas where there were no other signs of industrial activity and no evidence of habitation, and in those areas where the industrial waste was at its most concentrated, and therefore unlikely to be a location for residential areas, the main finds of valuable imported stonewares were made. Yet another explanation was invoked to help meet these latter circumstances. O'Connor suggested that the mixture of industrial waste and ceramics arose from the use of imported wares in rituals associated with iron-smithing, and Harrisson surmised that the scattering of slag outside industrial and residential locations was linked to an iron-working cult in which bits of slag were used as offerings or talismans.

In contrast to these rather tortuous theories to explain the Santubong finds, Christie's reappraisal brings subsequent work at Santubong together with studies of other port centres elsewhere in South-East Asia at this time (Bronson 1978). It over-comes the problem of assuming a very large-scale export-oriented industry relying on large amounts of imported iron ore, and it places the Santubong industry in a local context of iron-working and smelting, which does not depend on the hypothesis that technology was brought in from either India or China.

Given the work of Treloar (1978), Christie points out that much of the iron slag is not slag at all. Very high in iron ore, the materials thought to be slag 'resemble very closely the types of natural concretions found in lateritic soils of Borneo, Sumatra and the peninsula' (1988: 14). In other words, the so-called industrial waste is, in large part, iron-bearing and iron-rich laterites, which were the very local sources of iron ore used by the iron-workers and smelters at Santubong. This explains why the materials assumed to be slag occur in non-industrial and non-residential sites. It was not taken there or deposited by 'iron-worshippers'; it occurred naturally. If this is accepted, then there is an overall conclusion: the industry was not as large as was originally supposed. It was a modest-sized industry, locally based and resourced. It was not serving a large international market, but instead it provided mainly for local Bornean needs (1985: 83).

The other problem concerns the occurrence of a large quant-ity of fragments of earthenware. Christie, following Treloar (1978: 131), argues that these were not crucibles, but nozzles or tuyeres attached to a simple piston-bellow system for heating the charcoal in order to smelt iron ore. O'Connor too sub-sequently re-evaluated the earthenware remains and admitted that his earlier interpretation was mistaken (1977: 7). This piston-bellow method of smelting local iron ores is found very widely today among the Dayak peoples of Borneo, such as the Kayans and Kelabits (plate 28); the interior natives were well known for their high-quality ironware, and the proposed technology utilized in Santubong squares with the relatively detailed nineteenth-century accounts of local Bornean iron-working (e.g. Crawfurd 1856: 159; Everett in Roth 1896: 236; Low 1848: 18–19, 158, 209; St John 1862, i: 122). In other words, the technology, once acquired, has persisted for a long period of time; it is a relatively simple method, and fits well

*Plate 28   Kelabit smiths using piston-bellows and stone hammers
for working iron*

with my suggestion that early Borneo coastal communities, though increasing in scale and complexity during the period prior to Islam, were still modest in size and extent in comparison with the large trading and agricultural states elsewhere.

Deposits of iron ore in Borneo are generally of high quality and their occurrence has been reported in various locations on the island, in such places as western Borneo, interior East Kalimantan and the upper Barito basin. This iron-rich ore can be smelted and worked by simple techniques. St John provides a brief description of Kayan methods:

I may remark that their [Kayan] ore appears to be very easily smelted. They dig a small pit in the ground; in the bottom are various holes, through which are driven currents of air by very primitive bellows. Charcoal is thrown in; then the ore, well broken up, is added and covered with charcoal; fresh ore and fresh fuel, in alternate layers, till the furnace is filled. A light is then put to the mass through a hole below, and, the wind being driven in, the process is soon completed. (St John 1862, i: 122)

Given the fact that high-quality ore occurred in Borneo in many widely dispersed locations, so that it could not support a large-scale intensive, concentrated industry, the simple local methods were entirely appropriate. The equipment used was quick to assemble and easily transported or made anew; skills were basic; and techniques were flexible in terms of the level of ore supplies, local demand and the time required for smelting.

Christie, in explaining the high quality of iron goods such as bush knives and swords, which was remarked upon by several European observers, indicates that

The pit or 'bowl' bloomery process . . . produces a low-carbon iron 'bloom', usually referred to as 'wrought' iron, through a 'direct' or single-stage process. (1988: 7)

This native technology would not have provided sufficiently high temperatures to produce molten metal for casting, but, given the high-quality ore used, it was enough to permit impurities to be floated off or beaten out. This direct process produces a tough, formidable iron, ideal for making weapons.

The settlement at Santubong, then, was serving a local market in the hinterland and in the port centre. To obtain forest items from the interior, which were highly valued in Asian trade, the coastal communities exchanged their locally made iron weapons and tools, as well as pottery, beads, and later, in the case of Brunei, brassware (Bronson 1978). In return for these tropical commodities, centres such as Santubong then imported goods from China and India, mainly for use in the port and its environs. Christie notes that these imported goods – porcelain, stoneware, silks and other textiles –

played a major role in maintaining the internal stability of early coastal states. Most of these items were consumed either in the immediate region of the port or at the major district centres on the lower course of the river largely by the ruler's clients and supporters who comprised a large portion of the capital's population. (1985: 77)

These items from India and China were used in systems of social prestige and stratification in coastal settlements; rulers and senior administrators built up clienteles by distributing luxury goods to supporters and by displaying their wealth. Early on, Chinese porcelain and stonewares, especially jars, were imported, but from the thirteenth to fifteenth centuries ceramics began to come in from mainland South-East Asia, particularly Annamese monochromes and Siamese Sawankha-lok wares (Chin 1980: 13).

The manufacture of iron itself eventually penetrated into the interior, but this probably occurred some centuries later. Furthermore, imported Chinese ceramics and other goods do not appear to have found their way into the interior to any extent prior to the fourteenth century. When they did they also entered into tribal prestige networks and were kept as sacred heirlooms (B. Harrisson 1986). Dayak oral traditions abound with stories of illustrious heroes going in search, on journeys of adventure, of valuable porcelain, especially jars, and beads.

Descriptions of the state of P'o-ni prior to the advent of Islam confirm this commercial exchange of forest products for imported prestige goods (Hirth and Rockhill 1966). A Chinese account of the twelfth or thirteenth century indicates that this Bornean state produced four varieties of camphor, yellow wax, lac wood and tortoise-shell in return for trade-gold and silver, imitation silk brocades, brocades of silk-floss, silk lustrings, glass beads and bottles, tin, ivory armlets, rouge, lacquered bowls and plates and celadon porcelain.

P'o-ni is assumed to have been founded by the seventh century AD (Irwin 1967: 3; Leake 1990: 1, 3, 4). It may be the state referred to early on as Vijayapura or Sribuza (Brown 1970). What we do know is that P'o-ni sent envoys to the Chinese court in AD 977 to present tribute to the Emperor in the form of camphor, tortoise-shell, ivory and sandalwood (Hirth and Rockhill 1966: 157). Later missions were sent in AD 1082, 1370 and 1405. In AD 1082 the ruler of P'o-ni was possibly called Sri Maharaja or Maradja. It is also the case, as the finds at Santubong demonstrate, that the kingdom, or at least the court, had been subject to Indian influence.

The *Chu-Fan-Chi*, compiled by Chau Ju-Kua, on the Chinese and Arab trade in the twelfth and thirteenth centuries (Hirth and Rockhill 1966), reports that the 'king' of P'o-ni was a Buddhist. His residence was covered with the leaves of the nipah palm. The king went barefoot, wore gold jewellery and cloth of cotton. The economy was based on the production of hemp, rice and sago; the inhabitants had fowl and fish, made cotton cloth and alcoholic drinks from the sap of a palm tree and from coconuts. Clearly the royal household commanded some wealth: gold household vessels were reported, and the wives and daughters of rich families wore sarongs of 'fancy brocades' and 'melted gold coloured silk'.

As I have said, whether the capital of P'o-ni was early on at Santubong or Brunei Bay is difficult to establish. Given the iron industry at Santubong, Christie has suggested an early centre there, with presumably the focus of the state shifting later to more or less the present site of the Brunei capital.

Excavations have been undertaken at Kota Batu, the presumed site of the palace of the Brunei (or Burni) ruler visited by Antonio Pigafetta in 1521 (see below). The Harrissons undertook work there in the early 1950s, and the Brunei Museum has subsequently conducted archaeological investigations there and at another nearby site in the Brunei Bay area at Kupang (Bellwood and Matussin 1980; Matussin 1981). At Kota Batu ceramic assemblages of both imported Chinese and local pottery were discovered dating to the later fourteenth century, after Santubong had declined. Bellwood confirms the likelihood of this site as the capital. Kupang has revealed earlier occupancy from the tenth century. Locally manufactured pottery is in the tradition of Solheim's 'Bau-Malay' earthenwares, and they are closest to the Santubong materials. In the lower levels of the excavation there were fragments of paddle-and-anvil earthenware; plain, undecorated ware was common, though some comprising such items as storage jars, cooking pots and double-spouted vessels was paddle-impressed or incised, stamped and carved. In later levels there is more imported Chinese ware of the T'ang to early Ming periods. The Kupang site was abandoned from the mid-fourteenth century, presumably to be superseded by Kota Batu.

With regard to the local earthenwares Bellwood and Matussin remark that

manufacture in two or more important entrepot locations, such as the Sarawak River Delta and Brunei Bay seems most likely. (1980: 173)

Obviously there were close contacts between these centres along the north-west coasts of Borneo (Matussin 1981). But it was eventually the Brunei Bay area which was to rise to prominence. These port centres, showing Indianized features, and which were also found in other coastal locations in western, southern and eastern Borneo, were the predecessors of the Islamic sultanates. However, these later Muslim states continued the same patterns of trade as Santubong and Brunei Bay, importing prestige and other goods from China and elsewhere in return for hinterland forest products such as camphor, and manufacturing metalware, pottery and beads locally in exchange for interior goods.

The coming of Islam

The scale and nature of change among Borneo's peoples was to be very different with the arrival of Islam. Prior to conversion the coastal areas of the island were presumably inhabited by people of what we now refer to as Dayak ethnic groups: along the north-west and north-east coasts, Kadazans (Dusuns), Muruts, Bisayas, Lun Bawangs; on the west coasts the Bidayuhs and the ancestors of the Ibanic and other Malayic groups; on the south and south-east coasts the Barito-speaking Dayaks, and, in the east, the Kayans. Gradually some of these people either converted to Islam and, in effect, changed their ethnic affiliation, or like certain of the Iban groups withdrew inland. As Hudson says of southern Borneo, from the seventeenth century one can witness the retreat of Dayak culture in the hinterland of Banjarmasin, and the expansion of Muslim Banjar Malay culture and settlement (1967b: 55).

It is difficult to determine precisely when Islam established itself firmly on the coastal margins of Borneo. It is likely that Arab and Persian traders were travelling in South-East Asian waters by the eighth century AD. But it was definitely Indian Muslims who had the greatest influence on the western regions of the Indo-Malaysian archipelago, and Islam came to the area largely through the medium of Indian trade (Hall 1968). However, it is not until the thirteenth century that we begin to have evidence of the appearance of Muslim states in such places as

Sumatra. Then, following the establishment of the Muslim
trading state of Malacca as the Oriental spice emporium on
the margins of the Malayan Peninsula from the early fifteenth
century, we witness a rapid expansion of Islam and the Malay
language and culture along the coasts of Borneo (Andaya and
Andaya 1982; Turnbull 1988). During the fifteenth century
Muslim Malay traders, missionaries and teachers were visiting
Borneo ports as vessels from Malaya and Sumatra plied between the eastern Indonesian spice islands and the Malayan
Peninsula. Another channel of conversion must have been
trading contacts between Java and western and southern Borneo, following Javanese conversion to Islam and the visits of
Javanese traders, and later their settlement in the coastal ports
of the island.

Nevertheless, it was not until later that we have certain
evidence of Muslim states in Borneo. The Brunei rulers had
apparently still not converted to Islam by the fifteenth century
(Leake 1990: 7–8). But in order to maintain and promote their
trade and political influence it was judged practical and strategic by local South-East Asian rulers, many of whom had,
prior to Islam, adopted Hindu and Buddhist statecraft for
the same reasons, to assume the religious faith of the increasingly powerful Muslim traders and the states which they
represented.

There is some dispute about the period when a specifically
Muslim dynasty was founded in Brunei (Hall 1968: 241). Some
writers and official historians in Brunei point to an early date
in the fifteenth century. Muslim tombstones discovered at Kota
Batu have been dated from then. On the basis of dynastic
genealogies, some writers go even further back to the early
fourteenth century or before. However, Ludovico Varthema
of Bologna, who visited Brunei probably in 1504 or 1505,
reported as follows:

We arrived at the island of Bornei . . . The people are pagans and are
men of good will . . . In this island justice is well administered, and
each year they despatch a great quantity of camphor. . . . (in Nicholl
1975: 3)

Furthermore, in a letter from the Portuguese Captain-General
of Malacca to King Manuel I of Portugal dated 6 January

1514, it was indicated that

There came from Burneo to this city [Malacca] three junks . . . The King is a pagan but the merchants are Moors [Muslims]. (in Nicholl, p. 4)

Then from the Book of Duarte Barbosa, who was Secretary of the Portuguese factory at Cannanore on the Malabar coast from 1500 to 1516 or 1517, and who wrote in about 1515, we read that

the island called Bornei, which much abounds in provisions . . . is inhabited by pagans, who have a pagan King and a language of their own. (in Nicholl, p. 5)

It is not until the description of Brunei in about 1515 by Tomé Pires that we hear that the 'islands of Borneo' are

almost all inhabited by heathen [but that] only the chief one is inhabited by Moors; it is not very long since the King became a Moor. (in Nicholl, pp. 6–7)

These European accounts, which suggest that the conversion to Islam of the ruler of Brunei occurred at the earliest in the second decade of the sixteenth century, certainly contradict the royal genealogy in the Brunei Book of Descent, which was apparently commissioned by the fourteenth Sultan, Muhyiddin. This claims that the pagan ruler, of a Dayak ethnic group, who was called Awang Alak Betatar, became a Muslim and took the name Muhammad (Leake 1990: 8). Yet again information from the Portuguese in the first quarter of the sixteenth century suggests that the fifth or sixth sultan was on the throne at that time, and therefore to square this information with the royal genealogy the first Sultan Muhammad would have had to be ruling Brunei some 200 years before.

These conflicting claims are unlikely to be resolved satisfactorily, but it may be the case that there were two neighbouring port centres in Brunei Bay in the sixteenth century, one pagan, the other Muslim. Pigafetta's account of Brunei in 1521 points to the existence of two cities, the larger one inhabited by heathens, and the other by Muslims. Pigafetta says 'The heathen king is as powerful as the Moro king, but not so haughty' (in Nicholl 1975: 11).

Be that as it may, it does still seem that it is the sixteenth century which marks the foundation of a number of Muslim dynasties around the coasts of Borneo. Veth, the Dutch scholar, refers to the establishment of the Muslim states of Sambas, Sukadana and Landak on the west coast in the sixteenth century (1854, i: 193; Irwin 1967: 3). The ruler at Banjarmasin, Pangeran Samudra, became Sultan Surian Allah or Suriansjah, and conversion to Islam there took place possibly around 1530, but no later than 1588 (Hudson 1967b: 61). Among other Muslim states reported by Europeans were Kutei in south-eastern Borneo, and Kotawaringin, in the south-west (Irwin 1967: 3; Meilink-Roelofsz 1962: 100–1).

Brunei, the most important sixteenth-century state, was described as a place of some wealth and sophistication, but Bassett has warned against exaggerating the size and impressiveness of the capital (1980). Although Brunei rose to prominence in the sixteenth century, benefiting from the transfer of some trade there from Malacca after the Portuguese seized the spice capital in 1511, reports in the early sixteenth century indicate that Brunei was only sending three junks annually to Malacca. Bassett suggests that a few features of the Brunei capital appealed to such observers as Pigafetta, but, in any case, the Brunei port would have probably appeared as much more impressive to a sixteenth-century European than it would have done to an eighteenth- or nineteenth-century Dutchman or Englishman (p. 20). Here are brief extracts from Pigafetta's record of Brunei in 1521:

[w]e went to the king's palace upon elephants . . . All the streets from the governor's house to that of the king were full of men with swords, spears and shields . . . [we] entered a large hall full of many nobles, where we sat upon a carpet . . . [the hall] was all adorned with silk hangings, and two windows . . . with brocade curtains . . . The men in the palace were all attired in cloth of gold and silk which covered their privies, and carried daggers with gold hafts adorned with pearls and precious gems, and they had many rings on their hands . . . There is a large brick wall in front of the king's house with towers like a fort, in which were mounted fifty-six bronze pieces and six of iron. (in Nicholl 1975: 9–10)

Brunei, at that time, was exporting meat, fish, rice and sago to Malacca, along with forest and other luxury goods, honey, wax, rattan, pitch, cowries, camphor, gold and pearls (Meilink-Roelofsz 1962: 84–5).

In the later sixteenth and especially into the seventeenth century, Banjarmasin to the south also began to increase in importance, particularly with the shift of Chinese interest to there from Malacca. It exported camphor, along with diamonds, gold dust, bezoar stones, animal hides, rhinoceros horn, peacocks, parrots and nutmeg. Southern Borneo also became an important source of pepper. In the seventeenth century it was grown on a piecemeal basis by the Dayaks, but as the Europeans, and especially the Dutch, began to try to establish monopolies of spice production and export, such traders as the Chinese looked elsewhere for regular supplies. It was then that the Muslim Banjarese began to take up regular pepper production in the lower Barito basin, expanding at the expense of the Dayaks and converting them to Islam, as pagans and Muslims came into increasing contact in the areas of pepper cultivation (Hudson 1967b: 65ff.; Meilink-Roelofsz 1962: 262).

Islam in the hinterland

As an ethnographic example of the process of the expansion of Islam into the interior, I shall examine the Kapuas region of West Borneo. We shall leave consideration of the structure of Bornean Malay states until chapter 7 when we will use the Sultanate of Brunei as our case-study. As I have said, there must have been some settlement in Bornean ports of Muslim traders from other parts of the archipelago as trade expanded: Malays from the west, Javanese from the south, and subsequently such peoples as the Bugis from the east. The Bugis were especially influential along the east coast of Borneo, and in parts of the west coast. But the main ancestors of the present-day Brunei, Sarawak, Kapuas, Banjar and Kutei Malays are Dayak converts to Islam.

Following the establishment of the coastal sultanates of Sambas, Sukadana and Landak in west Borneo, smaller Malay states emerged along the Kapuas river at major strategic confluences for the control of upstream trade. Probably Sekadau and Sintang were founded sometime during the seventeenth

century (Enthoven 1903, ii: 672–4). Beyond Sintang there were
the smaller states of Silat, Suhaid, Selimbau, Jongkong and
Bunut, although, as we would expect, myths relating to the
early period of these states are often contradictory (i, pp. 135–
6). Thus, it is difficult to use them to determine with any
precision when these political units emerged. However, the
furthest upstream state, Bunut, was definitely founded by
Abang Barita, a Malay trader of Dayak descent from Selimbau at the turn of the nineteenth century (i, p. 94; Bouman
1952: 56). We can assume then that the downstream states
probably went over to Islam in the eighteenth century at the
latest.

The ruling families of these different states claimed relationships with each other through kinship and marriage (Enthoven
1903, i: 128, 158), and clearly conversion took place partly
through pagan leaders marrying into the families of Muslim
rulers elsewhere. From evidence in the nineteenth century, the
capitals of many of the upriver Malay states appeared to be
modest in size. This circumstance leads us to an issue which
has been raised many times in relation to the identification and
description of South-East Asian state formations. The emergence of so-called 'states' was, in many cases, a gradual process. Thus, it is often difficult to determine whether what is
referred to as a state in local oral traditions and in some of the
secondary literature is indeed a large-scale socially stratified
political unit possessing a formal hierarchy of offices, with a
certain level of control of peoples and territories by a hereditary ruler, his family and his officers. The ability to tax one's
subjects is also an important indication of political strength; it
entails some division between rulers and ruled, some stable
form of subordination and control over the use of force in a
given domain, and a degree of functional division of administrative responsibilities.

Often the 'early states' were not, in effect, states at all and
were little more than stratified small-scale societies, usually
with a recognized hereditary chief or leader, having authority
among a federation of village communities. The situation is
made even more confusing when these leaders styled themselves as kings or rulers (*rajas*). Rousseau says of the Muslim
states of Borneo, 'While small and relatively weak, coastal

sultanates had the trappings of states . . .' (1990: 284). The Sultan of Gunung Tabur in eastern Borneo, for example, had a very modest income derived from the delivery of birds nests from the nomadic Basap, and, in Sambaliung, the Sultan lived in a bamboo house like anyone else . . . [b]ecause of the weakness of the state apparatus, revenues were not collected regularly. (p. 285)

According to van Lijnden, in the 1840s the number of households in some of the capitals of the upriver Kapuas states only amounted to about 50 at such places as Selimbau (1851: 573). It is highly likely therefore that, in the case of these states which we shall now consider, they were small outliers of the larger and more powerful domains such as Sintang and Pontianak, further downriver (plate 29), and, in most cases, would not have qualified as states in the true sense of the word. They were certainly much smaller than the large coastal polities such as Brunei and Banjarmasin, involved in international trade.

The upriver Malay rulers reckoned their power not so much in terms of territory, which was to a significant degree uninhabited and economically undeveloped, but by the number of Dayaks under their authority from whom they could expect

Plate 29   The palace of the Sultan of Pontianak

tribute, and who could be taxed. Therefore, Dayak communities did, wherever possible, often move out of the reach of a Malay ruler, if he was perceived to be too exploitative. Rousseau notes that Dayaks of the Mahakam traded in Sarawak or the Kapuas or Barito when relations with nearby Kutei were tense. Furthermore, the paramount chief of the Kenyahs in the Apau Kayan did not recognize the downriver Sultan of Bulungan as his overlord, and maintained relations with the Sultan of Brunei to the north (1990: 289–90, 294). Thus, although nominally boundaries between political units were marked by natural features such as rivers and watersheds, in practice these were ill-defined and in a state of flux. Often competing rulers claimed sovereignty over the same communities, and local village leaders tried to play one sultan off against another, and sometimes refused to deliver goods.

The ability to exercise power over various surrounding populations was therefore often uncertain, and yet, though fluid, subordinate–superordinate relations were established. The position of the Kapuas Malay settlements at the mouths of the main tributaries meant that they could control the flow of crucial trade goods. The Dayaks especially relied on the Malays for supplies of salt, and, to a lesser extent, for such items as tobacco, iron, brassware, cloth, porcelain plates and jars, pots, firearms and beads, some of which were important prestige goods in Dayak society. To increase their wealth the sultans also 'encouraged entrepreneurs to engage in the collection of jungle produce' (Rousseau 1990: 286), and they were given land to settle on, with titles and official positions. Malay rulers could also use their slaves to collect jungle produce on their behalf, and they tried to establish monopolies on such items as opium with which they traded forest goods (pp. 285, 286).

What is more, Muslim rulers, by skilfully arranging marriages with the leading families of neighbouring communities, could also exploit the situation of endemic hostility and feud between different Dayak groups. They allied themselves with certain Dayaks against others whom they wished to suppress or punish. For example, Abang Tajak, a Selimbau *raja*, launched raids against unruly Malohs, as did Abang Tella of Selimbau in the 1820s, using friendly Dayak mercenaries

(Enthoven 1903, i: 157–61). A Malay ruler could also sometimes call on assistance from other neighbouring states through his kinship links and alliances with their ruling families. Very rarely did these *rajas* keep a standing army, but instead relied on the mobilization of allies and clients. They also had greater access to firearms and ammunition.

According to much of the nineteenth-century Dutch writing on West Borneo the relations between the Malays and their Dayak subjects were mainly exploitative. There are several references to the 'ruthless' and 'cunning' practices of the Malays in their trade with the 'docile' Dayaks (Blume 1843: 109; van den Dungen Gronovius 1849: 359; van Höevell 1852: 187, 191). Yet this view needs some qualification, and it should be remembered that European ambitions could only be realized if Muslim rulers were dominated and controlled; European opinions were therefore hardly impartial in this tension between the Islamic world and European Christianity (e.g. Bassett 1980: 41ff.).

It is true that some Dayaks were subject to various kinds of relatively heavy taxation (King 1976c: 99). There were two main kinds of levy, the *hasil* and the *serah* (Enthoven 1903, i: 193; Veth 1856, ii: 337–9). The *hasil* was a direct, fixed head or door (household) tax paid in kind, and the *serah* was, in practice, a system of forced trade whereby the Dayaks delivered such items as rice and forest products in return for downstream trade goods at grossly inflated exchange rates (van Lijnden 1851: 632–3). Defaulting on the levies usually resulted in an individual being taken into debt-slavery (Veth 1854, i: 337–9). Dayaks captured in raids also became slaves, and sometimes Malay expeditions were organized with the sole purpose of taking slaves. On special occasions, such as births, marriages and deaths of the Malay ruling family, the Dayaks tied to the ruler also had to provide certain goods and services (Enthoven 1903, ii: 790–2; Veth 1854, i: 339–40).

On the other hand not all Dayaks were subjects of a Malay state. There were *mardaheka* or 'free' Dayaks, including such groups as the Ibans and the Malohs, who were located in some of the more remote northern regions of the Kapuas basin. Many refused to pay tax or tribute and they retained much of their traditional culture. In contrast, the *serah* Dayaks near

Sintang and in the low-lying southern hinterlands of the Kapuas Malay states, along such accessible rivers as the Silat,
Suhaid, Selimbau, Embau and Bunut rivers, were generally
subject to taxation. There were also Dayaks in the Melawi
area, in the vicinity of the Sultanate of Sintang, who were
categorized as *serah* such as the Lebang, Linoh, Pajak and
Keninjal (van der Willigen 1898).

It is therefore clear that Islam and Malay culture and language significantly penetrated various regions, and large numbers of pagan communities were Malayized. Even so, it should
not be assumed that all these converted Dayaks were coerced
into embracing Islam. Some enjoyed harmonious relations
with Malays, intermarried with them and therefore established family relationships, placed themselves voluntarily under the authority of a Malay ruler to ensure protection against
other hostile Dayaks, and joined Malays in raids against
others. Nevertheless, relations with Malay and Islamic culture
resulted in profound changes. As we have seen, those Dayaks
who did not convert to Islam but came under Malay influence
experienced linguistic change. Some of those are probably the
so-called Malayic Dayaks of western Borneo. Cense and Uhlenbeck say of these changes

. . . we may take it for granted that the process of extension of those
languages which resemble Malay – both structurally and as regards
their vocabulary – at the expense of earlier languages, must have
created a completely different situation in the course of time.
(1958: 13)

For these Dayaks who did become Muslim the changes were
profound. Usually it resulted in a change in ethnic affiliation,
and over time a redesignation as Malay. Of course, during the
transitional period one would find some communities, groups,
families or individuals combining traits from both Muslim-
Malay and Dayak cultures. Longhouse domicile was eventually commonly abandoned in favour of single-family dwellings.
Consumption of pork and sometimes of alcohol ceased. Thus,
hunting wild boars and keeping domestic pigs, which were
important elements in the traditional Dayak economy, declined. Usually converts moved away from shifting agriculture
to trade, inland or coastal fishing, administration and small-

scale industries. Aspects of material culture – costume, decorative arts (such as woodcarving and weaving) – were transformed. Worldviews changed. Muslims followed the tenets of their faith, saw themselves as part of a wider community of believers and were tied into Muslim-Malay political systems, which comprised state formations spread across the South-East Asian island world.

Let us then return to look in a little more detail at these processes in the Kapuas basin. Competition between Malay rulers in the area for subjects and converts can be seen in the case of the various Dayak groups in the southern tributaries. The Seberuang Dayaks, for example, an Iban-speaking group who lived along the Seberuang river, were subject to taxation by the Malay rulers of Sintang up to the mid-nineteenth century. Subsequently the Seberuangs were claimed by Pangeran Haji Mohammad Abas of Selimbau, who considered them to fall within his sphere of influence. Possibly to escape the demands of these Malay rulers some of the Seberuangs had moved out of their homeland even before the 1850s, and were subsequently to be found scattered in various tributaries of the Kapuas (King 1976c: 96). In the 1870s, it was noted that the Seberuangs had abandoned some of their traditional ways and many had adopted Malay dress (Tromp 1879: 112).

What is more, in the 1890s Enthoven reported that Malay settlements were to be found extensively along the neighbouring Silat river, and only a few longhouses of Silat Dayaks remained in its middle and upper course (1903, i: 185). It was said that they had been subject to one of the early rulers of Silat, Pangeran Agung, who had suppressed them (Bouman 1952: 70). The situation is similar with regard to the Suhaid Dayaks of the Suhaid river: they had been heavily Malayized, and had long been taxed by the Malay ruler of the Suhaid state at the river-mouth. For a time they had also fallen within the sphere of influence of Silat. Suhaids, along with Suhaid Malays, who were presumably Dayak converts to Islam, were often mobilized by the Suhaid ruler against the Ibans, who engaged in headhunting raids against the state (Enthoven 1903, i: 170, 180–2, 216).

In the eighteenth century, the Malay state of Selimbau became increasingly powerful. At one time it claimed hegemony over those Dayaks in the region of Selimbau town, the populations along the Embau river, the Kantu' of the Empanang to the north, and some communities in the Bunut river basin, although some of these communities must have been subjects in theory rather than in practice (Bouman 1952: 73–4; Enthoven 1903, i: 141–2, 170). Selimbau also fought against but did not suppress various Maloh villages to the north.

In the mid-nineteenth century, Pangeran Haji Mohammad Abas, the ruler of the state and a fervent Muslim, energetically spread the Islamic faith to the Embau and Bunut rivers, and at that time the large community of Embau Malays emerged from converted Dayaks, some of whom continued to live in longhouses (Bouman 1924: 194; Enthoven 1903, i: 162, 205–6, 210; Veth 1854, i: 54). In the region to the south of Selimbau there were peoples called *orang-pengaki* or Pekaki Malays (Bouman 1924: 185; Enthoven 1903, i: 168–9), who were Islamized Dayaks. These too remained in longhouses, and apparently continued to follow some Dayak customs, including drinking ricewine and eating pork.

The last Malay state to be established in the upper Kapuas was Bunut, which emerged in the early nineteenth century. Its capital originally comprised Islamized Embau and Bunut Dayaks and under its ruler, Abang Barita, a sizeable Malay population came into being from the mid-nineteenth century in the Bunut river basin and its main tributaries, the Boyan, Tebaung, Semangut, Sebilit, Mentebah and Suruk (Bouman 1924: 194–5). Nevertheless, some upriver Dayaks, although acknowledging the ruler's sovereignty, did not pay taxes (Enthoven 1903, i: 108).

Relations of mutual support and political interest between Malay rulers and leading Dayak families are appropriately illustrated with regard to the Maloh Dayaks of the upper Kapuas. Malohs were closely involved with the affairs of the Muslim state of Bunut. Abang Barita, its founder, was of part-Maloh descent. His father, Abang (Patih) Turan, was a Maloh aristocrat who had embraced Islam on a visit to Selimbau and married a woman from the Malay ruling family of Suhaid. Abang Barita married a daughter of the Malay *raja* of Selimbau and took the title Panembahan Adi Paku Negara (King 1985a: 59–60). One of Abang Barita's daughters, Dayang

Suntai, then married Laksamana, a Maloh aristocrat from the Taman subdivision (Enthoven 1903, i: 96–7) and the successor to Barita, Abang Suria, his son-in-law, had a grandfather, Abang Harun, who was a Maloh from the Embaloh river.

According to Maloh oral tradition and information from Enthoven (i, pp. 172–8), the Malay state of Jongkong, downstream of Bunut, was, in part, established by converted Maloh Dayaks who had initially divided, under the leadership of a local aristocrat, from their relatives on the Embaloh river. Their leader took the Malay title Raja Kiyai Patih Uda. The father of one of Patih Uda's successors was a Maloh aristocrat from the Palin river (i, pp. 158, 166).

Obviously the conversion process in the circumstances described above owed much to the decisions and actions of native Dayaks, and it was not the simple result of coercion or positive proselytizing by Malay rulers. Some Maloh aristocratic headmen must have seen that it was to their advantage to ally with Malay *rajas*; the relationship was usually cemented by marriage. Either the *raja* would himself take a Dayak wife, or offer a daughter in marriage to a Dayak aristocrat. In this way the Malay *raja* secured allies and ensured trading relations. From his side the native aristocrat might enhance his economic and political position with the prospect of external support, protection and access to trade goods. The same kinds of relations between native chiefs and Malay rulers have been reported from other parts of Borneo. Rousseau notes, for example, that some Modang chiefs of the Mahakam converted to Islam 'in order to please the Sultan of Kutei' (1990: 83), and Bock noted in the later nineteenth century that Raja Dinda, a Modang chief, paid yearly tribute to the Sultan (1881: 52, 65).

One impetus for the conversion to Islam of native aristocrats was conflict in a Dayak village between competing and ambitious individuals. To enhance the chances of success an aristocrat might seek an alliance with Muslim outsiders, or alternatively the loser in a power struggle might decide to express discontent with the prevailing order by moving away, sometimes with his followers, marrying into Malay society and converting to Islam. In stratified Dayak societies there was clearly a proclivity for marriages between high-ranking natives and leading families from outside, whether Dayak or Malay. Even low-ranking villagers, unhappy with their lot, might turn to Islam for salvation. Conversion also resulted from contacts between local Dayaks and Malay traders, forest collectors, entrepreneurs and officials who visited surrounding villages. Some Malays even settled in or near Dayak communities and married locally (Rousseau 1990: 286–7).

Obviously Islam and Malay culture varied in significance for different individuals and groups in Dayak society. What it did was provide an alternative or a different set of values, behaviours and possibilities for the prestige-seeking and power-conscious Dayaks, or for those who were dissatisfied with their own social and cultural conditions. In that sense it reinforced and accelerated divisions and conflicts in Dayak societies. Overall, of course, Islam, and to a much lesser extent Hinduism and Buddhism before it, resulted in increasing differentiation in Austronesian societies, and, in particular, was associated with and consolidated the divisions between state-based and tribal societies.

Nevertheless, the processes and rate of conversion to Islam in Borneo were obviously affected by European intervention. When Europeans first came into contact with the coastal communities of Borneo they were confronted by a series of Muslim states, which controlled the main trade routes, and which dominated the movement of forest produce from the interior of the island. As we have seen, Islam continued to expand well after Europeans established themselves in this part of the world, but gradually the European presence had an effect both on the Muslim states and on tribal societies, particularly from the nineteenth century onwards. In the next chapter we shall examine in detail the European period, and its consequences for Bornean societies and cultures.

5

Europeans and Borneo: From Early Trade to Independence

European trade and commerce

Although the Europeans established no firm territorial presence in Borneo until the nineteenth century, there had been European contacts with South-East Asia from the early sixteenth century. The increasing involvement of Europeans in trade, their attempts to monopolize certain items of commerce, particularly spices, and their intervention in local politics by supporting some rulers or factions at the expense of others, gradually came to have important consequences for Bornean societies and patterns of trade.

Be that as it may, the marginal position of Borneo in relation to the great trade routes, its uninviting and difficult environment and the small and scattered population, resulted in little direct European intervention there until well over 300 years after the first European traders came to this part of the world. In much of the period of commerce and trade, prior to the setting up of colonial administrations, the Europeans were still only one set of traders competing with others, both natives such as the Malays, Javanese and Bugis, and outsiders like the Chinese and Indians (van Leur 1955). Yet over time the Dutch and the British in Borneo were to gain an unrivalled ascendancy. Before then local processes and events continued to be of most significance – the conversion to Islam, the establishment of Muslim states, native migrations through the interior and the eventual settlement of most of the island.

The Portuguese were the first Europeans to establish commercial relations with Borneo, most especially Brunei. After the defeat of the Sultan of Malacca at the hands of the Portuguese commander, Alfonso de Albuquerque, in 1511, some of the trade of this spice emporium shifted to Brunei; so much so that it enjoyed a period of rising prosperity, territorial expansion and increasing political power in the sixteenth century (Meilink-Roelofsz 1962). Brunei power extended both to the west coasts of Borneo and north-eastwards to the Philippines. Brown also suggests that 'Many of the Muslims fleeing Malacca perhaps went to Brunei' (1970: 141). With the transfer of Chinese interest from Malacca, the southern Borneo port of Banjarmasin also began to attract more trade from this period, and commanded some Dutch commercial attention in the seventeenth century.

The Portuguese from their base in Malacca visited Brunei, especially for camphor, and Bruneian traders went regularly to Malacca, but, as we have seen, Brunei did not generate a vast amount of trade. Apparently relations between the Portuguese and Bruneis were generally amicable. The main Portuguese commercial interests lay elsewhere in the eastern Indonesian spice islands, and Brunei was no military threat to them (Leake 1990: 16ff.). The other early European power in the region, the Spanish, initially had little contact with Brunei. However, with the progressive Spanish subjugation of the Philippine islands to the north, and Spanish perceptions of the political danger of Brunei influence among Muslims in the southern Philippines, the two powers came into contention. The Spanish adopted an increasingly hostile attitude towards the sultanate, demanding that it recognize Spanish authority in such places as the Sulu Islands and allow Christian missionaries into Brunei territory. A consequence of this hostility was a Spanish attack on Brunei in April 1578 and a brief Spanish occupation of the port (Brown 1970: 142). The Spanish interest in the southern Philippines did result in the gradual weakening of Brunei influence there during the seventeenth century, but the Spanish inability to exert full control over the south led to a partial power vacuum there. Eventually the Sulu Sultanate itself emerged as a power to rival Brunei in the later eighteenth century, bringing parts of northern Borneo, which were formerly under Brunei dominion, within Sulu's domains (Warren 1981).

Despite these relations between Brunei and Europeans in the sixteenth and the first part of the seventeenth century, Irwin remarks, no outside power 'succeeded in establishing permanent dominion over Brunei or any other part of Borneo' (1967: 4). This was a task eventually left to the Dutch and British. Dutch fleets of the East Indies Company (Verenigde Oost-Indische Compagnie, VOC) began to arrive in eastern waters at the end of the sixteenth century. Admiral Olivier van Noort visited Brunei in December 1600–January 1601, and trading relations developed. However, Brunei was not a major interest of the Dutch; instead they concentrated on Banjarmasin and the pepper trade between there and the Dutch foothold in Bantam in west Java. In 1603 the Dutch based a factory at Banjarmasin to coordinate the pepper trade, but conflict broke out leading to a Dutch attack against the sultanate in 1612, and the Sultan fleeing inland (Irwin 1967: 4).

The Dutch came to be the major European power in the archipelago in the seventeenth century after their defeat of the Portuguese and the taking of Malacca in 1641. Throughout much of this period the Dutch attempted to control pepper exports from Banjarmasin; they also established themselves at Kotawaringin. But in 1669 their commercial interest in southern Borneo dwindled and they did not renew it until the eighteenth century. Lindblad says 'Violence, treachery and disappointment haunted the attempts of the VOC to wrest control over the pepper trade from the Banjarese sultan' (1988: 8).

Dutch attempts to establish a firm commercial presence on the west coast of Borneo also came to nothing. Their interest was in the gold and diamonds produced there. They established a factory at Sambas in the early part of the seventeenth century, and a settlement at Sukadana further south, both of which foundered. It was extremely difficult to ensure that the sultans complied with the terms of the trade contracts and the Dutch did not have the resources or manpower at that time to support a permanent military presence there. However, in 1698 the Dutch sided with the Sultan of Landak in a war against

Sukadana, resulting in the latter's defeat. Their involvement came about through their alliance with the Sultan of Bantam in west Java, who had met the request from Landak for his support. Bantam claimed certain rights of sovereignty over the western Borneo coast.

This precarious foothold which the Dutch had in Borneo gradually changed from the mid-eighteenth century, when they erected a fort at Tatas Island in downtown Banjarmasin in an attempt to enforce their pepper contract with the Sultan. In 1787 they also intervened successfully in an inter-dynastic struggle within the sultanate, and in theory at least, assumed territorial control through their surrogate, Sultan Nata (Lindblad 1988: 9). Nevertheless, by 1767 Nata had resumed administrative responsibility in the south.

In the latter part of the eighteenth century the Dutch had, as in the south, intervened strategically in an inter-native dispute on the west coast. In 1772 they had supported an adventurer of Arab descent, Abdu'r-Rahman, who had set himself up as leader of the settlement of Pontianak near the mouth of the Landak river. He was to challenge the authority of the Raja of Landak, and, in the event, the Dutch recognized Abdu'r-Rahman as Sultan of Pontianak and located a factory there. They did so on the grounds that the Javanese Sultan of Bantam had ceded his rights in western Borneo to the Dutch. The Dutch, in turn, supported Abdu'r-Rahman against the rival neighbouring states of Sukadana and Bugis-dominated Mempawah.

Eventually the internal corruption and maladministration of the VOC led to its collapse, and together with the problems experienced by the Dutch in Europe towards the end of the eighteenth century, increasing commercial competition from the British and other Europeans in the archipelago and the temporary occupation of the Dutch East Indies territories by the British between 1811 to 1816, this stalled any further Dutch initiatives in Borneo until later in the nineteenth century (Ricklefs 1981). Irwin says

By the close of the [eighteenth] century, the only visible evidence that the Dutch East India Company had ever exercised authority in the island at all was one small Government fort at Tatas on the south coast. (1967: 7)

The British too, in the form of their own East India Company, had attempted to establish footholds around the coasts of Borneo in the seventeenth century, mainly to compete with the Dutch in the spice trade of eastern Indonesia. They had founded factories at Sukadana, Sambas and Landak in the seventeenth century and Banjarmasin in the seventeenth and eighteenth centuries. However, by the later eighteenth century British interest had turned to India and to the trade in tea, raw cotton and opium with China. Thus, the British came to see the northern Borneo coasts as potential staging-posts on the trade routes between India and China. In this connection, they became increasingly involved in the affairs of the north-east coast and the Sulu archipelago, wedged between the spheres of influence of Spain and Holland.

This region was envisaged particularly as a point of distribution for British and Indian goods to the Indonesian archipelago, and as a means to attract Chinese junk trade in search of marine and forest products. As Warren argues, the growing importance of the Tausug-dominated Sulu Sultanate from the second half of the eighteenth century rested on its role as a regional emporium and point of exchange for British and Indian goods on the one hand and Chinese on the other. It also attracted Bugis merchants who were based on the east coast of Borneo in the Sultanate of Kutei and in the small realms of Berau and Bulungan, and who connected up Sulu commerce with the eastern Indonesian spice trade.

The British were attracted here especially because of their need to acquire local trade goods with which they could exchange Chinese tea and silk from Canton and thus limit their shipments of silver to China (Bassett 1971: 1). They could trade British and Indian commodities, especially opium, lead, iron, gunpowder and cannon for South-East Asian items attractive to the Chinese market.

In 1761, a servant of the East India Company at Madras, Alexander Dalrymple, made an agreement with the Sultan of Sulu to establish a factory in his domains. In 1763 the British flag was raised on the island of Balambangan off the north Borneo coast, and in 1773 a factory was founded. At this time the Brunei Sultan had also tried to encourage the British to locate themselves at the island of Labuan off Brunei Bay to, in part, ensure British protection against Sulu hostilities (Brown 1970: 145). The British at first accepted the offer, but eventually withdrew, as they then did in Balambangan.

With regard to Balambangan it was Dalrymple's vision that

this unimposing uninhabited island could become a regional trade centre through Chinese immigration and settlement, diversion of the junk trade from Batavia [the Dutch capital in Java] and Manila, and provision of a local market for Bengal manufactures especially to the enterprising Bugis traders to the south. (Warren 1981: 18–19)

Unfortunately the factory did not realize Dalrymple's ambitions; it was badly managed, and it was sacked by hostile Sulu forces in 1775 (Bassett 1971: 28). Britain was preoccupied with affairs in India, and wary of intruding too much into the domains of the Spanish to the north. However, they had outmanoeuvred the Dutch in this region of Borneo. What is more, British involvement in the Sulu region had undoubtedly stimulated the expansion of Sulu commerce. It had resulted in Sulu-generated slave-raiding along Borneo's coasts and further afield partly to acquire the manpower to gather marine products for the trade with China.

Overall, the results of three centuries of European commercial contact had not been particularly marked. The Europeans had obviously affected trading patterns, and, in part, had been instrumental in the rise and fall of coastal states and their political fortunes. Spanish and British activities, for example, contributed to the decline of Brunei's position in north-east Borneo and the southern Philippines, and the emergence of the Sulu Sultanate as a regional power. The Dutch too had played a part in the establishment and expansion of the Sultanate of Pontianak at the expense of other west-coast states such as Landak. Obviously the interior natives were supplying goods for these commercial networks but they were little affected, if at all, by European contacts.

European colonialism

It was not until well into the nineteenth century, with the maturing of industrial capitalism in Europe, the enormous increase in wealth and power which this entailed and the technological advances in European military capabilities, transport and communications, that Borneo was drawn into wider Western imperial systems. There was an increasing European need for raw materials and control of their sources, access to markets, and avenues for investment, as well as an intensification of competition between the European powers for resources. Ultimately this led to territory in Borneo being carved up between regimes protected by Britain in the north, and the Dutch colonial state in the south. But as Irwin notes, the two European powers viewed Borneo rather differently (1967: 10). For the British the interest was mainly strategic, to protect British shipping along the sea routes to China. The British therefore wanted to secure the northern coasts against competition, without the need to encumber themselves with the administration of territories. The Dutch, on the other hand

always thought of Borneo in relation to Java, and hoped, when circumstances allowed, to make it part of the Netherlands India . . . . (p. 10)

Partly for these reasons, the Dutch colonial government was the direct agent of incorporation in southern Borneo, while the north was brought into the British imperial system by indirect means.

Following the return of their Indonesian possessions in 1816, after the brief British interregnum, the Dutch began to reassert their earlier claims to sovereignty on the southern and western Borneo coasts. Yet even so, Borneo played a much smaller part in Dutch aims and policies than the vitally important island of Java. The first task facing the new Dutch Commissioner for Borneo, Mr Jacob d'Arnaud van Bockholtz, was to re-establish relations with the important sultanate of Banjarmasin. This was done in 1817, with the cession of territories to the Dutch and concessions on the exploitation of gold, diamonds and timber. Then, in 1818, the sultans of the two west coast states of Pontianak and Sambas acknowledged Dutch sovereignty there. As a result, Dutch Residents were assigned to Pontianak, Sambas and Banjarmasin, and Assistant Residents to Mempawah and Landak.

Nominal contact also commenced with the interior. In the 1820s, both the Government Commissioner, L. C. Hartman, and Georg Müller, the Inspector of the Interior Provinces, travelled into the upper Kapuas basin, and we begin to get our first reports of the native tribes there (Veth 1854, i). After this promising start little more was done until the 1840s. The crippling war which the Dutch had to fight against local resistance in Java between 1825 and 1830 sapped Dutch strength (Ricklefs 1981: 112–13), and, although they maintained Residents at Pontianak and Banjarmasin, Sambas was reduced to an Assistant-Residency, and a Dutch official presence in Mempawah and Landak was removed altogether. As Irwin notes, the task for a relatively weakened Dutch administration was enormous:

Piracy had to be suppressed, trade had to be stimulated, revenues collected. There were innumerable treaties to be made with the petty kingdoms around the coasts, head-hunting Dyak tribes to be pacified and civilized, powerful and independent Chinese mining communities to be brought into submission. (1967: 51)

Nevertheless, Dutch capacities and resources improved from the mid-nineteenth century, and it remained their priority to operationalize their claims to sovereignty in Borneo, keep out other Western powers, especially the British, and establish an environment for trade and commerce so that profits could be realized and an administrative presence financed. Thus, traditional political systems which sustained piratical raiding and inter-tribal feuding and headhunting had to be transformed. Certain ethical considerations also played a part in European objectives. The notion of a European civilizing mission is well known. Perceived barbaric institutions such as slavery and severing heads could not be tolerated.

Christian missionaries were also an essential part of the Western enterprise, in company with administrators and traders. Conversion to Christianity was to have a profound effect on the cultures of interior peoples (plate 30). But the introduction of churches and priests was not merely guided by religious and ethical aims; political and economic motives were also at work. Religious conversion was an effective means to undermine the power-base of the Muslim sultanates; these would

Plate 30   Lundu Anglican Church in Sarawak

lose followers and access to labour resources. It was also seen to be an important way of establishing law and order, by reducing slavery and headhunting, and socializing European subjects, partially at least, into the culture of the dominating power. Military action alone would have been insufficient to pacify hostile tribes.

A key event which led to a reinvigoration of Dutch interest in Borneo and an increasing involvement of the British in the north was the arrival of the English adventurer, James Brooke, at the Sarawak river in 1839. Brooke's objectives were, of course, exploration, and to increase scientific knowledge, but also to provide some advantage to British interests in the area (Crisswell 1978). As we have seen, the political position of Brunei had been in decline since at least the seventeenth century. It had been weakened by the rise of Sulu, and Dutch action on the west coast had led to the waning of Brunei's power there. Yet the Sultan's representatives still had authority along the north-west coasts from the Sarawak river to Brunei Bay, although in the district of Sarawak a rebellion of local Dayaks and Malays was under way against their Brunei overlords. Brooke successfully intervened on the side of the Brunei Governor of the district, Pengiran Muda Hashim, and, in return for his assistance in quashing the rebellion, was installed in 1841 as Governor of Sarawak, or popularly as the 'White' Rajah, by the Brunei Sultan, Omar Ali Saifuddin II (Baring-Gould and Bampfylde 1909: 73ff.). Clearly the Sultan hoped that through Brooke, he could secure British protection against his enemies, especially the Sulus to the north.

Brooke therefore occupied a position not dissimilar to others of the Sultan's regional representatives. But in 1842 he managed to obtain the rights over the territories in what is now the western region of Sarawak in return for an annual tribute to the Sultan, and, in 1843, secured them in perpetuity. From then on James Brooke took advantage of the weakened sultanate to extend his territories at the expense of Brunei. As someone of some position and influence he could and did call on the support of the British Navy to assist him in putting down piracy and headhunting, especially in the Saribas and Skrang areas, where Ibans, in alliance with Malays, had acquired reputations as fearsome raiders. But despite Brooke's desire for British government recognition and his request that a Crown Colony be established, Sarawak was only granted Protectorate status in 1888. Nevertheless, Brooke was appointed British confidential agent in Borneo by the Foreign Office in 1844 (Tarling 1963: 121).

By the 1880s James Brooke and his successor, his nephew Charles, had swallowed up Brunei possessions along the coasts of Borneo. The rebellious regions of the Skrang and Saribas were subdued and acquired in the 1850s; the important Melanau sago-producing regions between the Rejang rivers and Bintulu were brought under Brooke control in the early 1860s, and then the basin of the Baram river in 1882 (Crisswell 1978). The Brooke administration also penetrated inland, constructing fortifications to pacify war-like peoples such as the Ibans. In October 1863, for example, a great peace-making was concluded at Kanowit on the Rejang river between the Ibans of the lower Rejang and the Kayans of the interior (Freeman 1970: 134). The Kayans thereafter accepted Brooke rule. However, it was not until the 1880s that tax revenues were more effectively collected in interior Sarawak, when a fort was established in Belaga in 1884, and the 1890s that the Kayans and Kenyahs of the Baram area came under Brooke control (Rousseau 1990: 32).

During this period of Brooke expansion Britain had established relations with the Sultan of Brunei. In December 1846, the two parties signed an agreement ceding Labuan, an offshore island, to Britain. Labuan served as a coaling station and a convenient stopping-off point on the route between Singapore and China. It was also a base for combating piracy and countering the possible intervention of other foreign powers. The following year an Anglo-Brunei Treaty was signed (Leake 1990: 30) to ensure British control of trade along the northwest coast, free trade and access to Brunei ports, and to prevent the Sultan ceding territory to any other nation without the consent of the British government. James Brooke was appointed Commissioner and Consul-General to the Sultan of Brunei and the Independent Chiefs of Borneo in 1847 by the Foreign Secretary, and become the first Governor of Labuan in 1848.

The remaining regions of the north and north-east coasts were eventually to come within the British sphere of influence by an equally circuitous route. From the later eighteenth century, the domains of the Sultan of Sulu had increasingly become a focus of Western interest. Aside from the established powers in the area – the British, Dutch and Spanish – there were also merchants and traders from America, Germany, Italy and Austria. In the mid-1870s, Baron von Overbeck, Consul of the Austro-Hungarian Empire at Hong Kong, and sometime manager of the China opium firm of Dent and Company, acquired rights in a large part of these coastal areas, ceded by the Sultan of Brunei (Tregonning 1965). Von Overbeck went into partnership with Alfred Dent, the head of a London-based firm of merchants and son of his former employer, and together they managed to get Brunei officially to cede these territories to them; they concluded a similar agreement in 1877 with the Sultan of Sulu, who laid similar claims to these regions (Wright 1970: 126ff.). The foundation of the British position in the north-east was helped enormously by the decisive defeat of pirates by the British Navy in the Marudu Bay region in 1845.

Von Overbeck withdrew from his partnership in 1879, having failed to gain Austrian government support for his venture, and leaving the Borneo territories in the hands of Dent and his associates in London. In 1881 Dent's interests were acquired by a new body, the British North Borneo Company, one of its leading members being Dent himself. In the same year it obtained official British government recognition for its enterprise in northern Borneo by the granting of a Royal Charter (Black 1983: 30ff.). The Chartered Company administered what came to be known as British North Borneo, and along with Sarawak and the desperately weakened Sultanate of Brunei, was granted Protectorate status in 1888.

Despite Brunei's British protection, Britain did not prevent Rajah Charles Brooke from annexing the Sultan's Limbang territories in 1890, cutting a wedge into the heart of the sultanate and leaving it with two enclaves of land surrounded on all landward sides by Sarawak. Britain regularized these territorial arrangements and finally established a firm presence in Brunei in 1906. In 1905–6 Britain and Brunei signed an agreement for the placement of a British Resident in Brunei. The Sultan was to accept and act on the Resident's advice in all matters except those relating to Islam and Malay customs. The main tasks for the early Residents were to settle finally boundaries between Sarawak and Brunei, to establish a revenue-base for the administration by centralizing revenue collecting procedures and to reorganize administrative structures to take on new and expanding roles (Horton 1984: 12ff.).

After the 'period of neglect' in south Borneo, the Dutch began in earnest a forward movement there in the 1840s. This was to some extent a result of Dutch apprehensions at the activities of James Brooke in Sarawak and the assumption that he represented a reinvigoration of British imperial interests in the Indonesian archipelago. It was also presumably prompted by the adventures of James Erskine Murray, who made an abortive attempt in 1844 to expand British trade into the heartland of Dutch Borneo in the Mahakam basin and the Sultanate of Kutei (Saunders 1986).

The Dutch had been troubled by the British commercial presence in northern Borneo in the 1830s and, to forestall this, some officials had hoped for a Dutch arrangement with the Brunei Sultan; this came to nothing. In 1844 the Dutch appointed A. L. Weddik as the Commissioner and Inspector for Borneo, Riouw and Lingga, to establish, on a firm basis,

Dutch sovereign rights there. The Dutch promoted fresh initiatives to negotiate or renegotiate contracts and treaties with
local rulers, secure law and order and encourage scientific
exploration into the interior (Enthoven 1903; King 1991b:
114). One expression of this renewed interest was the extension of Dutch power into eastern Borneo. Up to the 1840s their
attention had been devoted almost exclusively to the western
and southern districts, and even then only to the coastal
margins. The Dutch began to negotiate treaties with the east
coast, which comprised a series of sultanates: from north to
south, Bulungan, Gunung Tabur and Sambaliung (which were
formerly part of the Sultanate of Berau, partitioned in 1770),
Kutei and Pasir. Indeed, in 1817 the Sultan of Banjarmasin had
ceded his claims to these eastern states to the Dutch, but they
had had negligible contact with the Dutch up to 1844 (Irwin
1967: 44ff.).

In 1846 Weddik was given the post of first Governor of
Borneo and its Dependencies. It was decided to establish a
unified administration with the capital at Sintang, some 300
miles into the interior. This was largely to warn off the ambitious and expansionist Rajah Brooke to the north, who had
also been establishing contact with various local rulers in
Dutch West Borneo. This move was meant to indicate Dutch
intentions to consolidate their control in the interior. But it
was premature because Holland still did not have the resources
or the infrastructure and transport links to sustain a capital
and a significant administrative presence in the interior.

Instead in 1848 two administrative divisions, each headed by
Residents, were formed – the Westerafdeeling (Western Division) with its seat at Pontianak, and the Zuider- en Ooster-
afdeeling (Southern and Eastern Division) with its capital at
Banjarmasin. Aside from these administrative rearrangements
the Dutch had to begin to examine the economic and commercial possibilities of the interior, and obviously mineral exploration was an early focus of interest. A Government Mining
Service was established in 1852, although as with the British
in the north, the Dutch had only limited success in exploiting
Borneo's coal deposits. There was local native resistance to it,
extreme environmental and transport difficulties and a lack of
labour to work the mines.

Of more significance were the goldmining areas of western Borneo (Cator 1936: 138–80; de Groot 1885; Jackson 1970). Chinese goldminers had been brought into West Borneo by local Malay rulers as early as the 1740s to exploit the rich gold deposits inland of Mempawah. They were a lucrative source of revenue for the Sultan of Sambas and the Raja of Mempawah. The deposits were concentrated in the areas between Mandor and Montrado. But by the mid-nineteenth century, the Chinese, numbering about 50,000 at that time, were organized into independent, self-governing *kongsis*, which, among other things, levied their own taxes, and smuggled goods such as opium, salt and gunpowder into the districts from Singapore. These *kongsis* were alliances of mining unions along with their farming and trading members and they had considerable political power (de Groot 1885). There was also much conflict and competition between rival *kongsis* for control of the commercial gold deposits, and this intensified as various mines became exhausted.

Tensions began to emerge between the Dutch and Chinese from 1850 when the Netherlands Indies Government tried to bring the *kongsis* under its administrative control and secure revenues from them. In 1854 the Dutch sent a large military expedition into the Chinese districts and quickly secured their submission (van Rees 1858). The Dutch subsequently abolished the *kongsis*, but gradually, as the gold deposits became exhausted, some Chinese communities moved away – some on to other interior regions to work gold, such as in Tayan, Sekadau and Sintang, or to Bau in Sarawak, others to take up cash-crop cultivation of pepper, gambier, coconuts and rubber, or trade and shopkeeping in upriver settlements.

In establishing their control in western Borneo the Dutch had to pacify and control the Chinese districts, but in the south they became involved in a protracted conflict in the Banjarmasin sultanate, specifically in a succession dispute. The candidate whom the Dutch chose to support met much local opposition, which resulted in the so-called 'Banjarmasin War'. From 1859 to 1864 the Dutch struggled to control the insurrection. However, the conflict did not officially end in the coastal regions until 1867, and it continued sporadically in the interior until 1905 (Avé and King 1986). To confirm their

position following the suppression of the opposition, the
Dutch established direct rule in the territories of Banjarma-
sin. Along with the imposition of direct rule in the western
Borneo mining districts, the Dutch had clearly indicated their
political and territorial objectives in the lands to the south of
Britain's sphere of influence.

Over the next half century the Dutch gradually extended
their political control into the interior, and, like James and
Charles Brooke to the north, they were involved in pacifying
headhunters and eliminating inter-tribal feuding. For example,
a great peace-making between hostile Iban and Maloh communities in western Borneo was concluded in the 1880s (King
1985a: 65). But it was not until 1895 that a Dutch administrator (*controleur*) was appointed to Putus Sibau in a newly
created Upper Kapuas Subdistrict (Onderafdeeling Boven-Kapoeas) in interior western Borneo (Enthoven 1903). Furthermore, it was only in 1900 that a *controleur* was posted to the
upper Mahakam, and in 1904 the Sultan of Kutei ceded this
region to the Dutch. Similarly in 1900 the Kenyah chief, Pingan
Sorang, welcomed the Dutch administrator van Walcheren to
the Apau Kayan, and in 1911 a civilian administrative post was
established (Black 1985; King 1989a: 17). Commenting on this
extension of Dutch power Rousseau notes that

For a long time, the Dutch colonial adminstration showed little
interest in central Borneo [but] [b]y 1909, Bulungan, the Tidung
lands, the upper Mahakam, and the Apau Kayan were visited regularly. (1990: 33, 34)

Along with pacification came Christian missions. Schools
were opened with instruction in Dutch, and basic medical
facilities were provided. By the second decade of the twentieth century a Roman Catholic Capuchin mission had been
established as far inland as the upper Kapuas basin; the same
mission had started in the Mahakam in 1907 (King 1985a).
An immediate effect was to slow down the pace of native
conversion to Islam. In addition, it enabled recruitment of
educated natives into the lower levels of the colonial administration. Schärer, for example, says of the Ngaju area and
the work of the Protestant church there, established in the
1830s,

The Administration increasingly attracted mission-educated Ngaju into the civil service, and appointed them as officials, for the purpose of its pacification policy, among strange tribes and on other rivers, in place of tribal functionaries who were no longer recognised. (1963: 2)

There were also indigenous syncretic religious responses arising from the extension of Dutch colonial administrative control and sometimes specifically from mission activity. Local prophets emerged who founded sectarian or cult movements. Probably the most well-known was the Bungan movement which flourished among the Apau Kayan Kenyahs in the late 1940s and then expanded to Sarawak. Its prophet was Juk (Jok) Apuy. It streamlined old beliefs and practices, removing the complications of ritual prohibitions, the restrictions of unfavourable omens and the need to perform animal sacrifices (King 1978c). Subsequently it declined in importance and has now been largely replaced by Christianity. Bungan was also initially a new religion of the commoner class, and it has been seen too as a reaction to inequalities in the central Borneo stratified societies: Juk Apuy attempted to democratize religion and do away with the 'religious legitimations of stratification' (Rousseau 1990: 202). However, aristocrats eventually managed to reintroduce into the Bungan movement aspects of the traditional religion which supported social inequality.

Bungan was one among many religious responses to change as the Europeans began to undermine and transform long-established ways of life. Elsewhere in Dutch Borneo millenarian movements emerged. Among the Luangan Dayaks in south-eastern Borneo, the so-called *nyuli* movement flourished in the 1920s. It was preoccupied with 'a return to the "golden age" of man's immortality as foretold in Kaharingan mythology' (Weinstock 1983: 118–19). *Nyuli* was derived from the local Luangan word *suli* meaning 'to rise up' or 'resurrection from death'. Thus, the central belief of the movement was the release of the souls of dead Luangan from the Afterworld, Gunung Lumut, and their return to the land of the living. On their return the ancestral spirits would introduce into this world all the 'glories of heaven' and bring back the sacred gong of immortality. As Weinstock notes, the *nyuli* movement was prompted by increased Dutch colonial interference in native life: administrative control and resettlement, land registration and surveys, forced labour and taxation (pp. 120–4). Other religious responses to change have been reported from the Mualang of Dutch West Borneo (Dunselman 1955) and from the Murut in British North Borneo in 1915 (Black 1983).

A final element of European intervention which is worth reporting is that of exploration and scientific discovery. With regard to the initial stages of establishing colonial rule, journeys of exploration were an important means of showing the flag, making contact with local leaders and collecting information and intelligence about economic opportunities. Given the vast territories involved, it was the Dutch who sponsored and organized the most impressive expeditions. Probably the most famous figure in late nineteenth-century Dutch exploration of Borneo was A. W. Nieuwenhuis. It was he who was involved in the great Central Borneo Expedition of 1893–4 into the upper Kapuas region. Nieuwenhuis, then medical officer in the Dutch East Indies Army, was responsible for ethnological investigations; other colleagues included J. Büttikofer (as the zoologist), H. Hallier (as the botanist) and G. A. F. Molengraaff (principally as the geologist). Nieuwenhuis was subsequently to make further journeys into interior Borneo in 1896–7 and 1898–1900. His writings provide a wealth of ethnographic information on the region, especially on the Kayans (1900, 1904–7); and Molengraaff's geological work is one of the best surveys of its kind which we have for parts of central Borneo (1900). But as Whittier has said of Nieuwenhuis's expedition to the Apau Kayan in 1900

His expedition had scientific overtones; the party carried out extensive mapping and made floral and faunal collections, but it was at base a political mission. (1973: 32)

Over the next several decades until the Second World War, the European powers contented themselves with consolidating their political and economic position, by establishing a firm and regulated administrative presence, promoting economic development, introducing transport, warehouse and dock facilities and improving welfare, health and community facilities in the form of schools, clinics and hospitals, although these latter were by no means generally available.

152 *Europeans and Borneo*

There were outbreaks of resistance and rebellion against European control. We have seen that some responses took the form of religious or millenarian movements. The Brookes in Sarawak had a difficult time combating Iban headhunting raids. The Dutch faced unrest among the Tebidah Dayaks in 1891 and the Ot Danums in 1896, in the Melawi region; Dayaks of the upper Mahakam were engaged in resistance against the Sultan of Kutei in 1905, as were the Segai Dayaks against the Sultanate of Bulungan in 1906. These Malay rulers, having concluded treaties with the Dutch, and with Dutch support, made increased demands on their subjects (Avé and King 1986: 24–5). Nevertheless, the Europeans ultimately secured respect for their rule, and instituted law and order, particularly through the institution of inter-tribal peace-making (plate 31). What Rousseau concludes for interior Borneo has general relevance to the whole island. He says

The main effect of colonial rule on central Borneo was the disappearance of headhunting and warfare by 1910–25. (1990: 35)

I shall be considering some of the recent changes affecting Dayaks more fully in chapter 10. But these processes of transformation were really set in motion during the European

Plate 31   The great peace-making at Marudi, Baram District, 1899

period, and it is useful at this point to outline the main kinds of change resulting from colonialism.

The consequences of European rule

Despite the relatively brief period of European government in various parts of Borneo, its effects were relatively dramatic overall. One set of changes of great significance occurred in indigenous economic organization. In particular, local agricultural systems, oriented mainly to subsistence production, became more and more drawn into an international market. As we have seen, Borneo peoples were no strangers to change; even from the first millennium AD, some had been involved in the export of forest products and the import of goods from such faraway places as India and China. But it was not until the late nineteenth and early twentieth century that more and more local people began in earnest to produce agricultural goods for the market, and spend more of their time on activities which were not concerned with meeting their own subsistence needs. As we know, one of the main cash crops early on was rubber. Lindblad, for example, says of south-eastern Borneo

Indigenous rubber formed the most conspicuous manifestation of an intensified interaction between the regional economy and international markets during the interwar period. (1988: 57)

From the second decade of the twentieth century onwards, the Banjarese of the Hulu Sungai region were especially active in rubber cultivation, interspersing closely planted rubber gardens with their rice paddies. In 1924, for example, the region boasted 33,000 individual gardens and 8.9 million trees (p. 63), and, by 1936, 49 million trees (p. 65). Other important areas were near Martapura, and from the late 1920s the Dayaks of the Mahakam and Barito began to plant rubber trees. But it was the Muslim Banjarese who really prospered. Lindblad again says of the mid-1920s

Thousands of bicycles and hundreds of motor-cars passed into willing Banjarese hands already on quayside at Banjarmasin. Millions of guilders were spent on rice, other foodstuffs and textiles, making the import trade via the regional capital thrive as never before. More than 10,000 pilgrims bound for Mecca assembled each season at the landing stage of the ocean-going steamers. (p. 70)

In the case of Sarawak the cultivation of such crops as coffee, cocoa and pepper was early on introduced into the Saribas and Skrang areas and led to increasing prosperity and evidence of modernization among the Iban communities there. Nevertheless, what this increasing dependence on world markets and prices meant for local people was a greater degree of economic uncertainty. Rubber was not such a problem; trees could be left untapped for long periods without damaging them if market prices were low or labour scarce. But locals were drawn into a monetized economy and came to need more cash to meet their rising horizon of needs. They required cash to pay taxes, buy rice and acquire various consumer goods which they had come to use and enjoy.

Involvement in a cash economy also meant a greater degree of contact with market centres and urban areas. The immigrant Chinese gradually took over the role of intermediaries between the international market and local producers. As we know, Borneo has had long-standing contacts with China, and Chinese merchants settled in small numbers in such port centres as Brunei and Banjarmasin. However, it was especially from the mid-eighteenth century that Chinese miners began to come into western Borneo in greater numbers. Then from the latter part of the nineteenth century and into the early twentieth century, with the economic opportunities provided by European activity and the peaceful conditions established by European government, a large immigration of Chinese took place from south-eastern China to such coastal centres as Kuching, Brunei Town (now Bandar Seri Begawan), Jesselton (now Kota Kinabalu), Samarinda, Banjarmasin and Pontianak. Chinese merchants also penetrated the interior of the island and serviced larger-scale commercial transactions at key trading points along the main rivers, while Malay and Dayak traders continued to provide points of contact for local, small-scale exchange. For example, by the 1890s there was already a settlement of about 100 Chinese in Bunut in the upper Kapuas. They had managed to wrest part of the trade in forest products from the Malays and were visiting such distant places as Putus Sibau to trade (Enthoven 1903, i: 92–3).

There was also a significant amount of economic enclave development. In Sarawak this had been restricted because the Brooke Raj carefully controlled large-scale economic enterprises, and, in large part, did not permit private plantation and mining concerns into the state (Cramb and Reece 1988). Economic development was mainly in the hands of Chinese communities and smallholding cash-croppers from various ethnic groups.

The situation was very different in Dutch Borneo. There, large enterprises were given access. In south-eastern Borneo, for example, during the 30 or so years from about 1880, the activities of foreigners were principally of a speculative, pioneering kind – immigrant Western investors and entrepreneurs became involved in estate crops, including tobacco, copra, coffee and rubber. This was followed by a period of consolidation and expansion from 1914 to 1942, characterized by such processes as monopolization and agglomeration in commerce, agriculture and mining. It saw the rise to dominance of large European-owned companies such as Royal Dutch Shell's Bataafsche Petroleum-Maatschappij (BPM) in refined and crude oil production, and the Borneo-Sumatra Handel-Maatschappij (Borsumij) in commerce, real estate and intra-regional trade (Lindblad 1988).

In the east-coast districts of North Borneo, too, large estate companies established themselves in tobacco and rubber cultivation, and the Chartered Company was itself involved in these activities (Avé and King 1986: 77–8). In Brunei the British Malayan Petroleum Company, as an adjunct of Shell, also began to exploit oil reserves near Seria in 1929 (Horton 1984: 25ff.). Even today Borneo suffers from enclave development. Major economic activities are concentrated in a few favoured coastal locations, particularly focused on natural-resource exploitation. Therefore, during the inter-war years, and with the particular exception of Sarawak, what one finds, in broad terms, is the emergence of the phenomenon of a dual economy (King and Parnwell 1990). This comprised a foreign-dominated, modern large-scale, capital-intensive sector, in-

cluding oil and coal production, commercial logging and plantation agriculture, and a largely indigenous, small-scale,
labour-intensive sphere, characterized by smallholder Malay
and Dayak rubber and pepper growers who were partly concerned with subsistence activities as well. Again, put very
simply, these two sectors were linked by Chinese intermediaries as traders, merchants, shopkeepers and moneylenders.
Thus, the economy also took on plural features. In other
words, certain economic pursuits became identified with particular ethnic groups (Fidler 1976).

What is more, profits or surpluses were generally extracted,
or 'drained' from Borneo at the expense of the local inhabitants. Lindblad documents this for south-eastern Borneo.

At its zenith, in the years 1919 to 1926, drainage averaged 69% of the
value of the total private product, which is without doubt very high.
During those days Southeast Kalimantan came to display many traits
of a stereotyped path of colonial economic development, the well-
known one leading to exploitation of national riches by aliens for the
benefit of aliens. (1988: 214)

Other features of this kind of economic system were a concentration on primary production and very little attention to
manufacturing industry; a narrow range of activities based on
a few basic commodities, and therefore problems of excessive
economic vulnerability in relation to world markets; and some
development of wage labour, although mainly based on the
importation of coolie labour from outside, especially China
and Java: in this situation local populations were partly integrated into the marketplace but also continued to retain a
stake in the subsistence sector. We shall take these issues up
again in chapter 10.

Apart from economic change, the greatest impacts on
Borneo peoples and cultures resulted from European-induced
political and religious transformations. In effect, the Europeans undermined and eventually eliminated the power-base
of the Malay sultans and local rulers. The only Muslim
dynasty to survive and re-establish its political power after
Independence was that of the Sultanate of Brunei. Initially
the Dutch in the south, and the British in Brunei, concluded
treaties and contracts with the Malay rulers. In Dutch Borneo,

systems of indirect rule kept the latter in place and the Europeans worked through them. These were considered to be 'self-governing states' (*landschappen*) in contrast to the regions in which direct rule was imposed (*gouvernementslanden*). Direct rule was seen by the Dutch to be suited to Dayak areas where there was no firm Malay administrative presence or effective sovereignty, or where there were unresolved territorial disputes between competing and neighbouring Malay states. However, ultimately the Dutch even brought the nominally independent regimes under direct rule: Banjarmasin very early on in the 1860s, and some of the small western Borneo states in the early twentieth century (Ozinga 1940: 85).

For the Dayak population the main political and administrative changes which confronted them were the more effective coordination and implementation of taxation systems, and the selection and appointment of indigenous leaders to administer justice on behalf of the Europeans. Among the stratified societies it was obviously the aristocratic chiefs who were confirmed as tax collectors and local administrators. In Dutch Borneo they were normally entitled to take a percentage of taxes collected. For example, in 1895 in the Embaloh area of the upper Kapuas, four Maloh aristocrats were selected by the Dutch to collect taxes, and one among them was appointed as the custodian of local customary law to ensure that law and order were maintained according to local principles (King 1985a: 63). Where egalitarian social systems operated, Europeans usually raised local headmen and regional war-leaders as their intermediaries (Freeman 1970, 1981). In this regard, and with European support, these individuals probably enjoyed greater power and influence for a time than they had ever done in the pre-colonial period.

Given Western intervention, traditional legal systems were also affected. What, in effect, happened was the establishment of two separate but interlinked legal systems, one based on Western law, the other on traditional law – Muslim in the Malay areas, and customary law in the Dayak regions. But for crimes such as homicide, Western magistrates meted out justice, and local legal systems came into operation for minor crimes or in such issues as domestic disputes or conflicts over property: legal principles governing such matters as marriage, divorce and inheritance were usually in the hands of local leaders. However, even here, Dutch and British administrators encouraged the codification of customary law, reorganizing it, and, as they saw it, rationalizing legal procedures and often introducing money values for fines (Heppell 1975; Richards 1963). What is more, Western concepts of property ownership began to be established. Different Dayak groups, for example, often operated different systems of land tenure and inheritance. Very gradually Europeans instituted the concept of individual private property, and they began the surveying, registration and titling of land (Porter 1967). As production of cash crops such as rubber became more important, and the land on which these crops stood, more valuable, individual families registered it, or took the tract of land out of the jurisdiction of the village community as a whole or out of communal or shared forms of tenure. Europeans also instituted categories of state land. Although the Brookes, for example, with their concern for native protection and welfare, preserved native forms of land tenure, which remained unregistered, they were nevertheless increasingly circumscribed (Hong 1987: 37ff.). Registration caused problems in systems of shifting cultivation where large tracts of land were left fallow and therefore considered by government to be state land, while for the farmers concerned they were part of a cultivation cycle and under various rights. The difficulties were even greater for forest nomads who did not permanently occupy or farm land, or for settled agriculturalists who used forested areas for hunting and collecting. This land could be taken over as state land and government reserved or protected land, without recognizing native claims (Colchester 1989).

Above all, European administration fundamentally changed both indigenous Dayak political systems based on inter-tribal feuding and headhunting, and Malay coastal polities, which, in part, relied on slave-raiding and piracy. A good deal of the energy and resources of the Europeans, especially in the early stages of their rule, were directed towards the elimination of headhunting and coastal marauding, by a variety of means: punitive expeditions, military patrols, fines and imprisonment, the conclusion of treaties and the institution of inter-tribal peace-makings. The overall result was to redirect power and influence to European administrations and the officials who represented them. The position of local leaders depended on the approval and support of Europeans, not on indigenous action and value-orientations. This, in turn, challenged traditional systems of prestige and authority. When prowess in war and warriorship were no longer means to secure positions of leadership, individuals looked for other avenues of advancement and influence – in the civil service, the church and entrepreneurship, and by acquiring educational qualifications and gaining experience in towns or abroad.

Other very significant consequences of European administration were the fixing of settlement patterns, the restriction of the physical movements of communities, the drawing of territorial boundaries between different groups, the institution of population censuses, partly to determine tax liabilities and facilitate administration, and the delimitation and definition of ethnic groups (King 1982: 23–43). As we have already seen, some Borneo peoples had been particularly physically mobile. The Ibans, for example, had had a long history of rapid and large-scale migrations across western Borneo. As Freeman notes, in Sarawak at the end of the eighteenth century 'the basin of the great Rejang river was a sparsely populated region' (1970: 130). During the next 150 years it was populated by Ibans moving in from the west and south. By the 1950s there were already over 100,000 Ibans living north of the southern watershed of the Rejang river (p. 131). Small bands of hunters-gatherers and horticulturalists in the area were killed off, assimilated or squeezed into or confined in certain territories. To keep the European colonial period into some perspective in relation to local processes and events, it should be noted that these migrations continued despite the presence of Europeans. Nevertheless, the Brooke government in Sarawak progressively restricted the expansion of Ibans into particular areas and began to stabilize interethnic relations. For example, the boundary between the Ibans and the central Borneo groups, especially the Kayans in the upper Rejang, was more or less fixed from the 1860s with the Great Kayan Expedition of 1863 (Rousseau 1990: 31–2). Ibans were also prevented by the Brookes from collecting forest products in inhabited tributaries of the Baram river, which also served to limit Iban expansion there. Both the British and the Dutch also encouraged some forest nomad communities to resettle and move into closer proximity to longhouses for ease of administration. Aside from the Brooke restriction of Kayan expansion down some of the rivers of Sarawak, the Dutch also controlled Kayan movements in the south. The Kayans and Segai-Modangs had moved out of the Apau Kayan area in the eighteenth century and had begun to settle the Mahakam basin and subjugate groups there. The establishment of Dutch administration in the upper Mahakam in the early twentieth century acted to stabilize local inter-ethnic relations.

Last but not least, Europeans not only introduced Western culture through the medium of schools and the use of European languages, but most importantly of all promoted Christianity. The Rheinische Protestant mission had already begun work in southern Borneo in the 1830s; the Anglicans were invited into Sarawak from the mid-nineteenth century. Roman Catholics began proselytizing in the upper Kapuas and upper Mahakam in the early twentieth century. Often European administrations allocated different denominations different regions for their work to prevent inter-mission conflict and competition. Obviously Christian conversion resulted in changes in pagan traditions. Large-scale funeral rituals sometimes including human sacrifice, agricultural fertility rites, omen-taking, the observance of particular taboos and prescriptions, and the cult of heads, gradually disappeared, were modified or changed quite radically in form and content. The social order, which was initially related to cosmologies, worldviews, rituals and symbolism was also affected. This was especially so for stratified societies, which were, in part, given religious legitimation; traditionally, various rites and symbols expressed aristocratic superiority and gave prominence to their special position.

We shall return to these issues in chapter 10. But to complete the historical examination of Borneo peoples, we need to say something about the events leading up to the political independence of the various parts of Borneo, before considering the main features of traditional societies, and the problems and prospects for them in the modern period.

Decolonization and Independence

Despite the fact that the Dutch and the British and their surrogates had their firmest and most extensive control of the Borneo territories by the 1930s, within a few years their seemingly invulnerable position was destined to be completely overturned. The Pacific War and the Japanese Occupation (1942–5) constituted a watershed for Borneo, after which things could never be the same again. The once all-powerful Europeans were rounded up and herded into POW camps. The Japanese presence left deep scars, especially in western Borneo. As a result of long-standing Japanese–Chinese enmity, large numbers of Chinese in the region were arrested and imprisoned. Many native resistance leaders were also jailed or executed. The Dutch East Indies was divided into three administrative regions. Sumatra was under the 25th Army, Java and Madura the 16th Army, and Borneo and eastern Indonesia under the Navy. Ricklefs says

The area under naval control was regarded as politically primitive and economically essential to Japan; it was governed in the most repressive manner of all. (1981: 187)

As the Occupation continued the economies of the Borneo territories were particularly badly affected. There had already been much war damage. The oil field areas in the north and east had been destroyed. Indeed the retreating British in late 1941 had sabotaged the facilities in Brunei and Sarawak to prevent them falling into enemy hands. Jesselton had been flattened by early Japanese bombing and Pontianak had been badly damaged before the invasion. During the re-taking of Borneo by the allies, Brunei Town had also been bombed. In general, rice was in short supply; coconut and rubber production had been seriously affected.

For the Dutch possessions in the south, immediate post-war political events were dramatic. The Indonesians fought a protracted war against the Dutch following President Sukarno's declaration of Independence on 17 August 1945. The Dutch were unwilling to give up their colonial territories, but after a long and bitter struggle they conceded, and the Republic of

Indonesia formally came into being on 27 December 1949. During the four years of the Indonesian Revolution, the Dutch had managed to retake and hold their Borneo (Kalimantan) possessions, and European administrators and troops had begun to return there in the second half of 1945, along with Australian troops who took the surrender in the Japanese naval area.

The Dutch set themselves against the idea of an independent unitary Indonesian Republic, which Sukarno had declared and for which he struggled. Instead they attempted to introduce a federal state which would retain links with the metropolitan country. They organized a conference in South Sulawesi in mid-1946, where there were native representatives from Borneo, to promote their plans. It was decided that Dutch Borneo should form one state within the federation, with the Dutch queen as 'symbolic head of a Dutch-Indonesian union of sovereign states' (Ricklefs 1981: 212). However, this proved impossible to implement. The Muslims of southern and eastern Kalimantan were very strongly in support of the Indonesian Republic. In May 1947, therefore, the Dutch created a separate state for West Kalimantan under the Sultan of Pontianak, which lasted until early 1950 when all of Kalimantan became part of the unitary Republic (Riwut 1958: 6).

Initially Kalimantan was constituted as a single province (*propinsi*) with its capital at Banjarmasin. But by the mid-1950s this proved to be administratively and politically unworkable and West Kalimantan was again established as a separate province, subdivided into administrative districts (*kabupaten*) and subdistricts (*kecamatan*). The other two provinces created were those of South and East Kalimantan. Subsequently, an additional province was founded in 1957. It was the culmination of a struggle by Ngaju Dayaks, who had been initially located within the Banjarmasin-controlled province of South Kalimantan, for administrative autonomy from the coastal Muslims. The province of Central Kalimantan, with its new capital at Palangkaraya, therefore came into being. It corresponded to the area previously referred to as the 'Great Dayak' under the Dutch administration, and was and still is very much a Dayak province run by and for Dayaks (Miles 1976). It represented the triumph of 'Dayak nationalism' against the domination of Islam, and one of the major unifying elements in the Dayak resistance was their pagan religion: Kaharingan (Weinstock 1983: 132ff.). They wished to enjoy the freedom to practice their own religion, and eventually also won national recognition for it. The first governor of the province was an eminent Ngaju Dayak, Tjilik Riwut, who had distinguished himself in the struggle for Indonesian Independence.

Independence came rather later to the British-protected Borneo territories. It was clear that after the devastation wrought by war and occupation, the relatively limited resources and skills of the Brookes in Sarawak and the Chartered Company in North Borneo were inadequate to the task of reconstruction. There was little in the way of nationalist consciousness or demands for Independence within these territories. Indeed, local political party formation did not begin in earnest there until the late 1950s and early 1960s. After the brief period of British Military Administration came to an end in 1946, full sovereign rights in both Sarawak and North Borneo were transferred to the British Crown. From then until 1963 they were therefore British colonies, although the direction of British policy was to proceed with post-war reconstruction and institute social and economic development so that ultimately these territories could be granted Independence. The form of that Independence was not really finalized until Tunku Abdul Rahman, the Prime Minister of the independent Federation of Malaya, formally proposed a wider Federation of Malaysia in May 1961, comprising Singapore, Brunei, Sarawak, North Borneo and Malaya. Sarawak and North Borneo did indeed receive their Independence within Malaysia two years later, and this arrangement has had a profound effect on the Borneo territories, as we shall see in chapter 10.

Finally, the Sultanate of Brunei, which had been included in the negotiations prior to Malaysia, decided to remain outside the Federation. Proposals for Brunei to federate with the other neighbouring Borneo territories had been discussed by the British as far back as the 1930s. The concept had appealed to the British as a way of forming a viable economic and political grouping, and it was revived in the early 1950s. But the idea of a Borneo Federation was overtaken by Tunku Abdul Rahman's Malaysia, and, of course, came to nothing.

Brunei retained its British Residential system until September 1959, when internal self-rule was instituted and a new Constitution promulgated. The British continued their responsibilities for defence, foreign affairs and internal security, and the medium of communication between Britain and the Sultan was now not through a Resident, but the High Commissioner (Singh 1984). In 1971 Brunei became responsible for its own internal security, and on 7 January 1979 an Anglo-Brunei Treaty of Friendship and Cooperation was signed and a date set for Independence. Brunei ceased to be a British Protectorate from 1 January 1984. Thus the remaining, but very small, part of Borneo achieved full autonomy, becoming a sovereign and independent state, while the other territories were merely parts of larger wholes, with their capitals, the centres of power and decision-making, at some distance from the island.

What I shall do in the next four chapters is to present a description of the main economic, social, political and cultural features of Borneo societies, having now established the prehistorical and historical contexts within which these peoples developed and changed. My account will be, in the main, a deliberately static one written in the ethnographic present, except where I refer to such institutions as traditional rank (including slavery) or headhunting and warfare, which have disappeared or been radically altered. In these cases I use the past tense. Even in my general descriptions it should not be assumed that Borneo societies have always been like this, or that they have been unchanging, or that the ethnic groups referred to as Iban, Kayan or whatever are internally homogeneous. I trust I have said enough already to confirm that the peoples under study comprise a complex ethnic mosaic, highly variable and subject to both internally- and externally-generated changes over a long period of time.

However, I wish to establish the main defining features of Borneo societies and I must therefore restrict myself to general characteristics, illustrated with case-studies. I cannot deal with all the variations and differences in detail. The materials are mainly taken from post-war anthropological and ethnographic studies and from my personal research experience of a number of societies in Borneo. This then is a synchronic treatment, a presentation of ideal-types. But following this attempt to capture the essential features of Bornean peoples, I shall return to address some of the real problems which these communities face currently, and the ways in which the modern world is encroaching on these ways of life.

6

Economic Systems

Introduction

It is very difficult to present a clearly delimited categorization of different types of economic system in Borneo. Usually one can identify activities and organization broadly characteristic of particular peoples, but often a given community will be involved in a range of economic pursuits. For example, some Iban longhouses depend on hunting and gathering, shifting cultivation of hill rice, fishing, cash-crop agriculture and labour migration for wages. Furthermore, there has invariably been socio-economic change and adaptation over time, so that, for example, some forest hunters-gatherers have settled in villages and adopted sedentary agriculture. Therefore, the following discussion is based on ideal-typical cases, and on generalizing and extracting the salient points and issues with regard to economies raised in the literature. What is clear is that despite the seeming diversity of economic activity, there are a limited number of major forms of environmental adaptation in Borneo: these are hunting-gathering, shifting cultivation, horticulture and marine fishing and collecting.

Although the discussion begins with hunters and gatherers, it is not meant to imply any evolutionary sequence, or any distinction based on less advanced and more advanced, or simple and complex economies. Just as some hunters and gatherers have over time adopted settled forms of agriculture, so it is reasonable to assume that, in the past, some agriculturalists adapted to a more mobile hunting and gathering lifestyle (Bellwood 1985: 132; Rousseau 1990: 218–19).

I would rather see these different economic systems as illustrating a range of adaptations to the natural environment of Borneo. In addition, these traditional adaptations have attempted so far as is possible to harmonize with and conserve the environment. A basic concern has been ensuring the sustainability of the economic activities so pursued. In other words, the traditional view of Borneo natives is that natural resources are held in trust for future generations.

Hunting-gathering

Information available during the past two centuries suggests that forest nomads, as we know them, have characteristically lived in the rainforests of interior Borneo. However, as we have seen, this might not always have been the case. Certainly during the pre-Austronesian period, hunters-gatherers were mainly located in lowland, coastal areas. Even today in the province of East Kalimantan, some groups of hunters-gatherers are found nearer the coast.

Forest nomads usually live in touch with surrounding settled agriculturalists such as the Kayans, Kenyahs, Malohs and Ngajus with whom they trade and are culturally related. Rousseau states, 'Central Borneo's nomads form a distinct socio-economic sector, but they are not a separate society' (1990: 216). Nomads and agriculturalists in Borneo have been interacting over a very long period of time, but contacts between separate nomadic groups are generally infrequent.

Nomads build a range of dwellings. There is no uniformity. Some are simple lean-tos of saplings, palm-leaves and tree-bark, others are huts, either on the ground, or on stilts; still others are built along the lines of the longhouses of settled agriculturalists. Sometimes, as in the distant past, caves are used for shelter and for the storage of valuables. An important consideration is that the dwellings should be built near a water supply. A nomadic group may use a base-camp from which they organize their forest trips in the surrounding area, before moving on to other tracts of forest to exploit. Others have more fixed settlements and divide up into small groups, usually two to three families which build temporary shelters in the outlying forest and forage and hunt from there.

The size of nomadic bands is also very variable. They may be as small as 30 to 40 people or up to 150 or 200 (Needham 1972). Their length of residence in a given territory can also vary. Some can move within an area for a considerable period of time; others move often from one region to another, sometimes migrating over great distances. During migrations nomads usually move over land, rather than use the rivers, although some make bark canoes for short-distance travel. In terms of territorial rights, some groups claim a given tract of forest to the exclusion of outsiders, while others do not, and exploit some of the same areas as other groups. Of course, until the more recent encroachment of settled agriculturalists into remoter regions, there was little demographic pressure or competition for resources.

The basic staple of hunters-gatherers is sago. One species which has been exploited by settled peoples in the coastal swamplands of Borneo is the *Metroxylon*, and this has formed the basis of the economies of such peoples as the Melanau of Sarawak. Inland, the forest nomads exploit the *Eugeissona utilis*; like the *Metroxylon* it has an edible pith which is processed into flour. The sago shoots are also eaten, along with other palm shoots. It has been estimated that a nomadic band of 25 people needs 20 palms per week for subsistence needs; most palm stands comprise 50 to 100 trees, of which half are usually mature. Therefore, it is assumed that a band has to move to another stand every week or two weeks (Sellato 1986: 461–2).

They also rely on forest fruits such as durian, rambutan and mangosteen, vegetables and fern-leaves. They gather honey from beesnests in such tall trees as the *tapang* (*Arbouria*) or *menggaris* (*Koompassia*); it is eaten as a sweetener. Aside from felling sago palms, men also hunt. Women gather products near the camp. A variety of animals are hunted and trapped. These include gibbons, macaques, civet cats, squirrels, reptiles and birds. Small tree animals and birds are commonly taken using the blowpipe and poisoned dart. Some nomads, such as the Western Penan of Sarawak, are well known as skilled users and manufacturers of the blowpipe. Larger non-arboreal animals like wild boar and deer are hunted on foot with spear and dog. There is a trade in good hunting dogs between nomads and agriculturalists (Hoffman 1983: 54). More recently shotguns have come increasingly into use (Avé and King 1986: 49). Some groups also fish using hook-and-line, cast- and floating-nets, harpoons and poisoned derris root (*tuba*).

Nomads are, to a large extent, self-sufficient, although they have had long-established trading links with settled agriculturalists. Hoffman (1983) has argued that the *raison d'être* of nomadic life is the specialization in forest hunting and collecting for the purposes of trade. He goes further by proposing that nomadic society arose specifically to serve the Chinese market with sought-after forest products. In other words, as commercial forest collectors, nomads are a specialist native group in close touch with settled agriculturalists. This view has recently been criticized. Nomads do trade, though some do so more than others. Furthermore, certain groups have acted as guides for downstream collectors. But it is not an absolute necessity (Rousseau 1990: 237–9; Sellato 1989b: 153ff.). Some nomads will over time come to depend on, for example, iron goods from agriculturalists, while others can manufacture their own. Some foodstuffs are also traded. Some nomads acquired a taste for rice and obtained small quantities from nearby farmers; tobacco also entered into trade networks. On the other hand, settled agriculturalists hunt and gather as well, and do not rely exclusively on specialist forest nomads.

Nomads may indeed not spend as much time or energy on collecting as settled agriculturalists would like. When they do so, it is in order to maintain good relations with farmers, and, over time, they have become partially incorporated into settled society. They cannot isolate themselves completely from cultivators, because, although there are vast areas of forest, the nomads are surrounded on all sides by village societies (Rousseau 1990: 241). Hunters-gatherers broadly complement the settled way of life by exploiting ecological niches which are not used to any significant extent by others. But specialist collecting for external markets is certainly not the explanation for nomadic society.

What we have been witnessing over the last century or so is

the progressive sedentarization of nomads. Usually as a first step they begin to cultivate sago, manioc, cassava, sugarcane and bananas, and then ultimately move on to rice. They also early on keep pigs and chickens (Sellato 1989b: 216ff.). In the development of agricultural systems in Borneo, we have suggested that horticulture must have been an early form of cultivation and that sago was probably a very early basic foodstuff. There are cases of nomads deliberately planting sago, and some of the now-settled agriculturalists, such as the Kajang, Berawan, Modang and Kenyah, also grow sago. As Sellato (1989b: 218–20) has argued, it is therefore misleading to contrast nomads with agriculturalists as ecological types; there would seem to be a continuum from nomadic society, through horticulture to rice agriculture.

Probably one reason for sedentarization of nomads was the desire of some agriculturalists more fully to control nomads, and bring some of them to live nearby to supply jungle produce. Subsequently in closer contact and with partial settlement, farming is adopted. In some cases, nomads moved closer to certain settled groups for protection to avoid attacks from others. Finally, European governments began to try to fix and stabilize nomadic society for ease of administration and control, and this policy has been continued by the independent governments of Malaysia and Indonesia.

Swidden cultivators

A rather different adaptation to the forest is slash-and-burn agriculture. It can, of course, support higher population densities than hunting-gathering, which is dependent on what is available in given tracts of forest. Swiddeners exert some control over their environment and use it for the purposes of food production.

It is a sad fact that popular myths about shifting cultivation are still entertained. Sometimes this is for political and ideological reasons on the part of governments. Cramb says

Initially, the polemic against shifting cultivation in Sarawak arose from perceptions which were clouded by the cultural bias of European colonial officials. (1989: 42)

A major aim of administrations is to secure control over populations and to bring them within the ambit of government. Bureaucracies, usually run by coastal urban populations, also have very little sympathy with ways of life which are considered to be backward and representative of earlier, primitive stages of human evolution. Cultural and economic biases also favour the perceived modern forms of plantation agriculture or of settled intensive cultivation of food crops.

Therefore, the main characteristics of shifting cultivation are evaluated negatively (see Cramb, pp. 28ff.). Swiddeners are charged with being wasteful of natural resources. They cut down forest, burn it and then farm the land. The critics of this form of cultivation argue that it is destructive of the environment, and causes forest degeneration and soil erosion. It also uses 'primitive' methods of cultivation. The tools, such as bush-knives and axes for clearing, dibble-sticks for sowing, knives for weeding, and small finger-knives for harvesting, are considered simple and basic. There is then no mechanization; no use of the plough or draft animals; no application of fertilizers. Swidden cultivators rely mainly on ash produced from burning the forest for fertilizer. They are also charged with being too mobile. They do not settle in permanent villages. Furthermore, their agriculture is thought to be inefficient – not particularly productive in yield, and only able to support low population densities. It is often contrasted unfavourably with what are considered to be the sophisticated forms of wet rice cultivation, either in low-lying areas or on terraced hill sides, which depend on systems of water control and intensive application of labour; these support high population densities and are usually associated with the high civilizations and large-scale political systems of the Hindu, Buddhist and Islamic states of South-East Asia.

Criticisms of shifting cultivation also often assume it to be a homogeneous, unchanging system of agriculture, unable easily to adapt to new circumstances. On the contrary, it is a very variable system of cultivation, and I can only sketch out its main characteristics here. The basic rationale of shifting agriculture is that rather than a rotation of crops to enable farming to be sustained over a long period of time without undue detriment to the environment, swiddeners rotate or shift their fields. They clear a patch of forest, farm it, usually for one or two years, leave it fallow to regenerate, farm somewhere else, and then they may ultimately come back to the same areas of land used previously to cultivate again (Freeman 1955).

The method of short-cycle cultivation and long-term fallowing recognizes important properties of rainforest ecosystems (Cramb 1989: 24–6). Nutrients are accumulated and stored in vegetation and in a small layer of topsoil; soils are generally of poor quality, thin and fragile. When exposed to heavy rainfall and high temperatures they are either rapidly eroded or are leached to such an extent that thick-rooted grasses such as *alang-alang* or *lalang* (*Imperata cylindrica*) take over and make it extremely difficult to control and cultivate the land. Therefore, farmers temporarily use a tract of land; they allow the vegetation to recover to minimize exposure to the elements and to inhibit intractable weed growth. Many communities have been able to sustain this system of agriculture on secondary forest land already within the fallow cycle, without needing to bring substantial areas of virgin or primary forest into the cycle each year (Padoch 1982). Although the Ibans of Sarawak, for example, have acquired a reputation as prodigal cultivators (Freeman 1970), Cramb notes that, in long-settled Iban areas, shifting cultivation has proved to be a sustainable system of land use (1989: 33). Indeed, among some communities sometimes as little as 5 per cent of the land cleared in a season is primary forest (S. Chin 1985).

During cultivation the soil is disturbed as little as possible. As Geertz notes (1963), a swidden, in many respects, 'apes' the surrounding forest. The soil is not turned; crops are not planted in neat exposed rows. Apart from dibbling and lifting weeds, the soil is not worked as such. The slashed and felled vegetation is burned, which releases ash for cultivation purposes and which breaks down the soil and makes it sufficiently friable for planting. Large tree stumps, logs and plant debris are commonly left in the fields and various tree crops are interplanted with rice to provide as much cover as possible and to reduce erosion and run-off. Furthermore, a variety of crops is intermixed; besides rice, these include cucumbers, gourds, mustard greens, beans, pumpkins, peppers, chillies, maize and taro; fruit such as banana, pineapple and pawpaw is cultivated; sugarcane is usually planted along with other crops such as cassava in a small patch of the farm following the harvest (Hudson 1972: 29). This practice utilizes the range of micro-environments and nutrients available; it spreads risks, because there is not over-dependence on a limited number of food sources, adds variety to the diet and helps to spread demands on labour.

Of course, shifting the fields and leaving relatively large areas of land fallow does limit the level of population which can be supported in a given area. But it is absolutely necessary environmentally. In addition, given the amount of labour invested in agriculture in relation to its returns, the system is relatively efficient. Shifting agriculture is 'land extensive' and not 'labour intensive', although demands on labour tend to be concentrated in particular periods of the year, for example at harvesting. Swiddeners are also engaged in other economic activities, in addition to farming, and therefore their dependence on the rice crop, though important, is lessened to some extent.

Certainly some shifting cultivators have been known to be physically mobile, migrating in the course of time over large distances. But one should beware of perceiving this as a necessary result of agriculture. Given the appropriate level of population, shifting agriculture can be sustained in a particular territory without requiring expansion or large-scale movements, although it may result in village settlements being moved within that territory. What is more, from the few studies that have been done, 'soil erosion and runoff from land under shifting cultivation are minimal' (Cramb 1989: 40).

Sometimes when population growth has resulted in pressure on land, it is automatically assumed by those critical of shifting cultivation that farmers will over-exploit an area, resulting in environmental deterioration. This can happen. But another response to population growth is not necessarily a reduction in the fallow period. Cramb has noted, among the Saribas Iban, that the annual area cultivated by shifting methods has been reduced to maintain or even increase the fallow period, while labour is diverted into cash-cropping or into off-farm work (p. 40).

Other regions of Borneo for which we have good data on systems of shifting cultivation which have been undertaken on a sustained basis over a long period of time, are in the Kapuas basin among relatively permanently settled Maloh peoples and among the Ibanic-speaking Kantu's. Where shifting cultivation is conducted on a long-term basis, it is often done so in lower-lying areas where some land is waterlogged or covered with standing water. This permits some attention to hill rice farming and also swamp rice agriculture. Among the Kalimantan Kantu' 'swampland is referred to as *tanah paya* and dryland as *tanah darat*; swamps are found in low areas along the main rivers, but small tracts can be found at the sources and along the banks of meandering side-streams. Wetland farms are called *umai paya*.' In contrast, the dryland swiddens are referred to as *umai darat* (Dove 1985a: 35). Swampland can be cultivated for sustained periods of time because the soil is not subject to leaching and erosion and does not require long fallowing. However, within any village territory one will find a range of micro-environments, depending on the elevation of the land, the soil type and the type of vegetation.

Shifting cultivators have an intimate knowledge of their environment. They obviously know where there are variations in soil quality. More generally they classify areas of forest suitable for clearing and cultivation according to the vegetation cover. The girth of the largest trees indicates whether the vegetation is adequate to produce sufficient felled and slashed debris to provide a good burn and ample supplies of ash-fertilizer. Massive, tall trees are either part of primary forest, which usually has not been cleared in living memory, or virgin rainforest which has simply not been exploited on any previous occasion. The length of fallow periods will obviously vary depending on such factors as the cultural practices and economic needs of particular communities, population pressure, soil type and terrain and the proportion of economic activities devoted to rice-farming. Some households, for example, may not need to devote too much land to rice cultivation because they are involved significantly in cash-cropping. Usually 10 to 12 years is sufficient time for a forest to regenerate between cultivation cycles. But some communities may leave land for up to 25 years. In regions of Borneo where shifting cultivators have been restricted in their physical movements by government, or where forests have been reserved or taken over for commercial logging, or where population has increased significantly and there are few alternative economic pursuits, the fallow period may be reduced to as little as four to five years. The vegetation, in these circumstances, will comprise only dwarf trees, saplings, bamboo, scrub, tangled vines and creepers and *Imperata* grass; ash from the burn will be inadequate, soil will be very poor and susceptible to leaching and erosion, and weed growth will be rapid and prolific. A vicious circle is then established of a deteriorating environment and a declining subsistence-base for cultivators. Be that as it may, shifting cultivation, given certain conditions, is not naturally or inherently destructive of the environment. It is usually as a result of outside pressures that the system begins to break down.

Overall, shifting cultivators have to come to terms with climatic and other kinds of uncertainty, and there is the lack of a clear seasonal pattern to these climatic factors. There will be effects on agriculture depending on whether the winds blow, how strong and from which direction; on drought, rain and flood; whether there is too much sun on particular days or it is overcast. For example, a good burn will depend on good dry, hot weather. Agriculture therefore attempts to cope with uncertainties; it counters risks as best it can, and tries to exploit environmental diversity.

As a result of its ecological requirements, shifting cultivation leads to dispersed settlement patterns. Longhouses and villages are usually some distance apart, scattered ribbon-like along rivers. Where the environment is rather more favourable, where soils are more fertile, terrain less steep and there are tracts suitable for swamp rice, then some concentration of settlement may occur, as in the Maloh areas of the upper Kapuas (King 1985a). Nevertheless, the need to keep large areas of forest under fallow means that a relatively large coalescence of population is unlikely, and, furthermore, that often households have to farm at some distance from the main village. During the busy periods of the agricultural cycle households may decide to build farm-huts or more substantial farm-houses on or near to their farm, to overcome the problem of a long journey to work. In the case of such groups as the Ibans and Kantu's, several households, if they are farming neighbouring areas distant from the main long-house, elect to come together to build a subsidiary longhouse (*dampa'*) near their fields. Shifting cultivators will also usually establish two or more fields in different tracts of land to spread the risks of cultivation and to exploit different micro-environments.

Usually individual households spend much of the time working their farms alone. But at certain busy times of the year larger groups are formed. Especially at the periods of clearing the forest, sowing, weeding and harvesting, members of different households may form cooperative work groupings. These generally lighten the burden of work since it is more pleasant to have companions with whom one can share the heavier, back-breaking tasks. These groupings are always formed on the basis of strictly balanced and reciprocal labour exchange between households.

Before examining the main phases of the cultivation cycle we have to address briefly a central element in rice cultivation, which we shall return to in chapter 8. Growing rice is not only a technical and economic operation, it is also a religious task. As we know, rice is a staple food; in some Bornean languages the general word for food is translated as 'rice' (King 1985a: 154). Rice agriculture consumes a significant amount of time and energy. Local languages have a rich and complex vocabulary concerned with rice-farming, the varieties of rice and their characteristics. A successful rice harvest provides physical, material, social and psychological well-being; its failure means hardship and distress. Rice is the main food for humans; its leftovers are fed to domestic animals; surpluses are converted into other goods through trade and barter.

Rice provides a link between the human and supernatural worlds. Knowledge of rice and its cultivation was conveyed to humans by the gods (Jensen 1974). Among the Ngaju rice can serve in rituals as a bridge between this world and the spirit world to bring spiritual blessings into this world for the benefit of humans (Jay 1991). Rice is therefore understandably treated with great reverence. Except in the normal procedures required to process it, rice should not be struck, abused, discarded or harshly treated. If it is unwittingly or deliberately harmed a ritual of apology and forgiveness must be performed.

Usually in Dayak cultures rice is thought to have spiritual properties similar to those of humans. In other words, it has a soul whose condition and contentment is responsible for the success or otherwise of the rice harvest. Even after the rice has been reaped and stored, it is believed that it can increase or decrease depending on the condition of the rice soul.

Clearing

Following the selection of suitable sites for farming, the first major operation is to clear the undergrowth with single-edged bush-knives. Usually cutting implements, including axes and adzes, are honed on special whetstones, and a ritual accompanies this task. Slashing the undergrowth can be undertaken by adult men, women and mature teenagers. The slashed vegetation provides the essential material for ensuring the ignition of the larger felled trees. It provides the lighter, more easily dried materials in contrast to the heavy trees, which require longer periods for drying and are more difficult to burn. Slashing the undergrowth also gives access and cleared spaces to the larger trees which are subsequently felled. For the Malohs of the upper Kapuas, the slashing phase usually takes place in May or June, though the period may well vary, to some extent, in different parts of Borneo.

Axes and adzes are then used to clear the large trees. This is a heavy task and is commonly reserved to men, especially if primary forest is being opened. Malohs undertake this operation in June and July. Sometimes, trees are particularly large, with spreading exposed buttress roots. To get at the main trunk, wooden or bamboo platforms have to be quickly constructed above the roots or a ladder set against the trunk. Among some peoples, such as the Ma'anyans, a line of trees is boxed, and not completely chopped through. One large tree at the head of the line is then felled in such a direction that it hits and fells the next tree, and so on, like a set of stacked dominoes (Hudson 1972). At the time of felling, and if the community also farms swamp rice, women normally clear coarse grasses in swampland areas.

Among some Dayak groups, and especially those which farm more often in secondary vegetation or in wetter areas, felled trees are usually trimmed (Dove 1985a: 122–3). In other words, the branches are severed, so that they create a denser mass of vegetation close to the ground. It also aids the drying process. If the weather is particularly dry before the burn, the vegetation will usually burn well anyway; but if there are heavy rains at this time, then cutting over felled vegetation can assist the burn, and provide a more even cover of ash.

However, in areas of primary forest, it is said that secondary cutting is usually unnecessary. The heavy branches of tall trees break off under impact. In any case, the size of the trees makes this operation extremely difficult and laborious and it is not considered to be worth the labour investment for the returns achieved. Secondary trimming is also a problem in more hilly, steeply sloping terrain.

Burning

Following a sufficient period for drying the debris, farms are fired before the onset of the monsoon. Among the Malohs, farms are usually burned in late August or early September. It is therefore crucial that there is sustained, hot, rain-free weather after clearing, and it requires coordination of neighbouring household farms, because of risk of fire in one farm spreading uncontrolled to others.

Burning not only provides the essential ash from the cleared vegetation and from the layer of humus on the forest floor; it also removes most of the obstructions to permit agricultural operations on the farm. Finally, the burn kills off or retards the growth of any living vegetation still remaining in the farm, which might compete with the crops, and it kills any germinating seeds which have established themselves following clearing. Therefore, the success of the burn is absolutely crucial to the success of the harvest. A prolonged dry period is even more important in felled primary forest which requires longer to dry out. In secondary vegetation, burning is usually easier. But if primary forest is very dry, it burns most fiercely and leaves a substantial layer of ash.

As Dove says, burning also 'represents an irrevocable point

of commitment' within the swidden cycle (1985a: 132). During or after field selection, and clearing, the subsequent use of the farm-site can still be postponed for a year or more, or delayed indefinitely. This is not so with burning. By then it is too late. Dove adds, 'Once a swidden is burned, it is always planted, weeded and so on, to the end of the cycle' (p. 132).

If farms do burn badly then certain redressive measures can be taken. Unburned or semi-burned matter is collected together, placed in piles and then torched again. Or at the planting phase, piles of insufficiently burned debris can be fired there and then. If there is much debris which is still wet and unburned, it may simply be removed from the swidden to enable farming to continue.

On swampland, slashed vegetation may be partially burned, but it is usually cleared away, or some of it may be mulched in.

Sowing

Sowing commences at the onset of the monsoon in late September–early October, and this stage is marked by major rituals to ensure that the sacred rice strains are content. Among such peoples as the Ibans and Malohs the sacred rice is planted in a prominent place, usually in the centre of the swidden. It is considered to be the 'base' or support of all the rice sown, and it is thought to have accumulated special sacred properties or spiritual powers from its ritual treatment from year to year. This special rice is stored separately; it is often distinctive in shape, size and colour, and is seen as the very font of fertility.

Dayaks have a great diversity of rice varieties, and those selected are usually sown in different parts of the field. They serve to exploit different aspects of the environment, and they are also intended to spread risks. Some, for example, are more suited to drier conditions, others to higher rainfall; some to dryland, others to wetland. Some are early-maturing, others late-maturing varieties. Glutinous rice is often sown in small quantities in a strip or demarcated area of the farm; it is used mainly for making rice-wine and cakes.

Sowing methods demonstrate remarkable similarities across Borneo. At the farm, males proceed ahead of the women, equipped with a long pointed dibble-stick to make holes in the ground. Females follow behind carrying woven seed-baskets which are hung over the shoulders or tied at the waist. They drop seeds into each hole. Those peoples who cultivate swamp rice usually transplant nursery plants at this time to the prepared field.

All shifting cultivators plant their fields to a variety of crops. They mature at different times of the year and therefore provide a regular food supply and spread labour requirements. They also give variety to the diet. Some seeds are sown in the same holes as the rice seed; others are sown separately, often at or around the perimeter of the field.

Among some Dayaks, sugarcane, as well as providing a sweetener or syrup in cooking, is processed and used for making a fermented alcoholic drink. Crushing sugarcane can be done by using a simple manual press, as with the Ot Danums, or sometimes more sophisticated rotating presses are used, comprising two upright cogged cylinders set slightly apart, supported by a wooden frame and rotated by horizontal bars tied at right angles to the cylinders. Cane is crushed by being pushed through the small gap between the cylinders, and the juice is collected in a pan beneath them.

Again in certain parts of Borneo, aside from drinks made from glutinous rice or sugarcane, some groups use the cultivated *aren* palm (*Arenga pinnata*) as a source of both sugar and alcohol. It can be made into a reddish-brown sugar. *Aren* palms store up large amounts of starch in their stems, which is used in fruit formation and is converted into sugar. The peduncle of the male flower is cut to release the sugary fluid. This is caught in jars placed beneath and can be drunk while still fresh; the juice ferments itself, but bitter tree-barks can be placed in the jar to aid fermentation and alcohol formation (King 1983).

Weeding and guarding the farm

Aside from a good burn, another process which is absolutely essential to a successful harvest is to keep weed growth in check. Weeds can quickly compete with and choke young rice plants, and, in a badly burned swidden, weeds are a special

nuisance. Weeding, which is a back-breaking task, is primarily
a female responsibility and is done with a small bush-knife or a
short-handled hoe. It begins in October and continues until the
rice flowers. To ease the burden, women prefer to work in
cooperative groups. There are usually two types of weeds
and weeding methods: those which grow from seeds or remaining root systems are uprooted or severed from the
ground; others such as bamboo regrowth or sproutings from
tree stumps left in the swidden are slashed with a bush-knife.

Other tending and protective measures involve guarding the
farm against the depredations of pests and wild animals. Dayaks use various birdscares to combat the rapacious rice-spar-
row (*Munia*), or they smear the vegetation in and around the
farms with birdlime. A variety of traps is used: spring-spear
traps equipped with sharpened bamboo to kill wild pigs or
deer entering the farm along paths, or snares, nooses and
box-traps to catch macaques and rodents. Rail- or brush-
fencing erected along parts of the farm perimeter also deters
animals such as deer and pigs. Guarding the crops requires
farmers to spend some time nearby in farm-huts or farm-
houses. Dayaks who farm in or near primary forest, rather
than secondary vegetation, are often especially skilful in the
manufacture of ingenious traps and snares.

Insect pests are a great problem for swidden farmers, and
before the introduction of modern pesticides there was only
limited action which could be taken against them. The most
serious threat is posed by rice bugs, mole crickets, grasshop-
pers, army worms and stem-borers. Coordination of the planting time is one recognized means to reduce insect infestation;
once farms are attacked, Dayaks may use traditional poisons
and burn *aloes* wood to emit an odour, or the sap of a species
of tree (*Gluta* sp.), the smoke of which is said to drive away
pests (Dove 1985a: 242–3).

Harvesting

This phase represents the culmination of the swidden cycle.
The Kantu's say, for example, 'After harvesting our year is
finished' (Dove 1985a: 265). Harvesting times vary but are
usually spread from the end of January through to April. This

too is an important time ritually. There is usually a presentation of offerings to the rice soul and spirits to ensure that they
do not desert the farm during the reaping. There is also
commonly a ritual first cutting and tasting of the rice confined
to a small area of the farm before the main harvest gets under
way. This period is covered by a number of ritual prohibitions.
Harvesting is undertaken by both men and women; sometimes
even children assist, and it is generally conducted in coopera-
tive work groupings.

The traditional reaping implement is the finger-knife. It
consists of a thin blade of sharpened iron, fitted at right angles
into a small wooden or bamboo dowel. The handle is held
upright in the palm of the hand, the cutting edge protruding
from between second and third fingers, and each panicle of rice
is cut individually. The stalk is held by the index finger while
the thumb encircles the handle at the top and the rice stalk and
touches the index finger; the second, third and fourth fingers
pass around the panicle, and, with slight pressure, pull the
stem against the blade.

Given that various kinds of rice are sown, and the fact that
these are normally located in different sections of the farm,
these are harvested as they ripen. There is thus a fixed pattern
to the reaping. It is not a haphazard activity. The harvested
rice is then placed in a harvesting basket, and when full the rice
is poured into large, deep carrying baskets. These heavy containers are eventually carried, usually by men, to the main
village or, if too far away, the farm-hut or -house.

Processing and storage

Before threshing, the rice is dried. It may be stored temporarily
in large bark-bins. The usual threshing method is to spread the
rice panicles on a large rectangular grill or frame of bamboo or
rattan which is placed over a threshing mat. Men then stand
on the frame keeping their balance with stout poles or by
holding straps attached to the house beams or rafters. The
rice is gathered up into heaps using the sides of the feet and
then treaded downwards, pressing the panicles against the
instep. The grains separate from the stalks and fall through
the square holes of the grill onto the mat below. The com-

pressed panicles are then collected and rubbed by hand against the frame to release any remaining grains. Sometimes women sit at the side of the grill with a small hand frame set at an angle and rub the panicles against this.

The threshed grains are then placed in large cordless winnowing baskets and taken outside. There the grain is slowly poured onto mats, while women create a draught by a rapid fanning motion with woven winnowing trays or specially plaited reed fans. This separates the empty and half-empty husks from the full grains. The waste is placed in winnowing trays and processed for a second time. Women move the trays in a brisk circular motion, periodically tossing the material in the air to separate out any remaining good grains from chaff. The winnowed rice is then dried thoroughly on mats in the sun prior to storage (plate 32).

Rice is commonly stored in large bark-bins, and a ritual is performed and offerings presented to ensure that the soul of the rice, and any guardian spirits responsible for it, rest contentedly. The rice may also be placed in bins inside the long-

Plate 32   Rice being dried on the open verandah of an Iban long-house

house or in separate rice-storage huts (plate 33). When needed the necessary quantities of rice are taken from the bins and pounded to remove the husks. This is undertaken with a large wooden pestle and a solid wooden base or mortar. The mortar is curved with a hole in the centre for the unhusked rice. Women usually stand beside the mortar, but sometimes, if the mortar is large enough, women may stand on its rim. A woman may work alone or in twos or threes; when working

Plate 33   Kenyah rice storage huts

cooperatively each woman strokes down with the pounder on the rice in sequence, in beautifully synchronized and rhythmic movements. After pounding, the rice is then winnowed again. Sometimes a circular tray with a mesh in the centre is used to divide the hulled rice, which falls through the mesh, from the grains which require a second pounding. Some Dayak groups also use special rice huskers; made from part of the trunk of a tree, it comprises two sections; the upper one is hollowed out and equipped with two horizontal handles, the lower part is solid, its upper end shaped into a cone with notches cut into it; the hollowed portion fits exactly over the solid base. Grain is fed through a hole in the top of the upper section, which is rotated backwards and forwards until the husks detach and escape via the notches.

When the rice has been taken in and the farming year is at an end, it is time for celebration and thanksgiving in Borneo. The spirits and deities responsible for agriculture are welcomed and feted. It is usually a time of plenty when there is the opportunity for relatives and friends to get together and for visits between members of different longhouses. It is also a time for young people to meet and for marriage ceremonies to be held. There is much display of fine costumes, dancing, sometimes masked dances, and singing.

Cash crops and other activities

As we have seen, shifting cultivators do not depend exclusively on hill rice agriculture. Some of them farm swamp rice; they grow a variety of secondary crops, and like the forest nomads, they obtain animal protein from hunting. Domestic animals are usually slaughtered and eaten on special occasions. They are more likely to be used as sacrifices in ceremonies, rather than eaten as an everyday source of food.

Although hunters-gatherers do fish, it is the settled agriculturalists who are well known for their adaptation to life on inland waterways and for skills in fishing. The most common device is the cast-net, which has a diameter of about five metres with the central part in a cone-shape to which a strong cord is attached; the net is weighted at its edges. It is thrown out over the water in shallows or in a pool, and the net sinks, trapping the fish beneath. Sometimes a broad flat net is strung out across a small stream; the fish are then driven downstream into it. Women often use simple scoop-nets, either long- or short-handled. Rod-and-line is also used with bait. There is a large variety of fish traps made from bamboo or rattan. Men often use fish-spears and harpoons; for night-time fishing special lamps to attract the fish are sometimes employed. The most well-known Bornean method of catching fish is the use of poisonous roots of *tuba*. Men construct a dam across a stream; then everyone – men, women and children – gathers a distance upstream, pounds up the roots to release the poisonous juices into the water; the stunned and poisoned fish are then caught at the barrier further downstream.

Among the cash crops which have been increasingly grown by swidden cultivators from the end of the nineteenth century, rubber is the best known. It is a tree crop which fits well into dryland shifting cultivation. It provides good ground cover; it grows on hilly terrain with poorer soils. It can be left untapped if rubber prices are too low or if labour is needed in other activities. It needs little maintenance, as long as tapping is undertaken with due care and undergrowth is periodically cleared from around the trees. Usually native rubber is a low-quality product, although over the last few decades government subsidies have been made available for replanting with new high-yielding stock. Primary processing methods are also simple. The latex once collected is simply rolled through a mangle into sheets and then dried in the sun before it is traded or sold on to a local dealer or shopkeeper. Because of lower prices over recent years, and more lucrative alternative activities, smallholder rubber production has declined in importance.

Another significant cash crop is pepper and in such places as southern Kalimantan, it has been grown for a very long time. This is a much more difficult crop to tend, although the returns are potentially much more lucrative than with rubber. If grown on sloping terrain the pepper bushes require terracing. The garden has to be kept free of weeds; ideally it needs a high fertilizer input, and wooden support-posts are needed to train the bushes. Pepper is very susceptible to such diseases as root rot and it is therefore a risky crop. For all these reasons the crop demands quite high levels of labour and capital input.

A tree crop which has gained in popularity in recent years is cocoa. It is a perennial and, like rubber, it needs less intensive labour input. It gives ground cover and so intercropping can be undertaken, but, when young, it benefits from shade, and some farmers have established cocoa gardens by interplanting in rubber groves. Other crops which are grown on a small scale are tobacco and coffee, mainly for local use.

As we shall see in chapter 10, government policies have led to the introduction of large-scale forms of estate agriculture in Borneo into which shifting cultivators have been integrated, either by resettling them, or undertaking *in situ* land development. The most popular crop is oil palm, which is much more suitably cultivated as a plantation enterprise, and generally provides good returns to the farmers. This is an increasing trend in Borneo as governments attempt to increase the income-levels of small-scale cultivators and wean them away from shifting agriculture.

Although the possibilities are clearly restricted, governments have also encouraged wet rice agriculture wherever there are suitable water supplies and terrain. In Borneo difficult countryside and extensive swamp areas render the construction and maintenance of irrigation works an expensive enterprise. In general, it is not a viable option in much of Borneo, and in the interior, tree and estate crops seem to be the most attractive options for government development policies.

Coastal economies

Sago production

So far we have been examining agricultural and other activities undertaken in the interior and based on adaptations to inland equatorial rainforest environments. Borneo also has extensive tracts of coastal swamps and these are obviously unsuitable for agriculture, unless they are drained. Some swamp and wet rice cultivation is carried out, but coastal dwellers, who are mainly Muslims, have depended on trade and also on the exploitation of the resources of the swampland forests, the lowland waterways and the inshore seas. Maritime products are plentiful: catfish can be caught using basket-traps, prawns with a scoop basket and fish of all kinds with cast-nets and hook-and-line. But the distinctive and particular adaptation of the coastal regions is sago cultivation, and this form of economic activity is best exemplified by the Melanaus of Sarawak. During the Brooke Raj, and even during the earlier period of the Sultanate of Brunei, the Melanau districts provided a most important source of revenue in the production and export of sago flour (Morris 1977, 1980). As we know, sago cultivation was probably the first major staple produced by the early Austronesians; we also have evidence that the Melanaus were in their present area of settlement by the later fourteenth century at least (Nicholl 1980: 189). Melanau villages were usually located on the raised banks of tidal rivers, and although this land provided the opportunity to establish fruit orchards, rubber gardens and rice fields, the main orientation of the Melanaus was to the surrounding swamp forests.

As the principal student of the Melanaus has said

The low lying swamps in which these [Melanau] villages are situated and the poor quality of the peat soil limits the economic possibilities open to the inhabitants. (Morris 1953: 11)

When Morris did field research among the Melanaus in the late 1940s and early 1950s sago production was very much a cottage industry. Subsequently the manufacture of sago flour was penetrated by outside capital, and Chinese middlemen and traders involved in the sago trade invested in the mechanization of the industry and established factory-based operations which progressively undermined the smallholding producers (Morris 1982). Production was based on household units, more specifically the husband-and-wife team. The male tasks were to clear, cut and rasp the sago palms; those of the female to process the sago flour.

Although sago will grow on poor peat soil, sago yields are much greater on the loam soils, which combine alluvial sand, peat and clay, found on the promontories of slowly meandering rivers and streams. The lowland species *Metroxylon* frequently reaches a height of over 12 metres; it throws up stems in succession from rhizomes, and it is easily propagated by suckers. But sago can also be grown from seed. The palms are harvested any time after about 12 years of growth when the stem is about five to seven metres high.

The palm as a commercial crop is planted on land cleared of lowland swamp forest. As in shifting cultivation the cleared vegetation is left to dry and is then burned. Suckers are planted in shallow holes, usually in September, October or November, but unlike rice agriculture, they can be put down at any time of the year. In the early stages of growth the young palms are susceptible to attack by monkeys, which like the soft flesh of the growing tip, or honey bears and wild pigs. In the first few years the garden is cleared and intercropped with vegetables. Subsequently it needs irregular clearing because 'It is easy for a garden to revert to jungle' (Morris 1953: 23).

Sago cultivation is not a seasonal activity like rice-growing. It demands a steady work-rate all year round in felling, rasping and processing. Customarily men fell the mature palms using a large bush-knife, and the rough trunk is smoothed off and divided into about 1.3 metre lengths and cut into logs with an axe or bush-knife. The logs are then rolled to the river, bound together to make a raft and floated to the village. At the village the logs are stripped with a bush-knife and split in two. The insides of the log are then rasped. Traditionally the logs were placed in an open trough fixed by upright posts to the beams of the workshed. They were then rasped by a sharp, curved adze-like implement called a *palon*. At the turn of the century a narrow board (*parut*) about two metres long, studded with nails, replaced the *palon*. The male workers would sit in line at the side of the trough, each with a log, holding it steady with one foot and scraping the pith inside. The shredded pith produced by traditional methods was very coarse, and it would have to be flailed using a flattened piece of wood. Subsequently mechanized rasps were introduced which were driven by an engine, and comprised two wooden circular wheels studded with nails and bolted to a spindle attached to a driving belt.

After rasping, the pith is then trampled by women, although sometimes men do undertake the task (plate 34). The pith is placed on a mat woven from sago palm leaves, which is in turn set on a wooden trampling platform, beneath which is a fixed

Plate 34   Trampling sago

ironwood trough for catching the raw sago as it trickles down the sloping draining boards from the platform. Water is ladled from the river on to the pith and is then treaded into it. As the water is forced through and the mixture dries, more water is added until the water running through is no longer a milky white colour with suspended starch. The bran waste is then disposed of.

Generally the small-scale cottage industry produces low-quality sago flour. The quality depends on the cleanness of the water, the fineness of the mat-weave, whether a straining cloth stretched on a wooden frame is placed on the trough under the drip boards, and the care with which the woman throws away the waste, because some can fall into the trough if it is handled carelessly. The wet flour in the collecting trough is then sold to a Chinese middleman. The trader washes it again, sun-dries it, and bags it for export.

Locally, households will also bake small sago biscuits; these are eaten with dried and salted fish. To make these the wet sago flour is mixed with rice bran in a wooden trough. The dough is put on a woven mat, usually made of nipah palm leaf. Two women take one end of the mat each and flap the dough backwards and forwards. This action produces pellets which are then strained through a sieve made of split reeds. They are baked on the top of large flat clay ovens in bakehouses.

Now the industry is fully mechanized with serious consequences for employment in the region. Both rasping and trampling are now factory-based mechanical operations, and Morris points out that even by the 1970s there was unemployment in the coastal areas (1974). The household unit is losing its involvement in the industry and the Melanaus are merely becoming wage labourers for others. However, even in Morris' time some owners of sago gardens would put them out to be worked, and the income from wet sago would be divided between owner and workers. There existed a variety of arrangements for the division of labour, and partnerships in the owning and working of platforms and bakehouses, as well as credit-and-debt relations with Chinese dealers.

What has happened subsequently is a concentration of capital, ownership and control, particularly with the involvement of Chinese middlemen, and the emergence of Melanau wage-workers, who have lost any stake in land or products, and are simply employed by others. We shall examine these processes in Borneo more generally in chapter 10.

Fishing and strand collecting

Another kind of coastal adaptation is illustrated by the Samal-speaking Bajau peoples of north-eastern Borneo, in the coastal areas and islands of Sabah and the Sulu archipelago (Nimmo 1972). These 'sea gypsies' or 'sea nomads' played an important and early role in the Brunei Sultanate; they were small-scale traders, outrigger boat-builders, marine gatherers and fishermen. The term 'Bajau' was applied to them by the Brunei Malays. They also spread further afield to eastern Indonesia and Sulawesi (Sather 1978: 172; Warren 1981). Today many have abandoned their previously mobile, roving lifestyle and have settled on land. However, some communities have for a long time practised mixed farming of wet rice, fruit and vegetables as well as cattle-rearing on land, and the term 'Bajau', although popularly used to refer to the boat-dwellers, refers to a wider grouping of linguistically related people who are land-dwellers as well.

The so-called 'Bajau Laut' or 'Sea Bajau' traditionally lived exclusively on fishing and gathering in the coral reefs of Tawi-Tawi, the seas around the Sibutu Islands and the tidal flats of Jolo and Basilan (Sather 1971). They were very little influenced by shore-based activities, living predominantly on boats and moving between anchorage sites. More recently they have been settling in fixed pilehouse dwellings over the sea.

As Warren has indicated, the Sea Bajau seek mother-of-pearl-bearing oysters, decorative shell and tortoiseshell, and *tripang* or sea-cucumber, of which there are some 60 species. However, it is especially the *tripang* species *Holothuria* which is sought either by diving for it or spearing it in shallow water (1981: 67). The Bajau Laut then fish and gather in the offshore reefs, coral terraces and shoals in the shallow shelf areas off the coasts of Sabah and the Sulu Islands. These regions are not owned as such by any group; they are exploited by Bajaus from various settlements. The main equipment for fishing comprises driftnets, either floated individually or linked up with the nets of other boat crews into circles. These may number 50 to 60 in one complex.

This fishing and maritime gathering economy demands a significant level of mobility and periods at sea of often several weeks. Sather points to the main unit of production as the conjugal family boat crew (*dabalutu*), comprising husband, wife and dependent children. He says

While at sea, family members carry on their everyday domestic activities entirely afloat, putting into shore only to collect additional firewood, to dry nets or take on food or water supplies, and their association with other families is limited to those with whom they are sailing or happen to encounter at sea. (1978: 174)

Therefore, married women, for example, live onboard the boat, preparing and cooking meals, looking after the children there, and cleaning and processing fish and other maritime products.

As a result of this mobility, the shore-based settlements (*lahat*) constitute relatively fluid social groupings. Conjugal families, linked by ties of kinship, friendship and mutual economic interests, do come together to form multi-family households (*luma'*) which occupy a pilehouse dwelling on-shore. These, in turn, are organized into household clusters, related through 'house leaders', which together constitute a village. However, the conjugal families are frequently moving off to fish and gather, and they break away from the house-hold, the cluster and the village, and may well then join up with other families elsewhere.

The movements of family boat crews are governed by wind and tidal patterns and the seasonal location of pelagic fish at various netting sites. At certain times, when tides are especially high, the usually exposed reefs are inundated and bring in fish from deeper waters to the rich feeding grounds. However, during the period of the north-east monsoon, with high winds and rain blowing on to the northern coasts of Borneo, fishing is made very difficult. Sather indicates that boat crews spend on average about four months of the year at sea, comprising about 20 to 50 voyages. A boat crew may fish alone, in small groups of two to six families, or in much larger drift-net assemblages drawn from several villages. In deeper waters outside the reefs, hook-and-line fishing is used.

Thus, overall social alignments in different fishing sites are very variable; membership is constantly changing, and this kind of economy does not easily lead to the establishment of permanent social groups. Although there is a tendency to cooperate with close kin, and family heads have a roster of fishing partners who are most frequently selected for coopera-tive fishing ventures, there is still considerable choice in the formation and activation of social ties. This issue of flexibility and choice in social organization is something which I shall take up again in the next chapter.

We have examined a number of ways in which Borneo peoples use and adapt themselves to the environment. Often European observers viewed these ways of life in rather negative terms. Shifting cultivation was seen as wasteful and encouraging unrestrained physical mobility. Hunting-gathering was thought to represent an early primitive economic form, in evolutionary terms. Small-scale coastal economies were perceived as generally inefficient and needing to be developed technologically. These attitudes are still very much the basis for certain current government development programmes. But what is often neglected is the fact that the traditional economic systems were generally in harmony and balance with the environment. They did not over-exploit and degrade the natural resources of the rainforests, swamplands and inshore coastal regions. Sadly this equilibrium has been increasingly upset since the establishment of larger-scale European enterprises in the twentieth century, and even more so during the past 20 years.

We shall now turn to consider the various major features of Bornean social and political organization. In this present chapter we have touched on certain aspects of social life as it relates to economic activity, and we have already provided some historical details of Bornean tribal and state systems. What I shall do now is consider the main characteristics of Bornean societies and some of the variations among them, illustrating these with case-studies.

7

Socio-political Organization

Introduction

In this chapter I shall continue to dwell on the subject of uniformity and diversity in indigenous Bornean societies. Social organization in Borneo exhibits a variety of forms, but there are certain basic principles of order which are found very generally across the island, and which allow some comparisons to be made. Bornean societies are usually categorized as 'cognatic' or 'bilateral' (King 1978a: 1ff.; Murdock 1960). This form of social organization places the peoples of Borneo closest to those of the Philippines and to the lowland majority populations of the maritime regions, such as the Malays and the Javanese. It distinguishes them from various of the hill peoples of interior Sumatra and societies of eastern Indonesia.

A cognatic system is one in which the ascription of statuses is based on relations traced equally through both the mother and father, or which theoretically allows for a choice to be made in affiliation between either the mother's or father's kin (Murdock 1960: 2–6).

I have yet to find a better summary of the various concomitants of cognation than the early discussion by Leach of the fundamental principles of social organization found among Sarawak peoples (1950); he proposed that, though observed in the limited context of Sarawak, these principles are probably generally valid 'for the whole of Borneo'. The features so designated are:

1 A 'personal kindred' comprising 'the whole body of an individual's [recognized] relatives' (pp. 61–2). In other words, it is a kinship circle focused on a given individual and traced outwards bilaterally through both the maternal and paternal lines.

2 A classification of categories of relatives which differentiates them in terms of genealogical levels (e.g. parental, grandparental) and distinguishes one's 'immediate family group' from other collateral relatives (pp. 57–60).

3 Ambilateral or ambilineal descent, whereby inheritance and succession 'at any point [are] as likely to pass to a female (or through a female) as to a male' (p. 62).

4 The presence of a politically influential 'house owning group' which is 'a small group of closely related families the members of which had a more direct descent linkage with the ancestral founders of the house (or village) than other members of the community' (p. 61).

5 Longhouse domicile.

Other important social features in Borneo, which have been indicated by others, following Leach's pioneering work, are the presence of 'small family' units (Murdock 1960: 2–7), or perhaps more appropriately small households, and the consequent absence of extended family structures, and finally, wider social groupings, which some anthropologists have chosen to designate as 'tribes' (Freeman 1970: 73–4), based on the communities which are located along a river or within the same river system (King 1978a: 26). Obviously the characteristic Bornean orientation to rivers, as the main arteries of communication, has led to social forms emerging in relation to them.

Leach's work and the detailed studies of Bornean social organization of such observers as Freeman (1955, 1960, 1961), Geddes (1954) and Morris (1953) began to be published in the 1950s and 1960s. They set down information on previously little-known social forms, which are very different from the kinds of societies studied in Africa by British anthropologists in the 1930s and 1940s. I do not wish to become involved in the complexities of the theoretical arguments in anthropology about the nature of cognation and such sociological concepts as the personal kindred, which then followed in the later 1960s and the 1970s and which have even continued into the 1980s (e.g. G. Appell 1976; Hüsken and Kemp 1991; King 1978a). Some of these academic disputes were hardly enlightening, but despite differences of opinion and perception, certain modest conclusions can be drawn for our purposes here.

First, there are similarities socially among a range of different ethnic groups in Borneo, although no one would maintain that some of the principles and features set down by Leach and others would apply equally and in the same way to all Bornean societies. Second, which logically follows from my last statement, there is also considerable social variation across Borneo, which has arisen because of different historical experiences, environmental constraints and possibilities, economic and political circumstances, migrations and physical mobility, inter-ethnic contacts and demographic variations. One of the most important distinctions among Borneo peoples, as we have seen, is between the relatively egalitarian societies such as the Iban and Bidayuh, and the relatively stratified or hierarchical societies such as the Kayan and Kenyah. Another significant variation is that between the small-scale political systems of the interior, based either on the village community as the basic political unit or a loose confederation of villages in the same river system, and the large-scale state systems which managed to integrate numerous communities along the coasts of Borneo. These coastal states rose and fell in power and influence depending on the skills and abilities of rulers, and their capacity to control trade routes and take advantage of links with large trading states elsewhere in the archipelago.

In order to indicate the kinds of variations in social organization between different kinds of society in Borneo, I now propose to sketch out the main features of certain selected case-studies.

Egalitarian societies: Iban and Bidayuh

It is well to remember that these classificatory categories are not absolute. No society is completely egalitarian, and the

Ibans, for example, recognize differences in status and prestige (e.g. Freeman 1981; Rousseau 1980). Furthermore, the societies do not exist in isolation. Contacts with others have led to changes in them; there are internal variations within them in response to different environmental circumstances; and so on. For example, the longer-settled Ibans of the Skrang and Saribas areas of Sarawak, who had been involved for a long time with stratified Malays in engaging in piracy and sea- and coastal-raiding for heads, developed, during the course of time, a more marked system of social stratification. Freeman (1981) has argued that, in contact with the Malay administrators of Brunei, some Iban leaders were ennobled and given honorific titles.

The main features of Iban society conform, to a large extent, to the general principles of a Bornean pattern of social organization proposed by Leach. The basic corporate unit of Iban society is the *bilek*-family, a small group numerically, usually of five to six members (Freeman 1970: 2ff.). *Bilek*-families comprise closely related cognatic and affinal kin, commonly a nuclear or elementary family of husband, wife and children, or a three-generation stem family of parents, one of their married children with spouse, and then their children. Ibans are strictly monogamous. There are no extended families in Iban society, an extended family being defined as a unit which comprises two or more married couples from the same generation residing together.

The *bilek*-family is united and defined on the basis of the occupation and sharing of a single compartment (*bilek*) in the longhouse. The compartment consists of a living-room (also called *bilek*), a loft (*sadau*), and adjacent sections of the roofed gallery (*ruai*) and open verandah (*tanju*) (figure 2). The members of the family group occupying this residential space are also referred to as *bilek*, acknowledging the intimate association between kinship relations and residential propinquity. One's effective membership of a *bilek*-family is therefore sustained by residence in a compartment, and an individual can only belong to one *bilek*-family at a given time. The family group then both occupies, and as a collectivity owns, this defined section of the longhouse. As one might expect, the boundaries of the *bilek*-family are also confirmed by addition-

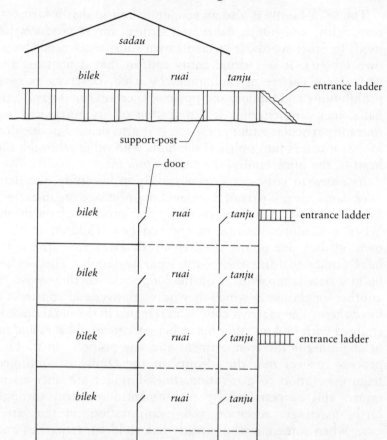

Figure 2   Plan and side elevation of an Iban longhouse

al criteria, arising from this sharing of space. The family is a domestic unit in that women prepare food for its members who share meals together; its members sleep in the living-room, with the exception of young bachelors, who customari-ly prefer to sleep outside on the covered gallery; children are socialized and brought up in the family. The *bilek*-family also owns other property besides the compartment, including fami-ly heirlooms and valuables, household goods, farming and other equipment, sacred rice seeds (*padi pun*) and a ritual whetstone; it has rights to particular areas of forest for farm-ing purposes.

The *bilek*-family is also an economic unit in that it farms its own fields, and hunts, fishes and gathers forest products for itself. In other words, it meets its own subsistence needs by its own labours. It is a ritual entity too, in that it finances and performs a variety of ceremonies by itself, observes its own prohibitions and taboos, and possesses certain ritual paraphernalia, including charms. It can cordon off its portion of the *ruai* for particular ritual purposes. It is also defined politically, in that it enters into political relations with others through the head of the *bilek*-family, the *tuai* or *pun bilek*.

As Freeman indicates very positively in his study, the Iban *bilek*-family is not part of a wider clan or lineage organization. What is more, it is kept small by the process of partition. When individuals mature, marry and have children of their own, all but one of the children break away from the natal *bilek*-family to form their own separate family. They either build a new compartment on the longhouse, or they move to another longhouse in which they have relatives and construct a *bilek* there. The married child who remains in the natal *bilek* is charged with looking after his or her parents in old age, and he or she inherits the compartment and any property in it. This process ensures that the identity of the family is continued from generation to generation. *Bilek*-families are also maintained and perpetuated by recruitment into them through birth, marriage, adoption and incorporation; in the latter case, when someone who already has children, remarries and moves into the *bilek*-family of the new spouse, his or her children are then incorporated into this new family. Another important feature of the *bilek*-family is that membership in it by birth is just as likely to be traced through the child's father as through the child's mother, depending, of course, on which parent is resident in their natal *bilek*. Freeman also found, having collected statistics on the location of residence after marriage, that post-marital residence is just as likely to be with the wife's parents as with the husband's parents.

Freeman's major conclusion is that the *bilek*-family is an autonomous unit 'both socially and jurally'. It is not part of a wider kinship unit. When partition occurs and a married couple divides from a *bilek*-family, the new unit so formed is also a discrete entity, and the estate of the original *bilek*, with one or two exceptions, is divided into two distinct parts. Despite the autonomy and independence of the *bilek*-family, it is part of a larger community, a 'confederation' of *bilek*-families, residing in a longhouse. What is it which gives this collection of separate but residentially joined units coherence? According to Freeman there are several dimensions to *bilek* interrelatedness within a longhouse.

First, as Freeman says,

> every individual belongs to an extensive bilateral grouping which may be termed a *kindred*; [it is] that cognatic category which embraces all of an individual's father's kin, and all of his (or her) mother's kin. (p. 67)

In this sense we are concerned with a complex network of interlocking relationships, focused on an individual. This circle of kin is not a bounded grouping; it extends 'indefinitely outwards' (p. 67). What is more, cousins may marry. Marriage is permissible for first, second or third cousins, or for any degree of relationship within the same generation and outside the *bilek*-family.

It is this bilateral network, reinforced or consolidated very often by intermarriage between close kindred members, as well as the practice of adoption of children between closely related kin, which provides the means by which *bilek*-families are interlinked within the longhouse. Cognatic and affinal ties are very dense and highly interrelated within the longhouse, although individuals in a given community have kinfolk in other longhouses as well, because kinship groupings are not circumscribed. What one usually finds is that many closely related kin, for example siblings or first cousins, tend to live in adjacent compartments of the house. Kindred ties carry with them the expectation of mutual obligations, assistance and support between relatives (Freeman 1960, 1961). Furthermore, related families living in close association under one roof also develop 'a sense of identification with the longhouse' (Freeman 1970: 126).

Thus, although the Iban have no corporate kin groups wider than the *bilek*-family, nor do they have a stratified society comprising defined social classes or ranks, the kindred, or in Iban, *kaban*, is a very effective mechanism for recruiting and

organizing larger collectivities of people. Apart from giving a
certain coherence to the longhouse, kindred ties which, of
course, extend to individuals living in different longhouses
scattered along stretches of the same river were also used
traditionally to mobilize large war expeditions against enemies. Freeman refers to these river-based groupings, which
call themselves by the name of the river along which they
live, as a 'tribe': 'a diffuse political structure', based on a
particular river system (1970: 73). Thus, Iban communities
along the Skrang river refer to themselves as 'We of the
Skrang', or 'Skrang people'. They used to come together to
wage war against and take the heads of their enemies in other
river systems.

More recently Freeman has reiterated the importance of
kindred organization in traditional Iban society. He says '[i]n
the classless society of the pagan Iban, kindred relationships
were pervasive' (1981: 63). As we can see, one of the major
functional advantages of a cognatic system, based on personal
kindreds, is its flexibility and adaptability. The kindred provides an individual with a network of relationships which he
or she can activate when the need arises, leave dormant, or, in
some cases, discard. Presumably in the traditional mobile,
migratory, egalitarian society of the Iban, involved in opening
up new areas of rainforest, founding new communities and
raiding and headhunting against other tribes in these territories, the kindred and the autonomy of the *bilek*-family provided
a mode of social organization ideally adapted to this lifestyle.

Apart from kindred relationships, a second element of longhouse identity arises from the sharing of a particular territory.
The constituent *bilek*-families of a longhouse do not collectively own land, for example. Rights in land are held separately
by each independent *bilek*-family. But all resident families do
have equal rights of access to the defined longhouse territory,
to the exclusion of members of other communities elsewhere.
They can use it for hunting and gathering, and, if not already
claimed, can open it for farming and establish rights over it.
The constituent families also have a common burial ground
(*pendam*), and, although each compartment of the house is
individually owned, the ladders giving access to the house also
belong to the community as a whole. Furthermore, even

though the longhouse is not a collective economic unit, various *bilek*-family members do cooperate together in agricultural and other tasks on a strictly reciprocal basis.

Thirdly, the longhouse can be seen as a defined community in a politico-jural sense. Longhouse identity is manifest in the position of the secular office of longhouse headman (*tuai rumah*), despite the fact that the Iban are an egalitarian society. Freeman notes that, over the years, government innovations have affected the nature of Iban leadership. From the Brooke Raj onwards, Iban longhouse headmen and also renowned warriors (*orang kaya*) and pioneers who had influence in several communities within the loose tribal organization were gradually incorporated into a formal hierarchy of administration; their positions were increasingly institutionalized as agents of government, authorized by state power, and, on the other hand, as representatives of their people in relation to the state. This situation has, if anything, been consolidated in the period of Independence, and social inequalities have been further generated by processes of modernization, commercialization of agriculture, urbanization and differential access to political power.

Nevertheless, and despite the exception of the more accessible Iban who had been partially incorporated into the Brunei Sultanate, there was traditionally no formal Iban ranking system. There was no centralized authority; no chiefs or aristocrats who could command tribute and formal respect and obeisance by virtue of acknowledged or hereditary positions of superiority. Ultimate authority rested in the *bilek*-family.

Jurally each *bilek*-family is a power unto itself, managing its own affairs and acknowledging no other family to be its superior, or master. (Freeman, 1970: 129)

In the past disputes were settled through kinship mechanisms, sometimes by force. Between communities where few, if any, kinship ties existed, situations of persistent feud and warfare existed. Nevertheless, Iban society cannot be characterized as anarchic. Behaviour and relations are regulated by a well-developed system of customary law (*adat*), backed by certain procedures for administering disputes within a community or by ritual sanctions.

The *tuai rumah* is a custodian and administrator of *adat* within a circumscribed social space. He cannot independently make decisions, direct a result or command others, but by his knowledge, oratorical skills, wisdom and judgement, he provides a medium, along with other recognized elders, for disputing parties to discuss their differences. Thus, he can influence the course of events and often summarize the sense of a meeting so that a dispute might be resolved.

One further important point needs to be made in relation to Leach's observation about the general feature of 'house owning groups' in Bornean longhouse societies, although, with regard to the Iban, Leach's term may not appropriately convey the kinds of rights and status which these groups hold. The Ibans certainly have a 'core group' of closely related *bilek*-families in each house, descended from the original founders of the community and therefore often enjoying rights to substantial areas of land. The longhouse headman is usually selected, in the context of a general meeting of adult house members, from this core group. In practice, headmanship often does pass from father to son, although it is not theoretically hereditary, and any suitable candidate, usually within the limits of the core group, can be chosen. Indeed, in theory anyone with the right qualities can emerge and accede to positions of leadership.

Finally, the Iban longhouse is defined in ritual terms, expressed in the position of the *tuai burong* or augur (literally 'bird elder'). The position may be occupied by the longhouse headman, or by a different individual. He is responsible for the ritual welfare of the house, and secures and interprets omens or signs conveyed by particular birds and animals before any major undertaking, such as building a new longhouse, migrating or commencing the next farming year. The omen birds especially are seen as messengers of the gods, providing advice and counsel, but it is the correct evaluation of these messages by the *tuai burong* which enables the Ibans to decide on the auspiciousness or otherwise of important activities and planned ventures.

The behaviour and actions of individual members of the longhouse also affect the community as a whole, both in a ritual and a secular sense. Ibans strive to maintain a harmonious relationship between their world and the world of spirits. Inappropriate behaviour, contrary to *adat*, can have serious effects for the longhouse in the form of supernatural punishment: illness, death, crop failure and floods, brought on by supernatural forces which are, in turn, activated by unthinking or unsuitable human action. If, for example, there is death or illness in the house, longhouse members also observe certain ritual prescriptions collectively.

Overall, then, Iban society provides an example of a small-scale political system. Its basic units are the family and the longhouse. The longhouse is, for most purposes, the highest-level unit in political terms. In the past, members from several communities could, on occasion, be brought together under illustrious warriors to embark on warfare and headhunting. But these raiding groups were not permanently constituted, nor did the leaders occupy permanent, hereditary positions in an institution of chiefship. Social inequality, which there was, was based on prestige, and constant competition to acquire it and outdo others. The autonomy of the *bilek*-family, the relative fluidity of leadership institutions and the flexibility of the personal kindred networks were all well adapted to the migratory, pioneering nature of traditional Iban society.

Let us now look at a society which demonstrates both similarities to and differences from the Iban case. The Bidayuhs of western Sarawak also have no formal authority structure, social classes or hereditary chiefs (Geddes 1954: 48ff.). The differences between them and the Iban appear to stem, in large part, from the greater degree of physical permanency of Bidayuh settlement over a long period of time in contrast to the mobile Iban. For example, there is a greater clustering of population in Bidayuh areas and more complex arrangements in relation to land. It is also unwise to generalize too much with regard to Bidayuh social organization since the main ethnographic material available comes from Geddes' study of the Sadong Bidayuh, and Bidayuhs are much more linguistically, culturally and socially diverse than the Ibans.

Geddes' overall summation of Bidayuh society as characterized by 'individualism and equality' (p. 48), also applies to the

Iban. Indeed, Geddes goes further: 'we are dealing with a society of democrats, if not anarchists' (p. 51). The headman, now called *tua kampong* by government, but previously referred to as *pingara* or possibly *pilima* (p. 48), is, as with the Iban, a custodian of *adat*, with no powers to command or direct others. Usually succession to office is confined to the 'core group', which has already supplied the current headman, though the candidate is officially selected at a village meeting, and, as with the Iban, suitability depends on the possession of certain personal qualities. Procedures for settling disputes are very like those of the Iban, and, although the regulation of social order seems to be informal, it is backed by *adat*, ritual sanctions and Bidayuh notions of shame and loss of public esteem.

The size and composition of the Bidayuh household is, in most respects, like the Iban case. The Bidayuhs also recognize a personal kindred, although in contrast to the Iban *kaban*, it is of a narrower range, only embracing first cousins, whereas the Iban kindred extends to fifth-cousin range. Geddes tells us that Bidayuh kindred relations are based on 'the sentiments developed by common family experience' (p. 14). The functions of the kindred are much the same as those of the Iban, but relations with non-kin appear to take on a somewhat greater significance among Bidayuhs.

The main differences between Iban and Bidayuh social organization are to be found in settlement patterns and land tenure arrangements. There seems to be nothing like Iban tribal organization, based on river-system groupings. Boundaries between sets of Bidayuh villages are much less easily defined. There seems to be a broader, though again poorly defined grouping, beyond the village unit, comprising a set of villages which traces links to an original or ancestral village, but this does not deserve the term 'tribe' (pp. 12–13). Furthermore, in contrast to Iban society in which a village community comprises one longhouse – in other words, village and longhouse are equivalent – among the Bidayuh the village (*binua*) is often made up of more than one longhouse (*ntangan*) or several longhouse sections (*ntupok ntangan*). This is obviously the result of a process of longhouse fission resulting in the establishment of subsidiary houses. But whereas new Iban longhouses establish themselves some distance from others, the concentration of Bidayuh settlement means that houses stay in close proximity to each other. In some cases, longhouses may separate out and ultimately form separate villages in their own right. But they still often retain certain links to a parent village. Village identity is expressed in the institution of headmanship, shared territory, and a measure of social solidarity, but with the process of longhouse and village fission, and the ultimate emergence of new independent villages, the boundaries between communities are often not so easily defined. Another element of village identity is the headhouse (*baluh* or *balai*), which is communally owned, and a focus of various social and ritual activities. The Ibans do not have such a structure, and their community activities are performed on the longhouse verandah.

Finally, Sadong Bidayuhs have a social grouping which Geddes calls a 'descent group' (*turun*) (1954: 59); it is an ambilineal or cognatic descent category comprising all the descendants, both male and female, of a common ancestor who first cleared primary forest and established rights in an area of land. It is not so much a 'group', if by that we have in mind a well-defined corporate unit; it is rather a category or collectivity (King 1978a: 18–19; Morris 1978: 46). An individual does not have exclusive membership in one *turun*, but belongs to many, and therefore there is no exclusive social interest in one set of kin. The *turun* only functions in relation to land rights; it operates an undivided estate, and there is a subsidiary set of procedures to determine who among a given *turun* can farm a piece of land at a given time, before it reverts back to the common pool. *Turun* are not therefore the basis of other kinds of social, economic or political relations or organizational forms.

What seems to have happened in the Bidayuh case is that they have developed more permanent residence patterns than the Ibans. With greater population densities, and the fact that they have been confined in certain areas by the more aggressive Iban who have settled to the east of them, there is pressure on Bidayuh land; a more complex arrangement for ensuring that everyone has access to at least some land has emerged in the institution of the *turun* (King 1978a: 18ff.).

Stratified societies: Kayan and Kenyah

There are some marked differences between the egalitarian societies and those with social classes, and, although all Bornean societies, the hierarchical ones included, are cognatic in that kinship and descent is reckoned in the same way as in Iban and Bidayuh society, the ways in which kinship operates and is manifested, and indeed its general social significance in ranked societies, differ. Most importantly, as Rousseau has said of the Baluy Kayan of Sarawak,

Kinship plays only a residual role among the Kayan, as it does in Western society [and] beyond the family it is not the basis of any grouping having an economic or political role. (1978: 87)

For Rousseau the most crucial principle of Kayan society is that 'Behaviour is determined on the basis of stratum ascription' (1978: 88). Thus, he does not devote much attention to kinship organization in his analysis of Kayan society, nor is there an equivalent of the Iban personal kindred. Among the Kayans there are very few kinship reference terms for relatives and there is a tendency to play down the distinction between cognatic and affinal kin (Rousseau 1974: 283). Among the Ibans, however, the difference between blood relatives and kin by marriage is more important and kinship reckoning is more extensive. The reason for this may be that, as a result of the preference for marriage between individuals of the same rank in hierarchical societies, so that members of the same class are very closely interrelated by blood and marriage, there is a tendency to conceptualize one's own class as an undifferentiated set of kin in relation to individuals of other classes (King 1991a: 15–31). In other words, in contrast to egalitarian societies in which distinctions between relatives are significant, in hierarchical societies it is differences between classes which are of utmost importance (King 1985a: 117ff.). These features appear to hold generally for ranked societies.

Nevertheless, there are similarities between egalitarian and ranked societies arising from the principle of cognation and longhouse domicile. Like the Iban, the Kayan household (*amin*) is the only corporate group in Kayan society, and its form and characteristics are much the same as the Iban *bilek*-family. One main difference is that the *amin* is generally larger in size than the *bilek*-family, often comprising a three-generation stem family. In the past, and in the case of other stratified societies such as the Kenyah, Maloh and Melanau, households tended to be large, even comprising extended families, partly because it was difficult for a young married couple to secede from the natal household and build a separate compartment at the end of the longhouse. In contrast to Iban longhouses, those of the stratified societies were traditionally large, more permanent, solidly constructed houses on massive ironwood piles, and it was difficult for young people to accumulate sufficient resources to erect a new compartment. What is more, given the fact that the relative physical position of households in the house was determined, in part, by considerations of rank, it was often difficult for a new compartment to be tacked on to one end of a house and still satisfy matters of social precedence and the need to position households of different rank in appropriate physical relationship to each other. Couples therefore often had to wait for long periods until the house was rebuilt or a new one constructed.

Finally, rank determines the form and content of a number of the features of cognatic kinship among stratified societies (King 1991a: 25–30). With regard to the range of collateral kinsmen recognized and the extent of genealogical knowledge, these generally differ according to rank. For example, Whittier says of the Kenyah that aristocrats have 'greater genealogical knowledge' (1973: 77), arising from the fact that they are much more preoccupied than commoners with maintaining rank status, wealth and property and selecting suitable marriage partners. In this connection, levels of bridewealth paid for a wife, choice of spouse and type of post-marital residence vary according to rank. Aristocratic bridewealth levels are high; aristocrats tend to want to bring wives to live with husbands because they are concerned to secure male succession to office and access to political power within their own village. Aristocrats also carefully consider the pedigree of potential spouses, and often marry partners from outside the village. This last practice is partly a product of the fact that there are only a few aristocratic households in a given village, and therefore the numbers of potential partners are small. But marrying into aristocratic households from other communities acts as a means of forging political alliances and extending one's prestige and position.

Given the importance of rank, one also finds that various social units in the stratified societies are not primarily based on kinship. The longhouse is not a kinship unit. Village membership requires the consent of the aristocrats, and, in contrast to the Iban, it is insufficient simply to claim a kinship link with residents of a community to which one wishes to affiliate. Nor can individuals leave a village without the permission of the aristocratic chief; in Iban society, on the other hand, the *bilek*-family is entirely at liberty to move elsewhere should it so desire. Yet again, unlike the Iban, traditional Kayan or Kenyah raiding parties were not activated by kindred ties but were mobilized and led by aristocratic chiefs.

Finally, and arising from the greater control which aristocrats can exercise over households and therefore over population movements, settlements tend to be rather more permanent and fixed in stratified societies. When migrations took place in the past they were organized by aristocrats; longhouses were very solidly built with heavy timbers, and village communities, as with the less mobile Bidayuhs, frequently comprised more than one longhouse. Even today, in the case of the Kenyahs, villages may consist of two, three or more longhouses, each with their own longhouse chief, as well as an overall village leader. Furthermore, in some cases, given greater permanency, there is a tendency for descent-based groupings to emerge, especially among the house-owning group of aristocrats. As well as commonly controlling areas of land together, aristocrats in a given longhouse or village often act together in a range of activities and have a shared interest in maintaining their superior economic and political position. In these circumstances, it is probably legitimate to talk about these longhouse- or village-based groupings of aristocrats as localized ambilineal descent groups. They would appear to have a much greater degree of coherence and corporateness than the Iban 'core group' of *bilek*-families.

Let us now examine in a little more detail the various dimensions of social inequality in stratified societies. It is useful in this regard to distinguish between three dimensions of hierarchy, which we can call 'class', 'status' and 'power' (King 1985a: 13ff.). Classes are generated by the economic processes of production, distribution and exchange, and defined with regard to the differential possession and/or control over productive resources such as land and labour. This is not to say that social classes in Borneo are exactly like those in Western industrialized societies – they are not – but they do entail economic inequalities (Rousseau, 1990: 215).

Secondly, status or prestige is concerned with social estimation, with the subjective evaluation or categorization of hierarchical positions relative to one another, and of the criteria on which they are evaluated. Status-levels are therefore indigenous categories of classification. Individuals occupying a particular class position do not necessarily have the same status, although economic criteria may be ingredients of prestige. The dimension of status generally refers to consumption patterns, manners and styles of life which are accorded higher or lower prestige (Morris 1953: 64; Whittier 1973).

Finally, there is the consideration of power and the political order. Again it may be closely interrelated with the economic dimension, wealth and ownership, but it is not the same thing. Power is about the ability to realize one's will against others; it is the application of coercion and sanctions, as well as the ability to manipulate people's expectations and desires contrary to their best interests. Clearly political leadership and decision-making are vital aspects of power.

Observers differ about which dimensions of inequality are most significant or basic in Bornean social systems. This is again partly the result of different analytical perspectives, as well as real differences between Bornean societies. I have tended to stress economic relations in my studies (King 1985a: 14–16), while Rousseau concentrates on the importance of political power in structuring Kayan social relations of inequality (1990: 199ff.). I would now suggest that both economic and political criteria are of at least equal weight and that it is difficult to determine which is, in practice, prior or basic in generating inequalities in Borneo. However, in a speculative reconstruction, I would still tend to emphasize control over economic resources as giving rise to inequalities, and this is very clearly seen in communities which managed to establish key positions in trade.

While there are social differences among the stratified societies of Borneo, there are broad principles of organization, which they share. Generally one can identify three main economic classes, viz. aristocrats, commoners and slaves, although this system has been subject to change through time. Among Kayan they are *maren*, *panyin* and *dipen* (Rousseau 1979: 215–17); among most Kenyahs *deta'u* or *paran*, *panyin* and *lipen* or *panyin lamin* or *ula'* (Whittier 1973: 69–70; 1978: 109–11). For the Kajangs they are variously *linau laja*, *maren* or *lajar*, *panyin*, and *dipan/dipen* or *lipien*; for the Malohs-Tamans, *samagat*, *banua* and *pangkam*. The aristocrats in a longhouse are very obviously Leach's 'house owning group'. In the past they commanded labour resources (slaves for farm and domestic chores, and corvées from commoners). Traditionally aristocrats usually had rights in more and better quality land than commoners, or at least, given their control of labour, the capacity to cultivate larger tracts of land; they accumulated agricultural surplus and trading profits, and translated some of these benefits into heirlooms and ritual objects. They did not, as a rule, have to undertake menial field labour; they also often supported impressive religious feasts. Historically some paramount chiefs had very large numbers of slaves, such as Kwing Irang, the Mahakam-Kayan chief, at the turn of the century (Nieuwenhuis 1907, ii: 96).

Usually the commoners formed the bulk of the population in a given community of between two-thirds to three-quarters of longhouse or village members. Commoners were free agriculturalists, exercising some control over their production, productive factors and the product of their labour. Periodically they had to work for aristocrats and deliver tribute to them (Rousseau 1990: 173–9). Slaves, however, were owned by aristocrats. Captive-slaves worked entirely for their masters and usually lived in aristocratic households as house-slaves. They were instruments of production and could be exchanged for goods or for payment of fines or bridewealth, or used as sacrificial victims in rituals. Bond- or debt-slaves could farm and live independently of their masters, but generally they had no land rights and no freedom of movement; they were at their masters' beck-and-call; they could not marry without their permission, and theoretically all the products of their labour belonged to aristocrats.

Obviously with processes of modernization in Borneo, these class distinctions are being undermined, but they can still be discerned in some communities, and, for some high-class individuals, the advantages of traditional class have been consolidated in that aristocrats have managed to secure education, qualifications and senior positions in administration, or set themselves up as entrepreneurs.

If we now turn to considerations of social esteem or prestige, we find a rather different hierarchical arrangement, which is interlinked with class distinctions, but is not precisely coincident with them. Given the fact that status is concerned with indigenous categorization, we should not be surprised to find that members of a society might disagree about what constitutes high or low prestige. This is especially so in a situation of rapid change in which older secular and religious values supporting the privileged position of aristocrats are being undermined and increasingly replaced by new considerations of status based on such things as modern education, white-collar employment, and Western religion and modes of dress. Nevertheless, when aristocrats clearly had political power in the past, their values could more easily be imposed on others, and traditionally there was a broad consensus in status-ranking in stratified systems. Four status levels were acknowledged in most central Borneo societies, and they still have some currency in local discourse. Among the Kayans these were the *maren* (ruling estate), *hipuy ok* (lower aristocrats), *panyin* (commoners) and *dipen* (slaves) (Rousseau 1978: 86; 1990: 165). The Kenyah case is rather more variable and complicated, but broadly there were *paran* or *deta'u bio* (big aristocrats), *paran iot* or *deta'u dumit* (small aristocrats), *panyin* or *panyin uma'* (commoners) and *panyin lamin* or *ula'* (slaves). If we take the Malohs, they had *samagat* (high aristocrats), *pabiring* (the middle rank or lower aristocrats), *banua* (ordinary villagers) and *pangkam* (slaves).

Because of the confusions in the use of different concepts to examine different dimensions of social inequality in Borneo and as a result of processes of change, it is sometimes difficult to distinguish status levels adequately in the literature. For example, this is the case with some of the work on the Kajang-Melanau (de Martinoir 1974; Morris 1953: 51ff.; 1980: 298ff.). Nevertheless, formerly the status criteria which were generally significant for expressing and confirming the categories of prestige in Borneo were social origins or birth, styles of life, personal and family names, genealogical connections, and a whole variety of symbols of rank which were enshrined in differentiated *adat* fines and bridewealth, ritual distinctions and seating positions in ceremonies, in material culture (heirlooms, ritual paraphernalia, clothing, bodily adornments and markings such as tattoos, ceremonial pictorial designs in painting, carving and beadwork) and in oral traditions (King 1985a: 16–17; Whittier 1973: 70ff., 141ff., 167ff.). Some of these elements are still used today by certain aristocrats to claim privileges. Of particular note in status systems was also the Kenyah graded scale of feasts (*mamat*) and rank insignia (Galvin 1966, 1968). Usually slaves did not figure in status terms; they were conceived of as 'non-people'.

These status levels were commonly regrouped into two broad ritual categories. For the Kayans there were the *kelunan jia* ('superior' or 'refined people'), comprising the *maren* and *hipuy ok*, and the *kelunan ji'ek* ('inferior' or 'bad people'), comprising the *panyin* and *dipen*. The first category was 'entitled to use some tattoo designs and ritual elements forbidden to the others', and was spiritually more powerful (Rousseau 1978: 86; 1979: 218). Among the Kenyahs there were the *deta'u* ('those of the right') and the *kelunan kado'* ('the many') (Whittier 1978: 110).

Distinctions were also established within status categories, and these were, in turn, a product of intermarriage and movement between levels. One vital mechanism of social mobility was inter-rank marriage, although ideally people married those of the same rank. Kenyah aristocrats, for example, were divided between *deta'u bio* or *paran bio* ('big aristocrats'), *paran lepo'* or *paran uma'* ('ordinary aristocrats'), as well as the 'small aristocrats' (*paran iot*) (Whittier 1973: 69–70; 1978: 109–11). There were also usually distinctions among the commoner or ordinary villagers, for both the Kayan and Kenyah, between the 'good *panyin*' and the 'bad *panyin*'; the 'good *panyin'* could demonstrate some links with individuals of higher rank (Elshout 1923: 207ff.; Rousseau 1990: 165). As another example, among the Melanaus there were distinctions between aristocrats: the *basa pengiren/pangeran*, who were descended from Muslim Brunei aristocratic families, and the *basa menteri/mantri*, ordinary Melanau aristocrats; and between freemen: the *basa bumi ateng* or 'true freemen' and the *basa bumi giga'* (Morris 1953: 54ff.).

Of crucial significance in this status scheme was the level below the aristocrats: the Kayan *hipuy* and the Kenyah *paran iot*. This level was an ambiguous one. Economically its members were part of the commoner class, yet in status terms differentiated from other commoners, and specifically in ritual and symbolism categorized with the aristocrats. They can be viewed then as either 'fallen aristocrats' or 'aspiring commoners'. Rousseau has said of the Kayan *hipuy* that it appears to be 'a residual category with no definite role' (1974: 389). He argues that, in his terms, these 'estates', based on jurally acknowledged status, are important

at the structural level; their presence is essential to the reproduction of the system as it protects the ideology which justifies the structure of inequality. (1979: 232)

One can therefore view this intermediate status-level as a means to accommodate social movements between ranks, and, by this means, keep the system of social inequality in being. The Kayan *hipuy*, for example, maintained the distance between aristocrats and the bulk of commoners. If aristocrats, who had fallen on bad times, could have become commoners in a very short space of time, then this might have led to the questioning of an ideology which made it appear as if aristocrats were sacred and intrinsically different from commoners. Again Rousseau says that the existence of this middle rank

makes it possible to regulate the ratio of dominant to subordinate classes without endangering the ideology of stratification. (1979: 230)

One therefore has examples of the interesting phenomenon whereby aristocratic households, which had declined in their economic and political position, and were in danger of being reclassified as of a lower rank, still claimed to be aristocrats because of their descent and genealogical connections, although the bases of that claim had been largely removed (King 1985a: 99).

Finally we come to the dimension of power. The aristocratic stratum was also a ruling class. A common feature of Bornean ranking systems is the terminological identification of aristocrats with chiefship or leadership. Among the Kenyahs, the word for chief or leader (*paran*) is also extended in meaning to refer to aristocrats; the same practice is found among the Kayans with the term *maren*. Traditionally, aristocrats monopolized the chiefly office, supplying longhouse, village and regional leaders (Rousseau 1990: 187ff.). Chiefs and closely related aristocrats were further demarcated by being given honorific titles. Kayans use the term *Laja'*, derived from Malay *Raja*.

Ideally succession to chiefly position was from father to son or from a man to his nephew. However, if there was no suitable candidate a man's son-in-law might succeed, or a brother or cousin, or even an adopted male, either from that village or another community, or sometimes even from a neighbouring stratified village of a different ethnic group.

In any matter of concern to the whole community, adult aristocrats, both males and females, played a dominant role in village meetings. The chief, as the representative of the aristocrats, had very little authority over other aristocrats. His decisions were, in effect, the collective judgements of the aristocracy. If insulted or injured, aristocrats could also initiate proceedings against others, and confiscate their property. Some aristocrats certainly did abuse their power in the past.

Traditionally, aristocrats were war-leaders, mobilizing forces to embark on raids for slaves and heads. They also negotiated peace-settlements between hostile villages; an important means of cementing an alliance or resolving conflicts was the arrangement of a marriage between the respective aristocratic families of the disputing factions. Indeed, aristocrats had an extensive inter-community network of marriage alliances, and, as Rousseau has argued, central Borneo chiefs played crucial roles in the management and control of the relations between villages.

One of the main reasons for community fission was conflict

between aristocrats; provided the contesting parties could muster sufficient support, the longhouse or village might be physically divided and a new settlement established. Communities could only be formed and maintained if they had aristocrats to lead them. Aristocrats could impose fines on their villages, and the fact that fines due to aristocrats were higher than those paid for offences against commoners meant that ordinary villagers might get into debt and ultimately become debt- or field-slaves. Slaves could be summarily executed if they committed an offence.

Formerly the movements of all non-aristocratic villagers were controlled by aristocrats. Longhouse and village size was usually a function of the political power, economic success and prestige of the chief. A fall in population through an epidemic, or the loss of subjects through conflicts and partition, could seriously weaken the position of a chief, and might ultimately lead him to subordinate himself to others.

Nevertheless, the aristocrats did not have a complete monopoly of power. There were usually experienced, influential, economically successful commoners who managed to acquire reputations in village affairs and were incorporated into decision-making processes. This wider political grouping, along with aristocrats, has been referred to as a 'political elite' (Rousseau 1974: 401–3), and, in effect, comprised a council of elders (King 1985a: 85). These individuals, who achieved positions of importance in politics, often tried to consolidate their position by securing marriages for their children with those of higher rank, or with enterprising households of the same rank. Mobility was also achieved through systems of status feasting, which could be used to translate economic success into acknowledged status.

As Rousseau has ably demonstrated, a stable and relatively developed system of social inequality existed for a long time in central Borneo, and social stratification has been and, to some extent, still is an important defining characteristic of the settled agriculturalists there (1990: 214–18). Nonetheless, these were small-scale political systems embracing either one village or a federation of villages. Because of communication problems and the distance between communities, it was difficult for a chief to establish firm and sustained control over villages outside his home village. Yet, with the more formal systems of hereditary chiefship, such groups as the Kayan and Kenyah did manage to produce paramount chiefs who exercised power and influence over several communities, using the network of marriage alliances forged by aristocrats. Be that as it may, the interior societies, with their limited resource base and dispersed populations, did not generate the large-scale state systems which emerged along the coasts of Borneo, and which we shall consider shortly by examining the example of the Brunei Sultanate.

Longhouses

Aside from such social elements as cognation, ambilineal descent reckoning, small independent families or households, and 'house owning groups', probably the characteristic feature of Bornean societies is longhouse domicile. But it is well to remember that not all natives of the island construct them. I have already mentioned that the Barito-speaking Ngajus, Ma'anyans and Luangans build individual multi-family houses, but not longhouses. Of the Ma'anyans Hudson and Hudson have said

Frame dwellings (*lewu'*) line the single village street. Older houses are large enough to accommodate several families, usually closely related. (1978: 215)

There is some dispute about whether the Ngajus have ever constructed longhouses. They certainly do not do so now; they have instead solidly built 'great houses' (*betang*), usually housing extended families. A stairway gives access, and is usually divided by a platform on which several carved wooden figures (*hampatongs*) would stand. What is more the hunters-gatherers of the interior, given their very mobile lifestyle, did not build longhouses, but instead temporary lean-tos, shelters and family huts, which could be easily dismantled or simply abandoned. Only under the cultural influence of settled farmers did some forest nomads adopt longhouse domicile.

Despite these exceptions the majority of Dayaks do live in longhouses, and have done so since ancient times. The architecture and layout of Borneo longhouses follow much the same sort of pattern across the island, although obviously there are variations depending on ethnic group, socio-economic change, availability of materials and so on (Avé and King 1986: 52ff.). The structure is usually divided into two parts: a rear section, comprising the family compartments, separated from each other by timber or bark walls, and a covered front section of the house. Longhouses are not an expression of a communal way of life; they comprise independent, physically separated families, which happen to live in the same residential structure under the same roof. Even the Kelabits, who may only have dividing panels of modest height between family living spaces, nevertheless have separate families or 'hearths'. The front part of the longhouse is, in effect, the village street, running the whole length of the dwelling, and giving access to each compartment through doors which open onto the gallery. Ladders usually run from both ends of the gallery to the ground below. Sometimes they may be placed at the front of the gallery.

While the compartments are private family spaces, identified symbolically and practically with females, the covered gallery is the public domain, and seen generally as part of the male world. An important focus of family life is the hearth where women cook the daily meals. Traditionally this was located in the compartment space against one of its walls, although now more frequently it is placed in a separate kitchen, connected to the living room by a walkway, and situated at the rear of the house. Toilet facilities may be provided there too. The compartment is where females spend much of the time while they are in the house. It is also where the family sleeps and where heirlooms and other family property are stored. Traditionally, valuable gongs, jars and plates would line the walls of the room. Increasingly one finds items of modern furniture in the house, whereas formerly people would sit and sleep on woven mats laid on the floor.

The gallery is the appropriate place for public meetings. It is where guests are entertained, where most major rituals are performed, where men spend much of their relaxation time or undertake daily chores such as repairing fishing nets and traps. Traditionally in most houses, the severed heads of enemies were hung near the main support-posts of the gallery, at which fires were lit at night. As we have seen, there were exceptions, such as the Bidayuhs who placed heads in the separate headhouse. Overall then, the gallery is identified with the exploits of men and with the male cult of headhunting. Another male preoccupation is cock-fighting; and cockerels are also tethered on the gallery outside the compartment doors.

Variations in longhouse forms are nevertheless considerable. As we have seen, for some groups such as the Ibans the village comprises one longhouse; for others like the Kenyahs and Malohs there are often multi-longhouse villages. Whereas Iban houses are usually raised a modest height from the ground and built of lighter woods and other materials such as bamboo, Kenyah and Kayan houses are massive structures, built on heavy ironwood posts with plank flooring, high off the ground. The central Borneo groups traditionally decorated their houses, particularly to designate rank. Important chiefs, for example, might have their compartment walls and heavy wooden doors, and even the rafters above and the adjacent gallery posts, carved and painted in elaborate motifs and patterns expressing aristocratic rank (see chapter 9). Sometimes the roof section of Kenyah aristocratic family compartments (*lamin*) would be raised higher than others, and the covered gallery outside the chief's residence would be wider and more spacious (figure 3).

In some houses, for example those of the Ibanic-related groups, the public gallery (*ruai*) usually has an uninterrupted passageway close to the compartment doors, which serves as a street. In certain cases, as among the Rungus Dusuns, the walkway is at a lower elevation than the rest of the outer gallery section. Bidayuh families sometimes construct the gallery at different widths and elevations and their longhouses and platforms are connected by bamboo and plank bridges and walkways.

The outer section of the Iban gallery may be divided into sections corresponding to separate family compartments, separated by low bamboo or wooden walls to form semi-enclosed spaces, where people can sit and chat, or work, and where guests can be entertained and accommodated. Among Malohs and Kenyahs, for example, the gallery is left open and not divided in this way. In addition, Iban houses usually have

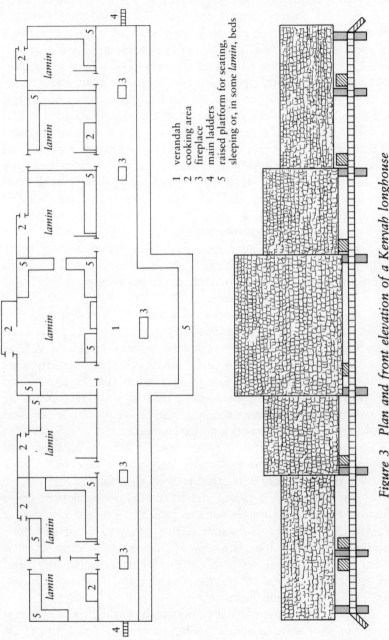

1 verandah
2 cooking area
3 fireplace
4 main ladders
5 raised platform for seating,
   sleeping or, in some *lamin*, beds

Figure 3 Plan and front elevation of a Kenyah longhouse

an open verandah (*tanju*) at the front of the house joined on to the covered gallery, access to which is gained by doorways from the *ruai*, which can be closed over at night. The *tanju* is used for drying rice, fish or various forest products. Clothes are also placed there to dry. Some ceremonies can be conducted on the *tanju* and processed rice might be winnowed there. Ibans customarily store their rice in bark bins in the house loft (*sadau*). For Malohs, however, rice bins are placed on raised wooden structures beneath the house, or in separate shelters where agricultural equipment can also be stored. Kayans and Kenyahs store their rice in separate barns on stilts near the house. For the stratified peoples who usually do not have open house galleries, drying and other activities in the open air can be undertaken on the ground in the vicinity of the longhouse or on separate bamboo platforms.

Another variation of house design is found among some Bidayuh communities and the Tingalan Dayaks of East Kalimantan; there, two rows of compartments face each other and look out onto an open verandah.

Longhouses are very functional dwellings. It is assumed that their *raison d'être* was traditionally defence. In the past when headhunting and raiding were rife, it was easier to defend one's community if it was gathered together in one structure. Houses were generally built much higher off the ground to make access for the enemy more difficult. Ladders could be drawn up at night. The vicinity of the house would be fortified with palisades, earthworks and trenches.

But the house, raised several metres off the ground and constructed of natural materials, also gives shade and allows cooler air and breezes to circulate to combat the oppressive heat and humidity. A raised structure also provides protection against flooding. Animals such as pigs and poultry can shelter under the house, and human refuse dropped from the floor above is consumed by the animals below, providing an efficient waste-disposal system. Various items can also be stored in specially constructed sections under the house – canoes, firewood, rattan and bamboo.

In the past, if people were physically mobile, it was much easier to cooperate in building a longhouse and fewer materials were needed if individual families shared dividing walls, support-posts, beams and access ladders. Finally, longhouses provide a most convenient social space for small-scale, closely-knit communities. They allow a measure of privacy while, at the same time, giving opportunities for communication and social interaction, and the holding of large public events. In other words, their physical structure partly gives expression to the social order, and, in turn, contributes to the maintenance of that order. There is an intimate interconnection between social relations and spatial arrangements.

The house, in an important sense, is the focus of a community's world: it gives form to that world; internally it embodies social and symbolic divisions and it provides external boundaries. The entrances or exits to the house, by means of doors and ladders, are especially important. They give access to the world beyond, to allow social interaction with outsiders and communication with the spirit world. But they are also points to be guarded, lest people from outside bring harm, or evil forces enter the house. Entrances are therefore often protected by guardian statues or demonic images carved into ladders to frighten away malevolent and often sickness-bearing spirits. These apertures in the boundaries of the house also figure importantly in religious life, in taboos or prescriptions, in the coming of invited gods and spirits to participate in house ceremonies and in journeys of the souls of the dead to the Afterworld.

Given the social, economic and cultural changes which Borneo is experiencing, some of the practices and values which give meaning to longhouse domicile have been modified or undermined. Thus, some individuals, groups and communities have abandoned longhouse domicile in favour of single-family dwellings. However, the longhouse has shown a remarkable resilience, a testimony to its social and cultural significance. In Sarawak, for example, in recognition of its continued importance, government agencies involved in resettlement or community development have constructed new longhouses for settlers using modern materials – sawn timber, glass windows and corrugated roofing. Some Dayaks have also taken it upon themselves to modernize their dwellings, while retaining the basic form and layout of the traditional longhouse.

State formations: the Sultanate of Brunei

The Malay principalities which, with the exception of Brunei, have disappeared in Borneo, were highly stratified polities with administrative organizations covering a large number of communities. They were cosmopolitan and were characterized by a greater degree of economic specialization than the Dayak communities. Their economic foundation was trade and the control of goods moving downriver from the interior and along the coasts. These states were therefore much more interested in the control of people and their activities, and the right to take tax and tribute from them, than in ownership of land. Territorial boundaries between states were usually very vaguely defined, especially as one moved further inland and away from the capital.

The focus of the realm was a Malay sultan or *raja*: a hereditary ruler who could confer on his appointed administrators titles and appanages. Sometimes various regions of the state were administered by royal or noble families, or they were granted as part of an administrative position to a non-noble official. These regions were thought of in terms of particular river basins or subdivisions of rivers. The degree of control which the ruler could, or indeed wished to, exert outside the immediate environs of his capital, of course, varied depending on the physical distance and access from the centre, the economic interest which the state had in the products of particular regions, the loyalty of the ruler's local representatives, the socio-cultural characteristics of the population there and competition from neighbouring states. These matters, in turn, depended on the success of the ruler in limiting intra-dynastic conflicts and personal ambitions in the court, and in conducting relations with neighbouring states.

I shall now describe the main elements of the traditional Brunei state. Many of these have disappeared during the past century, but certain features of the ranking system still find expression. In the traditional Brunei Sultanate three distinct forms of district or regional control were recognized (Brown 1970: 181). First came the *kerajaan* or the appanages of the ruling Sultan; second, *kuripan* or appanages of any other officials granted by the Sultan – if the office was vacant for any reason the rights reverted to the Sultan; and third, *tulin*, which comprised districts and peoples governed by hereditary rulers who had considerable autonomy but acknowledged some allegiance to the Sultan. The holders of these regions derived income from tax and tribute on the goods produced, including forest products, rice and sago.

At one time the Brunei Sultanate claimed sovereignty over large parts of the island. In reality, an administrative presence was maintained in limited stretches along the coasts, focused on important river mouths. Rarely did it extend inland, although, given the fact that the state controlled goods coming from and going into the interior, the government claimed more extensive rights than it in fact had. Even control over more distant coastal parts of the realm often depended on an uneasy alliance, expressed in terms of patron-clientship, between the Sultan and local rulers. In this way the Sultan's power was constantly kept in check by his officials and representatives, who might easily rebel against him, break away or offer allegiance to a rival. As we have seen, the polity was therefore unstable, particularly with regard to its vassals, and its control over remote interior peoples was slight or non-existent.

Different ethnic groups were also incorporated into the state structure and performed distinct roles within it. It was therefore a plural society or polity. In the Brunei state the Melanaus were sago producers; the Kedayans, rice-farmers; the Bajaus, small-scale traders and slave raiders; the Kayans, Lun Bawangs and other Dayaks, suppliers of forest products: and various Dayaks along with the Bajaus provided a 'volunteer army' (Brown 1970: 4). The government was dominated by the minority Bruneis or Brunei Malays. It was they who lived in and around the capital at the Brunei river, and had, as a whole, the highest prestige and greatest political power. They mainly inhabited the large water-villages, comprising wooden family dwellings built on stilts over the river, surrounding the Sultan's palace and the main mosque. The royal family and the nobility (*pengirans*) were generally of Brunei Malay stock, highly stratified and status-conscious. They had an elaborate system of administrative, ceremonial and ritual offices, with a complex hierarchy of honorific titles, linguistic usages and etiquette.

One's official position was very much determined by birth in the male line rather than achievement. There were very few promotions. As Brown says

One of the principal functions of the stratification system was regulation of access to office. Brunei's system of offices was apparently of 'Hindu' origin . . . but it also contained certain Islamic manifestations. (1976: 187)

The main distinction was between the nobility and commoners. Within these two strata there were further divisions based on genealogical closeness to officials. The 'core nobility' comprised 'nobles descended from current or recent Sultans or other high officials' (p. 186). The most important officials next to the Sultan were the four viziers (*wazir*), also from the core nobility.

Traditionally the viziers had particular ministerial functions; in order of precedence they were the *pengiran bendahara* (in effect, the deputy of the Sultan who ruled the land or the interior); *pengiran di-gadong* (responsible for finance and the treasury, particularly with regard to taxation); *pengiran pemancha* (the mediator of the State Council); and the *pengiran temenggong* (the military leader, especially of sea forces). However, although these senior officials were ideologically charged with special functions, in practice no office was necessarily linked to a particular function, and apparently these duties changed quite frequently (Brown 1970: 106).

Brown points out that because of the decentralized nature of the Brunei state, the senior officials might have little to do at a state-wide level, other than formulate general policy. The appanages and private domains were independent in many respects; indeed, the viziers too would have had administrative responsibilities for their own personal domains, which were usually extensive.

Below the core nobility were the commoner nobles (*pengiran kebanyakan*) (p. 186). These were appointed as officials with the term *cheteria*, a Hindu-derived term for the warrior caste. They too had appanages assigned to them and domains to administer and they were differentiated according to the level of their official positions. Nevertheless, there was much disagreement about this official order of precedence and therefore the rank status associated with it. The only overall agreement was that the highest *cheteria* was the *pengiran shah-bandar* (literally: 'the ruler of the port'), charged with the supervision and administration of foreign traders and visitors.

Below the nobles were those of non-noble rank, and the highest of these were the aristocrats (*awang*). It was these who undertook much of the day-to-day administration on behalf of the nobles and played a vital role in the functioning of the state. The non-noble officials were termed *menteri*, and the highest of them enjoyed the honorific title *pehin*. They were divided according to secular and religious responsibilities in the capital, with a further sub-group serving as district officials. Some of these latter were probably not Brunei Malays. Because the *pehin* were vital in the efficient administration of the state, they tended to be associated more directly with administrative functions; they were usually answerable directly to the Sultan, although some were subordinates of noble officials. Nevertheless,

The formal distinction of all *pehin* was that like all noble officials they were inaugurated with ancient and sacred formulas called *chiri*. (Brown, 1976: 188–9)

These *chiri* comprised various Sanskrit, Arabic and old Malay words.

Below the aristocrats were commoner Bruneis, and from these a whole host of miscellaneous officials or *menteri* were appointed. Then at the lowest levels of the official hierarchy was a large category of non-Brunei, usually non-Muslim, non-Malay local officials, who were usually referred to as 'land chiefs' (*menteri darat*). Although these were very low in Brunei status terms, they usually had high prestige among their own populations. These would have included, for example, Iban and Kayan leaders who were given Malay-derived titles such as *penghulu*, *temenggong* and *pemancha*.

At the very bottom of the hierarchy were the village headmen (*ketua kampong*) who were responsible for the basic constituent units of the state: the village communities. These comprised headmen of Brunei villages or wards within the capital of the court, and Dayak villages in the various outlying domains of the state. The mass of the population, mainly

Dayaks, were then classified merely as subjects, dependents or clients (*hamba*). Very finally, there were slaves (*ulun*), commonly owned by nobles and senior officials, and acquired through capture, purchase or indebtedness. These undertook such menial chores as household work. But as Brown says, even 'the various pagan peoples of northwest Borneo seem to have been, in the Brunei view, little differentiated from slaves' (1976: 187).

Most of the Malay wards in the capital at Brunei Bay performed specialist functions. Some were fishing communities or strand collectors, then there were wards of palm weavers, wood workers, textile manufacturers, rice processors, and traders. Of special importance were the metalsmiths. As we have seen in chapter 4, the coastal states played a vital role as pivotal points in Bornean trade, exchanging interior forest products (or upstream goods) for locally made products (or downstream goods). The coastal port centres specialized in the manufacture of iron implements, ordinary brassware, and later some silver goods, such as basic jewellery and other adornments for the interior Dayak market. Furthermore, the specialist smiths made high-quality items for the court and its nobles and other officials, and these tasks were often associated with aristocratic households. Thus, the capital also had wards of blacksmiths, silver-smiths and brass-smiths. These were caste-like occupational divisions, handing down skills from parents to children. Of special fame were Brunei brass products, particularly cannons, kettles, pots and other vessels (plate 35). These were traded widely into interior Borneo, and kept as heirlooms by Dayak communities.

Increasingly as trade and commerce expanded, other Asian merchants came to settle in the port. Of these the Chinese were the most important, and with later Chinese immigration during the British Residential period, they now comprise about 25 per cent of Brunei's population. The Chinese and small numbers of Indians and other alien groups were incorporated into the Brunei scheme of things as commoners, and some were given commoner offices and appropriate titles.

These then are the main social and political forms in Borneo, presumably developed over time from the first Austronesian

Plate 35   Brunei cannon

communities which came to the island. One can see clearly that certain environmental adaptations have been very important in giving rise to these variations in organization so that we have examples of different kinds of society in Borneo. These range from the small, mobile band organizations of the forest nomads through the longhouse- and village-based societies of the Dayaks, which themselves have differentiated into both egalitarian and stratified social systems, to the traditional Islamic coastal states – highly stratified and status-conscious. These latter were part of an international economic, political and religious community, internally differentiated in terms of specialist functions and with a marked division of labour, particularly coincident with ethnic differences.

The casual observer could be forgiven for assuming that these differences between Bornean societies have been the result of migrations of different groups of people to the island, or of evolutionary change from simple band societies through agriculture to large-scale complex state systems, or of the importation of foreign models and cultural artifacts from India and China in particular. All these explanations have been utilized to varying degrees by European writers. But I would prefer to invoke a more straightforward explanation in terms of the emergence of a set of alternative social forms from an original society exploiting the different economic and environmental possibilities of the island. Without doubt these internally generated adaptive responses were also affected by outside influences from other parts of Asia and from Europe. But these merely consolidated or modified what was already taking place locally. Those communities which could take advantage of strategic locations for the control of trade had the economic resources to develop stratified state formations. Those that specialized in rainforest hunting and gathering had to keep social and political forms to a minimum to aid mobility and a flexible response to meeting food needs from the forest, which could only support very modest population levels.

The most variable systems are the structurally intermediate ones: those of the Dayak agriculturalists. Nomadic societies and coastal state systems comprise the fixed end or polar points in a socio-political continuum. Some Dayak communities tend towards the nomadic end of the continuum either in their economic activities or their social order, or both. Others are closer to the stratified polities of the Muslim port centres. There is no single reason for this. The variations between Dayak societies must partly be attributed to different environmental adaptations and to variations in resource availability, but also to their relations with other communities and ethnic groups, with forest nomads and coastal Muslim states, and to historical circumstances, such as the penetration of Islam in Borneo and the establishment of colonial rule. Presumably some Dayaks could, by controlling some trade locally in the interior or exploiting a particularly favourable resource-base, develop a stratified social order. Some who did, of course, 'became Malay' with conversion to Islam, and they adopted fully the 'state model' of organization. Others, like the Kayans, developed stratification, but remained as Dayaks. Still others, like the Ibans, opted for a more mobile, migratory existence, and to sustain a pioneering and aggressive lifestyle, eschewed hierarchy in favour of a relatively egalitarian, competitive and prestige-achieving rather than prestige-ascriptive society. Some societies may well have adopted a ranked social order in contact with other stratified communities; others may have been more influenced by neighbouring egalitarian societies.

The examination of Bornean socio-political organization decisively illustrates one of my main preoccupations in this book: Bornean unity and diversity. To continue with this theme, I wish now to move from the more materialist considerations of environment, economy and socio-political adaptations, to the cultural spheres of religion, symbolism and worldview. But, in what follows, I shall indicate some of the connections between economic activities, rainforest habitats and indigenous conceptions of the world.

8

Worldview and Religion

Introduction

We have already seen that Borneo cultures are seemingly very diverse in their religious beliefs and practices. Yet beneath the surface of cultural variation, certain conceptions about the world and the place of humans within it are strikingly similar, as are the principles which structure this worldview. My assumption is that these conformities go back to the culture of the early Austronesian settlers of Borneo. Nevertheless, these uniformities are expressed in different ways in traditional Bornean religions. Some groups place great emphasis on funeral rites and the relationships between the living and the dead; others stress the importance of the cult of heads and the rituals of fertility and life-giving powers associated with them; still others have elaborate ceremonies which punctuate the agricultural cycle.

Yet, as Sellato notes, myths concerning the creation of the world and the first human beings are very similar across many Bornean groups. He says:

In the beginning, there were only the skies and the primeval waters, inhabited by godly beings, respectively male and female. (1989a: 35)

All Dayak groups either recognize a principal deity responsible for creation, which is comprised of two parts or aspects, sometimes separately named; or two main and separate deities. What is important is the principle of dualism which structures the native conception of the cosmos. It involves the union of the two aspects of the deity or the two deities, representing the heavens, skies or Upperworld on the one hand, and the primeval waters, earth or Underworld on the other.

The representation of this duality is also achieved by associating symbolically the Upperworld with birds, usually the hornbill or the hawk, and the lower world with the serpent or the mythical dragon. This dual conception of the cosmos is also expressed in the association of the skies with maleness and headhunting, and the Underworld with femaleness and agriculture. Both head-taking rites and agricultural ceremonies are central parts of a religion directed towards acquiring and increasing fertility, and what some observers have called 'life-force'.

However, it does not necessarily follow that the creator deity, or other of its manifestations, is omnipotent and plays a central role in everyday religious life. Its position and status may vary between different ethnic groups. It is most noticeable among the Ibans, for example, that, although there is a creator deity, commonly referred to as *Raja Entala*, and certain dual symbolic dimensions, there is a pantheon of deities which has overriding importance in the everyday affairs of the Ibans. Nevertheless, even among these deities two are of special importance: the 'bird-god' or deity of war, *Sengalong Burong*, and *Pulang Gana*, the deity of the earth and agriculture (Jensen 1974). Among the Ngaju, on the other hand, the creator deity is conceived of as comprising two aspects, and divided into two separately named entities: *Mahatala*, symbolized by the hornbill, and *Jata*, identified with the water serpent; these two play a vitally important part in the religious life of the Ngaju (Jay 1991; Schärer 1963). The senior deities or deity are credited with establishing a framework, a set of rules and procedures for conducting social and religious life. They also bequeathed the main institutions and customary practices, including headhunting and rice agriculture, to human beings.

Dayaks also recognize important ancestor deities or spirits, whose exploits are usually related in epics and legends, and again these are often headed by two main figures, one male and one female. This Dayak oral tradition, including myths of creation, obviously relates to a spiritual plane of existence, which is intimately interrelated with the world of human beings, but separate from it. This spiritual realm connects humans to their origins and to the very beginnings of time. Although supernatural beings are now separate from humans, they were, in ancient times, living together with them. Dayaks identify certain geographical locations and natural features with the life and events of the deities and spirits. These places may also be linked to oral traditions about the early physical migrations of peoples in Borneo. Often the abode of the gods is located on a particular mountaintop in Borneo, or the Land of the Dead associated with particular mountains and rivers. The Ibans and Malohs have the Mandai river and Bukit Tilung or Telung in the upper Kapuas area as the location of their Afterworld; the Kadazan, perhaps quite naturally, have Mount Kinabalu in Sabah, the Luangan of south-eastern Borneo, Gunung Lumut (Avé and King 1986: 34).

Thus, the Dayaks generally conceive of their world as in two main parts: one above and one below, interrelated but separate from the human world. Aside from the deities and principal spirits, this cosmos is inhabited by all kinds of spiritual entities – some benevolent, some malicious, some both, depending on their mood and the actions of humans. There are very common media among Dayaks for communicating with the spirit world. Some of these are available to all ordinary mortals, others are the responsibility of ritual specialists who have esoteric knowledge and particular expertise in handling relations with the supernatural.

An important general medium of contact is through dreams and dream experiences. There is a common belief among Dayaks that humans have a soul, which can enter or leave the body, usually through the fontanelle. It is especially during dreams that an individual's soul departs and has all kinds of adventures and contacts with spirits. That is why dreams and their interpretation are important for everyday affairs to enable an individual to evaluate whether his endeavours are likely to succeed or fail. Dreams are also an important mechanism of religious innovation and change, since one's dream experiences can produce wholly new ideas and practices (Freeman 1975: 284–7). They are not, in other words, controllable to any extent by social institutions or special practitioners. If, during sleep, one's soul strays too far, or gets lost, or is captured by evil spirits, this then directly explains human sickness, because the body is deprived of its spiritual essence or energy. If the soul cannot be recovered then death will inevitably result. The link between life and death is conceived of as the journey of the soul to the Afterworld. This journey of the dead is ubiquitous in Borneo. In funeral ceremonies, bards or chanters recount the journey, so that the soul is properly and appropriately conducted to its last resting place (Metcalf 1982). The soul then translates into an ancestor spirit which is remembered by the living, and from time to time is called upon by them, honoured and provided offerings to ensure its continued benevolent interest and its practical assistance to its living relatives.

Another important general medium of human–spirit contact is by means of messengers. As we have already seen in the case of the Ibans, Borneo peoples hold to the importance of signs or augurs from the gods, usually communicated by birds, but also by certain animals. Dayaks recognize special individuals who are able to interpret the behaviour, calls and appearance of forest birds and animals, in their various occurrences and combinations, so that the purposes and guidance of supernatural beings are correctly made known to humans. Divine and spiritual guidance can also be realized through certain divinatory procedures, such as the 'reading' of the livers of sacrificed pigs. The configuration and condition of pigs' livers are given meaning through divination to signal that an event will be auspicious or inauspicious.

Another avenue for spiritual encounters is the institution of shamanism and spirit mediumship. These ritual practitioners are considered to have special powers, usually to cure spiritually induced sickness, such as soul-loss. Shamans can enter into relations with spirits through trance, and send their souls out to contact the supernatural, or send spirit helpers to accomplish the task for them. Spirit mediums go into trance and become possessed by spirits; that is, they provide the channel by means of which spirits communicate with the human world concerning spirit-induced sickness. These practitioners operate at the boundaries between two worlds or dimensions, and therefore are frequently seen as ambiguous and marginal beings. This status is often expressed in their sexually ambivalent roles and characteristics. Transvestite priests are common in Borneo; for example, traditionally the Ngaju *balian* (Schärer 1963) and the so-called 'female' *manang*, or shaman among the Iban, who is, in fact, a male spiritual curer who dresses as a female (Graham 1987: 90ff.). It is these specialists who have an intimate knowledge of the cosmos, its different parts and the deities and spirits associated with them. Often these ritual practitioners have a history of mental illness, or physical illness from which they have recovered, or are perceived in some way as 'deviant'. Many are called to the profession by dream experiences and other encounters with spirits.

Indeed, aside from dreams, individuals sometimes report chance contacts with spirits in the forest who communicate with them, giving them warnings or advice. On occasion, someone may go deliberately to a remote place in the forest or to locations known to be inhabited by spirits to seek counsel and support. Either in dreams or in other encounters, supernatural beings also endow humans with special gifts: these are usually talismans or amulets which are deposited in the forest by spirits and to which humans are then directed. They include particularly stones, beads and pieces of wood, bamboo or bone. Of course, families also pass on these magical objects from one generation to another.

Thus, humans are constantly in touch with the supernatural. It is an ever-present reality for them, and, in their daily affairs, individuals have to be mindful of the relations between this world and the spiritual plane of existence.

Fertility cults

The worldview of the Dayaks is activated and given expression in rituals. Important sets of ceremonies are concerned with sustaining and promoting life, success and prosperity. On the premise that physical well-being and good health, material prosperity and one's general fortunes have something to do with spiritual strength and the maintenance of appropriate relations between humans and spirits, much religious cerem-

ony is directed to these ends. There are two major fertility
cults which encapsulate these concerns: one is associated with
the world of men and male symbolism, the other with females
and female symbolism.

The cult of heads has an intimate relationship to the promotion of human fertility, well-being and bountiful harvests. The
early popular European notion of headhunting as a barbaric
practice, symptomatic of an evolutionary stage of primitive
savagery, has long been put aside. For example, in the 1930s,
Tillema, in reflective mood, said of headhunting

I do not in any way wish to justify the custom, but I must say that it
was in no way founded on cruelty or lust of blood, and it seems to
me regrettable that when this custom, which was to a certain extent
based upon ethical conceptions, was abolished, we did not attempt
to replace it by some other conception of spiritual value. (1934: 4)

Certainly headhunting was part of inter-group feuding and
warfare, territorial expansion and competition for resources.
In that sense, one might argue that it was an expression of
political relations between groups. But these processes, although providing a context for headhunting, do not directly
address the question of why it was that heads were severed and
ritually treated.

We know that the cutting of enemy heads and bringing them
back to one's home village as trophies was a vital element of a
complex of beliefs and practices about the soul, life and death,
and fertility, and, even though the practice was eliminated by
the European powers, many Dayak communities continue to
perform rituals which require the use of skulls, and hold beliefs
which acknowledge the power of severed heads. A long debate
in scholarly circles has been concerned with the identification
of the mechanisms or agencies which connect headhunting to
fertility.

Some scholars, for example, Hutton (1938) and Izikowitz
(1985 [1941]) have argued that indigenous beliefs locate the
human soul, or the concentration of 'soul-substance' or
'soul-stuff', in the head. By capturing a head and bringing it
back to one's community, one accumulates more soul-substance or life-energy, which contributes to one's own and
one's relatives' and neighbours' well-being. Thus, there is a

spiritual element which is transferred from one community to another and which is responsible for 'fertilizing' humans, crops and animals. One community's loss is another's gain, so that one's enemies' well-being and vitality are correspondingly weakened. This constant desire to accumulate energy or vitality in excess or make up for its deficiency explains the rationale for head-taking. This may help in turn to explain why the capturing of a head was necessary to end the mourning period of a prominent villager. In other words, it compensated for the loss of a person to the community both socially and spiritually. An accompanying rationale was that the victims of headhunting, or at least their captured souls contained in their heads, acted as servants of the deceased in the Afterworld.

Other writers have argued that the view that there is an agency of fertility, a soul-substance, rather like ether, is one which has been imposed by scientifically-minded Western observers; it is not an indigenous conception (Needham 1976). Instead the act of severing heads and carrying them back successfully as trophies of bravery and endeavour is quite simply a sign that the gods look on that community with favour, and therefore endow it with material and spiritual gifts. There is no medium or agency as such which *directly* connects heads with fertility.

Yet other writers have drawn attention to the phallic connotations of the head, and the fact that a head trophy is a symbol of the generative power of nature (Freeman 1979). It is therefore linked symbolically to the rice cult and the fertility of crops. In support of this view, Freeman draws attention to an Iban allegory which recounts that the head, when split open, contains not soul-substance or a life-force, but seed.

It may well be the case that in Borneo, and elsewhere in the South-East Asian world, the reasons for headhunting vary, and different peoples choose to emphasize certain dimensions at the expense of others. What is clear is that it is a kind of sacrificial act, which establishes contact with the spiritual world, and is part of Dayak conceptions of the cosmos and their place within it. At a minimum we know that in a religion which stresses the life-giving powers of certain relationships between the human and spiritual worlds, headhunting is one means of activating a relationship and deriving benefit from it.

What is also obvious is that head-taking is an important sign of male achievement and prowess. For men the taking of a head and the participation in a successful raid is a means of acquiring prestige, earning respect and ensuring one's eligibility as a worthy potential marriage partner. Thus, there is also a close link between male and female motivations and aspirations in the context of headhunting. Females would joyfully welcome their menfolk and the severed heads back to the village and receive them in ceremony and dancing. As an initiation into manhood, successful warriorship entitled one to wear or use particular adornments or ritual paraphernalia. Iban men, for example, had special motifs tattooed on their hands. For the Malohs, men could wear rhinoceros hornbill feathers in woven rattan war bonnets, and Kenyahs and Kayans might wear the carved casque of the helmeted hornbill on their headdresses.

The equipment of war contributed to this view of men as involved in the wild and the dangerous, in the deep forest and on journeys away (McKinley 1976). They wore birds' feathers; war jackets for those of prowess and rank were made of the skin of such animals as the clouded leopard, bear, tiger-cat or *orang utan*. Large wooden shields, frequently painted with demonic images to frighten the enemy and scare away their spiritual helpers, were also decorated with the hair of victims. Swords and spears might similarly be adorned with tufts of human hair. Fangs of animals might be used as ear decorations. Special protective amulets sometimes carved of wood, or of beads, animal teeth, bone or stone would also be worn.

The cult of heads also required the production of other cultural artifacts. Important ceremonies to do with promoting one's own general success and military might as against one's enemies focused on certain ritual paraphernalia: for example, the Iban hornbill carving in the famous 'Bird Ceremony' (*Gawai Burong*) to weaken the enemy; the Kenyah carved poles (*belawing* and *keramen*) to mark successful headhunts in the context of the major graded prestige feasts. Severed heads were also decorated, carved or inlaid, and skulls appeared as motifs in such objects as wood-carvings and woven textile patterns.

The close relationship between headhunting and sacrifice

can also be seen, to some extent, in the treatment of slaves among the stratified societies of Borneo. Among Ngajus, for example, slaves were ritually sacrificed, particularly in funeral ceremonies. Similarly among the Kayans, Kenyahs and Mal-ohs, slaves were killed in funeral rites for prominent aristo-cratic villagers, and, in addition, at the commencement of the construction of a new longhouse, when the first support-posts of the aristocratic chief's compartment were erected. The underlying conception of human sacrifice, as in headhunting, was one of renewal, and harnessing and increasing life-energy and therefore well-being. As Sellato says

Human sacrifice and the taking of human heads pertains also to the notions of fertility. Sacrificing a human life is the highest offering to the gods . . . the need for a human victim arose whenever the welfare of the community was materially or spiritually at stake . . . Life . . . is regenerated through the destruction of life. (1989a: 34)

It is also interesting that in societies with a slave class, there appears to have been rather less head-taking, since human sacrifice was an alternative in various rituals, whereas among the egalitarian Iban without slaves, heads were eagerly sought after.

The other fertility cult, this time associated much more with the world of women, is that to do with agriculture. Dayak rice farmers invariably assign spiritual qualities to their rice (Jensen 1974). It is after all their source of life. Just as the major male contribution to a successful harvest is the capturing of fertility-enhancing heads, so the contribution of females is both in their substantial practical contribution to rice agriculture and in the knowledge which they bring to bear in such matters as the selection of seeds. Although men do participate in various stages of the rice cultivation cycle, agriculture is closely identi-fied symbolically with women: the growth and ripening of rice is associated with female pregnancy and the female anatomy; rituals of agriculture are linked to that part of the cosmos which is identified with women. Sellato too notes that rice festivals

may feature parodies of sexual intercourse; ritual transvestism – women dressed as men, dancing a pretence of taking enemies' heads . . . . (1989a: 31)

The combination of the male head cult and the female rice cult provides the most powerful source of fertility and prosperity. Men venture into the wild and unknown to capture or to confirm fertility and well-being endowed by the gods; women apply their best endeavours to the tamed and domesticated processes of fertility enhancement in successfully producing the staple foodstuff.

Because rice is considered to possess a soul like humans, because its fertility depends on its spiritual condition and because its welfare is watched over by rice spirits and a deity of agriculture, various ritual prescriptions surround it, and ceremonies have to be performed to ensure that the soul of rice remains content. Rice is therefore treated with reverence. Even after the harvest when the rice is stored in bark-bins, it is believed that it can miraculously reduce in quantity if its soul is not resting contentedly in or near the bins. The Malohs place special 'guardian stones' in their rice bins, which are thought to contain spirits which can protect the stored rice.

One of the most direct kinds of identification between the spiritual qualities of rice and humans is seen in the Iban belief that the souls of deceased Ibans eventually dissolve into dew which falls to earth and is then taken up by the ears of rice, which are, in turn, ultimately consumed by humans (Jensen 1974).

Each stage of the rice cultivation cycle is punctuated by rituals. These primarily comprise the taking of omens to determine whether the activity in question will be auspicious or not, the imposition of taboos to ensure that the rice soul is protected and the giving of offerings to ensure that the soul and other relevant spirits and deities are looked after. Especially important is the protection of the rice against disease-bearing spirits; sometimes protective carved wooden statues are placed at entrance points around the fields, or, as with the Kayans and Kenyahs, frightening carved and painted wooden masks are worn and dances are performed to scare away harmful spirits.

Aside from Dayak preoccupations with life-enhancing rituals, other major religious ceremonies revolve around death. Indeed, funeral ceremonies and the ritual paraphernalia involved in them are among some of the most impressive in the religious life of Bornean peoples. The dual division between male and female, Upperworld and Underworld, life and death are also manifested in funeral rites and conceptions of death and the Afterworld.

Death ceremonies

How do Bornean peoples deal with the fact and the reality of death? The loss of a social person to the community also entails a spiritual loss. Both the social and the cosmic orders are disturbed and placed in a situation of imbalance. Death cannot simply be accepted; it must be managed in some way and institutionalized. The potential dangers associated with death arise if the dead person's soul is not appropriately treated and does not formally arrive at its appointed place in the Afterworld. Therefore, death, in normal circumstances, is surrounded by certain prescriptions: a suitable period of mourning for the deceased, procedures for the correct treatment of the corpse and its soul, ensuring that the body or its remains are stored properly in a culturally acceptable structure above ground or in a grave, and providing the deceased with property, and sometimes companions, to take along with it to its new home. Finally, a ceremony or a set of ceremonies has to be held which marks the passage of the recently deceased into the Land of the Dead, and which establishes or reaffirms a boundary between those departed and those who remain. The journey of the dead is conceived of as just this: a passage from this world to another world, overcoming various obstacles on the way until the other side is reached.

All Borneo peoples, however, sometimes have to cope with death in circumstances which are conceived to be, in some way, special or abnormal. Sudden death is a particular problem: death in childbirth, violent death in a headhunting raid, suicide or certain unfortunate accidents (King 1976a). The belief is that, in these cases, the person's soul may become a malevolent spirit, which returns to harass and inflict misfortune on the living. Usually 'bad' deaths are treated differently from 'good' deaths. Sometimes the corpse is laid to rest in a separate place from the village graveyard. It may be summarily dealt with, without ceremony, or in a shortened ritual.

Nevertheless, in normal cases, death is not something to be feared as such or pushed to the side. In a sense, it presents other opportunities: the spirits of the dead, if treated properly, can be beneficent, providing support, guidance and taking a continued interest in human affairs. Especially renowned warriors, chiefs, skilled weavers and shamans are usually thought to have special relationships with the spirits which enable them to excel in various spheres of secular or religious life. Periodically feasts of the departed spirits are held to renew contacts with the dead and seek their assistance.

The Land of the Dead is a world apart. Not only is it separated from this world by a long journey, but it is distinctive because it is, in some respects, the opposite of this world, where black is white and night is day. Although modelled on human existence in that spirits are believed to conduct their lives like humans – they live in villages and longhouses, and farm, fish and hunt – it is also a world of plenty, without poverty or misfortune. One of the main purposes of death ceremonies is to ensure that the soul of the departed finds its way successfully to its appointed abode, and that it is treated properly. If it is not it could lose its way and become a malevolent spirit.

These are then the basic ideas underlying death in Borneo. Although there is a large variety of Dayak funeral practices these can be divided into two main kinds (Huntington and Metcalf 1979). There are those Dayak groups such as the Iban, Kayan and Kenyah which dispose of their dead in a single set of ceremonies; there are others such as the Barito groups, and several small populations of Sarawak like the Berawan, which perform what is technically called secondary treatment of the dead. As we have seen in chapter 3 this latter practice is likely to have been a very early Austronesian cultural form, and Metcalf argues that it is found among small, dispersed populations in northern Borneo, which have been submerged by other more numerous and aggressive migratory peoples such as the Ibans and Kayans moving in from other regions (1976).

In primary funerals, although the corpse may be kept in the house for a while, it is, within a defined space of time, laid to rest. Usually following death it is washed, cleansed, dressed and placed in state in the household's compartment or on the longhouse gallery for the living to mourn over. It is sung to; guarded and protected, in case, for example, the corpse is carried away by evil spirits; and fed, usually in a defined space marked out by sacred cloths or other ritual objects. It may then be carried from the house in a coffin and buried, as in the case of the Ibans; or in the case of a Kayan or Kenyah aristocrat, placed in a large decorated house-like family mausoleum on heavy support-posts, or in a jar and set in a cavity in a tall carved funeral post. Mourning prohibitions continue to be observed thereafter. In the stratified societies, the death of an aristocrat was accompanied by a large feast and traditionally a slave was sacrificed. Nowadays animal sacrifice is likely to be performed.

In secondary funeral practices, on the other hand, the corpse is usually placed in a temporary resting place, either buried or in a structure above ground. Weinstock says of the Luangan:

In the past, the body of the deceased was often kept in, or under, the house in a sealed wooden coffin until after putrification of the flesh. (1983: 52)

Eventually, and there may be a gap of some years, the bones are disinterred and ritually treated in a major ceremony; then the remains are placed in their final resting place, in a jar, or in an ossuary, or large tomb house above ground, or they may be buried. This is usually performed only for wealthy or prominent villagers. Not everyone would necessarily be given a secondary funeral and they might be laid to rest immediately following the first ceremony (Metcalf 1982).

The Ngajus hold a *tiwah* ceremony during which the remains of several people are collectively cremated and placed in a small hut-like structure on stilts. Similarly the Ma'anyans construct a wooden frame raised on an earthen mound for cremating the exhumed bones in the context of a great feast; the ashes are then placed in a special carved ironwood box (Hudson 1966).

Views of the natural world

Oral tradition is the medium used by the Dayaks to expound their views about life and its meaning, about its relationship to death and about the reality of life after death. They contemplate the relationships between humans and human spiritual existence and the spirits which inhabit the natural environment – the forests and rivers, the mountains and caves, the abode above and beneath the earth. The Dayaks perceive these supernatural beings to be ambivalent – just as is nature in their experience. The river, for example, is a vital element in village life – a provider of water for drinking and of food supplies such as fish, as well as acting as an important medium of transport. The Dayaks live near water; it is a constant influence in their lives. But the river can also destroy; it can burst its banks, flooding houses, crops and even taking the lives of humans and animals. The waters are also inhabited by spirits, and, in the case of the Ngajus for example, a deity, *Jata*. These have to be appeased and given offerings from time to time.

Humans are not, however, totally at the mercy of the caprices of spirits, nor do they believe that all disasters are the result of supernatural action. They have a continuous dialogue with the spiritual world through the various forms of communication which I have already mentioned, and they can manipulate supernatural beings to their own advantage. For example, the Dayaks will count on a good harvest if friendly relations have been maintained with the spirits and deities responsible for the earth, forest and rice; offence is avoided by following certain prescriptions and prohibitions and by presenting offerings and being ever-mindful of omens. Humans can avoid misfortune on a long journey by watching for signs presented by the spirits and by taking appropriate gifts to places in the forest or by the river. People can assure themselves of a successful hunting or fishing trip by observing certain prescriptions and by taking omens.

Nevertheless, humans will only have success if they employ their physical energies, skills and practical knowledge on their farms, and in hunting, gathering and fishing, as well as observing the supernatural context within which these practical activities are undertaken. A man can avoid the dangers of a long journey by preparing himself thoroughly, by observing the condition and the colour of the waters across or along which he is travelling, to avoid the onset of a sudden flood. An individual's catch from forest or stream will usually be greater if he knows and has trained his hunting dogs well, and if he employs appropriate hunting and fishing methods as well as skilfully-made equipment.

Dayak religion cannot be dismissed as superstition, nor does it encourage fear and anguish of the supernatural; still less does it cultivate fatalism. It is a rational response to the world in which rainforest dwellers live; it helps them to explain and come to terms with nature; it helps give meaning to existence; it is born out of contemplation of life and nature; it is a stimulus to further knowledge. Like all humans the Dayaks search for physical, psychological and a measure of material well-being. Much of Dayak thought and ritual is therefore concerned with the maintenance and promotion of life in its widest sense.

When we examine in chapter 10 the modern changes which Borneo peoples are experiencing, we shall see that the transformations of traditional habitats, and particularly the destruction of the rainforests, not only affects native people physically and materially, but also spiritually and psychologically. It is not only livelihoods which are altered, but the whole related cultural complex, including religion, upon which human identities and confidence are based. Government development programmes seem to neglect these non-material dimensions of social change.

Let us finally examine various concrete ways in which Dayak cultures are expressed in art forms and material artifacts before considering recent changes in native ways of life.

9

Material Culture

Introduction

Dayak material culture is obviously influenced by their world-view and their preoccupation with life, death, fertility and protection. Many motifs and patterns express the dual division of the cosmos and various elements of the cosmology, or the world of deities and spirits and the journey to the Land of the Dead. Some also reflect and express differences in social status and rank.

Dayak cultural diversity is nowhere more obviously displayed than in material culture. This diversity is linked to quite marked regional specialization in arts and crafts, which, in turn, has meant the development of a high level of local skills. The close relationship which has existed from time immemorial between Dayaks and the natural environment has meant that they manufacture objects from a range of natural materials such as rattan, bamboo, bark and wood, from animal bones, horns and deer antlers and hornbill 'ivory', as well as from local and imported metals (silver, gold, brass, copper and iron) and from stone, clay, other minerals and beads. They are skilled in carving, painting, plaiting, weaving and forging. They have constructed massive sculptured ironwood posts to commemorate the dead, and exquisitely delicate jewellery in brass and silver. Objects such as Kenyah paintings may be ornate and complex in design; Iban and Bidayuh wood carvings of spirits and human forms can be plainly and simply fashioned with little embellishment.

Despite this diversity, however, there are certain common principles. Gill, for example, notes that, in Sarawak, artistic creations tend towards two-dimensional or low-relief ornament, with a limited number of forms, such as images of deities and spirits, and common motifs comprising anthropomorphic figures, demonic faces, serpents, dragons and birds, especially the hornbill (1968: 186–9). These principles have been established over a very long period of time, and what little survives of ancient Dayak material culture, presumably as part of early Austronesian culture, in stone sculptures, bone carvings, clay pots and cave paintings demonstrates continuities in form and decoration. Over a long period there has also been the spread, adoption and interchange of objects, motifs, ideas, institutions and craft skills, both within Borneo and with cultures from outside, especially India and China. Therefore, although objects of material culture undoubtedly help us to differentiate some ethnic groups from others, they are not a certain guide to tribal differences. One can identify Iban *ikat* weaving, for example, but other related groups such as the Kantu' and Mualang also execute it. Furthermore, similar motifs in painting, tattooing, beadwork and carving are found very widely across central Borneo among differently named peoples.

It is misleading to use the term 'primitive art' when referring to Borneo productions. It does not represent the achievements of some early evolutionary phase of development (King 1991b). Many objects demonstrate high levels of skill and sophistication. Nevertheless, the manufacture of decorative objects is not a specialized sphere of activity, which is the preserve of professional 'artists'. There is little art for art's sake in Borneo, and craftsmen usually manufacture items in their spare time. There is also an intimate interrelationship between the aesthetic, functional, sacred and secular aspects of material culture. Some objects in everyday use are aesthetically pleasing in their own right or reflect social status and rank, but are often decorated with images which in other contexts have religious significance. Other items are also produced which directly serve religious objectives and are used in ceremonies which are directed to the main concerns of Bornean peoples – with life, death, protection and fertility (Sellato 1989a: 35ff.). They are therefore considered sacred or powerful, being closely associated with the deities and spirits. Working with these patterns is often seen as a dangerous undertaking and the person so engaged needs ritual protection, sometimes by observing taboos, or by sacrifice and offering, or by wearing special amulets.

Two especially significant motifs across Borneo are the hornbill and the dragon or serpent. Often the dragon is associated with dog forms in a combined motif (see below). Others depict human forms, sometimes naturalistic or stylized, which variously represent deities, spirits, sacrificial slaves and severed heads to protect, scare away evil forces or enhance fertility.

Some motifs are particularly linked with the lower world, sometimes serving protective functions, but also as fertility symbols: these include crocodiles, lizards, prawns, crayfish, scorpions, turtles, fish, toads and frogs. The symbol of fertility *par excellence* is the tree of life, linking or combining Upperworld and Underworld, sometimes with skulls hanging from its branches. Plant motifs are often fertility symbols too: bamboo and rice shoots, and the lotus (King 1985b).

Some of the very powerful symbols can only be used or worn by those who are of sufficient stature, prowess and rank to withstand the spiritual forces which emanate from them.

Textiles and clothing

Weaving textiles is very much a female domain and knowledge and skills are passed on from mother to daughter. Traditionally many different Borneo peoples wove textiles. Some, like the Kenyahs and Malohs, produced plain cloths, but do so no more. It is the complex of Ibanic groups which is skilled in the weaving of decorative female skirts (*bidang*), jackets for both sexes (*kelambi*), loincloths and ceremonial cloths (*pua kumbu*). The cloths serve as ceremonial wall-coverings and they mark out sacred ritual spaces. In the headhunting past, females would welcome war-parties returning from a successful raid, and wrap the severed heads in the woven cloths. They are also used to wrap new-born babies in. These textiles, woven by especially skilled women, are believed to attract the beneficence and protection of the deities, and are therefore thought to contain or carry supernatural power, which may benefit those who are associated with them. Therefore, the weaver needs a strong soul to be able to weave magical designs. It is instructive that renowned weavers of decorative cloths were traditionally accorded the same prowess in the domain of females as famous headhunters and warriors were in the world of men. The symbolic parallels between female weavers and headhunters are striking indeed, and illustrate the religious and social significance of textiles, and their importance for female prestige and qualities as a prospective bride.

Designs are incorporated by the tie-dye or warp *ikat* method, using a backstrap loom. The main motifs are given form by progressively dyeing areas of the background, usually in reddish-brown, indigo-blue, dark brown or black, to leave some warp in reserve (Hitchcock 1985). This technique is very widely used in the maritime South-East Asian world. Tie-dyeing produces a blurred, almost otherworldly effect. Iban patterns are many and varied. They comprise, among others, naturalistic or stylized anthropomorphic designs, zoomorphic figures, including birds, crocodiles, and invertebrates, as well as flora – leaves and creepers, ferns, and non-representational lozenges, keys, spirals, dentates, zigzags and border stripes (Haddon and Start 1936; Munan 1989: 65–83). Other decorations may be added to the weave, such as pieces of embroidery or needle weaving on the edging or important parts of the garment. Various groups such as Kayans, Kenyahs and Rungus Dusuns are well known for sewing imported fabric onto plain cloth.

Although it is rarely seen now, bark was the traditional material for clothing; it was widely used in Borneo and was an ancient element in Austronesian culture. Lengths of dried and beaten bark were skilfully stitched together to make hats, jackets, skirts and loincloths. Usually the material comprised the inner layer of the trees *Antiaris toxicaria* (*ipoh*) or was from the *Artocarpus elastica* (*tekalong*). Natural fibres, and more recently pineapple fibres, were used to stitch across the grain of the bark to strengthen it. Plain bark-cloth was often opposed to decorative clothing in that it often had to be worn by a widow or widower after the death of his or her loved one, and could only be discarded when the mourning period and the various taboos imposed during it were set aside in a ceremony. Nevertheless, barkcloth could also be painted and stencilled with elaborate motifs as in the case of Kenyah female skirts and male loincloths; they were also decorated with coloured cotton-weave, or had pieces of coloured cloth stitched on to them. As well as tree bark, another traditional material was animal skin, often used for war tunics.

Plaiting

Plaiting skills are very widely developed in Borneo and a range of forest materials are available for use: rattan, bamboo skin, the leaves of the pandanus, nipah and sago palm, and bemban reeds. Some Dayak groups are acknowledged for their special work in making such items as patterned split rattan mats; the Kenyah *tikai lampit* is made from long half-round strips of rattan, fastened together with weave at the ends. Mats are very important for sitting and sleeping on, and for wrapping belongings in.

On patterned mats the motifs are picked out by staining some of the weave red, black or indigo. Many of the Penans and Punans make pliable, tightly woven decorated rattan baskets and mats in diagnonal weave, incorporating human and animal images. In Kalimantan the most famous mat-makers are the Ot Danum, who provide elaborate representations of their cosmology which depict sacred houses, Underworld serpents, particularly the snake-like *ehing*, hornbills associated with the Upperworld, human protective figures and the tree of life (*batang garing*).

Peoples such as the Ibans, Bidayuhs and Melanaus make geometrical designs in mats: rhombs, keys and spirals, and the Penans work a kind of tartan pattern into some of their mats. Certain key, spiral and other abstract forms in Penan and Punan weaving are said to represent rice plants, ferns and bamboo shoots, and are symbolic of fertility (Chadwick and Courtenay 1983).

The Bidayuhs make a more austere plaited four-sided basket (*tambok*), strengthened at base and corner with sticks. Its beauty is conveyed by the simple close weave, contrasted with strategically placed coloured vertical and horizontal bands. Normally, however, most Borneo peoples work in diagonal weave. Baskets are obviously used for carrying and storing objects. Small finely woven ones are commonly used for storing rice seeds for next year's sowing. There are medium-sized baskets carried at the waist for harvesting rice. The Kayan *ingan* basket, shaped as a cylinder, slightly flared at the top, and made from rattan in diagonal weave, is employed in carrying in the harvested rice for processing and storage.

There is a variety of Dayak sunhats of overlapping pandanus, nipah or other palm leaves, from the large, rounded rather flat Kenyah hats (*sa'ong*), covered with bead designs and pieces of coloured cloth, to the high conical coloured hats of the Bidayuhs, Muruts and Kadazans. Kenyah and Kayan girls often wear rattan headbands or small skull-caps. Men too wear woven caps, and sometimes a distinctive skull-cap with horizontal projections and decorated with hornbill feathers. In the past war bonnets were often of woven rattan, decorated with beads, feathers and sometimes animal skin.

A very unusual item, which is now very rarely used, is the woven rectangular seat-mat (*tikar burit*), which hangs from the rear of a man's belt. It was very convenient to sit on to keep dry and clean, and, in effect, served as a mobile travelling seat, often finely decorated in the weave, and embellished with beads.

Beadwork and painting

Beads used in jewellery or to decorate garments, containers, staffs and baby-carriers are very commonly found in Borneo. They were an early trade item and came from as far away as the Mediterranean world and the Middle East, but also from China and India. Ancient beads of carnelian, agate, glass, amber, jade, shell and bone are now treasured as valuable heirlooms, and such groups as the Kelabit, Lun Bawang and Sabah Murut make them into beautiful necklaces, bracelets, hats and the distinctive skull-caps (plate 36). These latter are heavy, made from large opaque glass beads and others such as

Plate 36 Kenyah girl wearing a valuable bead necklace

carnelian; they cover the head of a female, keeping her long hair under control.

Since European contact, and especially from the nineteenth century, Western bead manufacturers in Austria, Bohemia, Italy and Britain copied known favourites among the natives and used them in trade. More recently small opaque glass or seed-beads have been produced in such places as Singapore for Borneo and other markets. The main beads used for making motifs on objects are small monochrome beads in red, white, yellow and black. Bead decorations can be embroidered onto cloth, strung onto one continuous thread or interlaced on separate threads. This was customarily female work; among such peoples as the Kenyah, the man was responsible for setting up the pattern for the woman to follow. In the past it was carved on a wooden board; more recently it comprises a cut-out paper template fastened on to a plain board. Traditionally forest materials or pineapple fibres would have been used for stringing, and needles were made from bone or fish-bone or thorns. Increasingly during the later colonial period, metal needles and cotton thread were introduced.

Both Kayan and Kenyah beadwork is delicately executed. The most striking designs are used as symbols of aristocratic status. In Kenyah culture they comprise the displayed human form (*kalong kelunan*), the dog-dragon motif (*aso*), and the tiger and hornbill. The *aso* is usually depicted with the body of a dog, a dragon-like snout, curled fangs and horns (Haddon 1905). I have argued that the dog may well have been an ancient motif in Borneo symbolizing the Underworld, and that it has probably been assimilated to both Chinese and Hindu-Indian dragon symbols, also associated with the Underworld. Certainly the Chinese dragon was an important and distinctive pattern on jars imported into Borneo and kept as heirlooms and status symbols by native peoples. The main images in Kenyah designs are linked by sprouting tendrils or hooks, and spirals (*kelawit*). In contrast, Kadazan beadwork uses abstract key and rhomb patterns and conventionalized human forms. Some objects such as Kenyah baby-carriers are also embellished with animal teeth and tusks, shells, embroidered cloth and silver coins.

Motifs in beadwork are also found in Kayan and Kenyah

paintings on longhouse apartment walls, the charnel houses of aristocrats, and on war-shields (Whittier 1973) (plate 37). But the medium of paint allows a greater variety of images, many of them naturalistic and comprising all sorts of animals and birds and importantly the tree of life. These paintings are now seldom executed, but some Kayan and Kenyah painters have been employed by such institutions as the Sarawak Museum in Kuching to decorate the walls of their buildings.

The Ngajus, on the other hand, are known for their delicate and complex 'cult-drawings', which depict their cosmology. For example, they paint 'soul ships', which carry the dead to the Afterworld, usually in red, black and white on wooden boards; it is said that the board becomes the residence of the deceased's spirit until the grand funeral ceremony (*tiwah*) is held.

A number of Borneo peoples, such as the Ibans, Kelabits, Kayans, Kenyahs and Ngajus also traditionally decorated their bodies with tattoos, although this practice is rapidly dying out. Young Iban males, however, still continue to acquire tattoos as a symbol of their journeys and adventures away from home

Plate 37   The outer compartment wall of a Kenyah chief

working in coastal towns, construction sites and in the oil and gas-field areas of Brunei and Sarawak.

Tattooing is above all a mark of rank, prestige and achievement, but it can also serve as a protective device to ward off evil spirits. Furthermore, many Borneo peoples believe that the Afterworld is a reversal of this world, where, for example, black becomes white. Black tattoos are therefore illuminated in the dark; they are believed to shine brightly by supernatural means. Arm and leg tattoos on an aristocratic Kenyah female are said to assist the deceased woman's soul in finding its way to the Otherworld (Tillema 1989: 162).

Traditionally the use of tattoos was restricted to symbolizing particular events or successes such as taking heads or participating in a victorious raiding party, or to expressing aristocratic status. The signs of Iban manhood, courage and fighting prowess are the stylized frog motif on the throat, and tattoos on the backs of the hands.

The practice of tattooing was also adopted through cultural contact. Nomadic Punans and Penans living close to Kayans and Kenyahs used tattoos, and many Maloh silver-smiths in contact with Ibans would return from their journeys with large stylized hornbill patterns, rosettes and the common *aso* motifs on their arms, legs and shoulders. Tattooing is a painful ordeal. The designs are tapped in using a sharp needle fixed to the end of a hammer-like tool. Tattoo motifs are usually drawn on by hand and stamped on with a carved wooden block; the ink comprises soot mixed with fat or sugarcane juice.

Carving

Borneo peoples carve in wood, as well as in bone, horn and ivory, and they incise in bamboo. Usually a small, long-handled knife is used for intricate designs. However, it is the Kenyahs, Kayans and Berawans who have a deserved reputation for their work in wood (plate 38). They carve free-standing wooden human, *aso* and hornbill figures as well as incising these images in wood, animal bone and horn. *Aso* figures are also carved as legs for tables and supports for serving plates,

Plate 38   Kenyahs carving

prows of war canoes, on the hilts of swords and knives, on kitchen utensils and in 'hornbill ivory' earrings. Frightening anthropomorphic protective figures are placed at village and longhouse entrances or to guard ritual places or structures. With terrifying visage and in threatening posture, and sometimes armed with weapons, these sculptures scare away evil spirits from the village. The most well known are the Kenyah figures (plate 39).

Kayans, Kenyahs, Kajangs and others also construct elaborately decorated funeral structures and coffins. There is a range of forms depending on such considerations as the rank and status of the deceased and the type of funeral ceremony performed. There are charnel houses or family mausoleums (*salong*) with beautiful carved roof ridges and eaves, on one or more solid support-posts, as well as funeral posts (*liang, keliring, lijeng, kelirieng*) decorated with demonic images (*hudo'*) and scrolls (Stöhr 1959). Among the Melanaus, traditionally the remains of the dead were placed in a Chinese jar in a cavity at the top of the post. Carved designs on funeral structures, and the apartment door and support-posts of ar-

Plate 39   A Kenyah guardian figure at the entrance to a village

istocrats include elaborate animal forms – crocodiles, lizards, snakes, dogs, scorpions and simian-like creatures. Coffins are often in the shape of a boat or canoe, which appears to be an ancient cultural form in Borneo, but they may be further decorated with stylized hornbill or *aso* fretwork.

Both the Kayans and Kenyahs also carve elaborate demonic masks for use in agricultural ceremonies to drive away malevolent rice-harming spirits. They have a variety of forms, but are usually carved as dog-dragons, hornbills or pigs, with protruding eyes and fangs and other exaggerated features, and with large ears, usually carved separately and attached to the mask with rattan. They are painted in black, red and green. Crude masks are also made by the Ibans, usually anthropomorphic in form, and worn by women dressed as men who perform comic dances. The Ngajus make softwood masks, with frightening features, teeth bared and nose hooked, which are worn in the *tiwah* death festivals.

Especially distinctive Bornean sculptures are the sickness images (*bilum*) made by the pagan Melanaus. Carved from sago pith, these represent sickness-bearing spirits. They are usually human-like, squatting or legs crossed, with crosshatching on the body to produce a scaly effect (Chong 1987). *Bilum* have a variety of headpieces (crowns, turbans, horns, braziers); some have wings or protruding tongues. In the curing ceremony, the malevolent spirit would be coaxed or cajoled to enter its carved image which would then be floated downriver, or abandoned in the forest.

The most notable examples of Iban carving are the hornbill (*kenyalang*), traditionally in hardwood and unpainted, more recently in softwood, with elaborate, exaggerated casque and tail, and painted in green, yellow, red, white and black. As Zainie has noted, the *kenyalang*, the messenger of *Sengalang Burong*, the deity of war, is the focus of an important Iban festival, the *Gawai Burong* or *Gawai Kenyalang*:

. . . generally the hornbill images were paraded up and down . . . adorned with jewellery and offerings of food and placed on top of poles. The other festivities, eating, singing and dancing, continued through the night, during which time the spirit of the carved hornbill left its image, flew to an enemy longhouse, and slaughtered or greatly weakened all the enemy warriors. (1969: 25, 27)

Ibans also fashion 'pig sticks' – an effigy of a hunting deity (*tuntun*), mounted on a long stick, human- or monkey-like, crouching with head supported by hands, legs and arms flexed, elongated features and protruding eyes. These are used to attract game to the trap.

The most well-known wooden sculptures of Kalimantan are the Ngaju-Ot Danum *hampatong*, mainly associated with death rites, specifically the secondary funeral rites (*tiwah*) (Avé n.d.: 97–8). But, in effect, various forms are carved and serve different purposes. For example, there are sacrificial poles (*sapundu, sampudu, sepunduk*) with human or animal figures carved at the top, at which animals or formerly slaves were sacrificed during secondary death rituals. Frightening carved human sculptures were placed at village entrances to scare away evil and sickness-bearing spirits. Some anthropomorphic figures (*tajahan, kejahan*) represent the dead. Still other human forms comprise small carved amulets or charms (*karohei, karuhai* and *penyang*) or 'divine gifts' (Goldman 1975; Vredenbregt 1981: 34).

Another Ngaju wooden structure, also part of their funeral complex, is the *sandung* or *sandong*: this is an ossuary in the shape of a modest-sized house on posts. It holds the cremation remains, and is decorated with floral motifs and sometimes anthropomorphic faces which are guardian spirits. Next to the *sandung* is usually located the *sengkaran* or *sanggaran*, a funeral post, which supported a carved watersnake or hornbill at the top, and a jar placed on it with wooden spears; it was usually reserved for upper-ranking individuals. It is said to symbolize the unity of the cosmos and the tree of life. It is specifically the treasure of the deceased sent to the Afterworld. Another wooden structure is a high wooden pole or *pantar*, erected at a *tiwah* as a memorial for someone killed in war.

The Kayans, Kenyahs, Ngajus, Ot Danums and Bidayuhs are skilful workers in bamboo; they incise or whittle the tough surface of bamboo containers and quivers in low relief in tendrils, hooks, floral, human and other motifs. Tobacco pipes and musical instruments such as nose-flutes are also fashioned from bamboo. Ngaju bamboo tubes (*solep*) often depict *tiwah* funeral huts, dancing priestesses, gong players, trees of life, the Upperworld hornbill and Underworld serpent, sacrifices and offerings, coffins, *sengkaran* funeral posts and head trophies.

An early medium for carving was obviously stone, and there is ample evidence of stone-working in Borneo. Various Dayak groups which are, it seems, representatives of ancient Austronesian cultures, worked in stone, such as the Kelabits, Kadazans and the Pins. These latter were a long-established population of the upper Mahakam and were subjugated by the Kayans moving into the region. Rousseau says, following Sellato,

These Pin appear to have known horticulture, iron smelting, stone carving, and pisciculture; they may also have been in contact with Hinduism. (1990: 24)

Large stone pieces were either erected as dolmens or menhirs with little fashioning, or hollowed out to serve as resting places for the dead. Fashioning of stone usually comprised sculpting human forms of guardian deities or spirits in relief on the surface of prominent boulders, although some examples have been found of free-standing anthropomorphic statues thought to have been made by such groups as the now extinct Srus in Sarawak, who were killed off or absorbed by the Ibans.

Metalware

Many Borneo peoples are able to forge iron to make everyday utensils, tools and weapons. Increasingly from the nineteenth century imported bar-iron was fashioned, but there is an indigenous tradition, developed to a high level among such groups as the Kayan and Kenyah, of the smelting of good-quality local ores and the manufacture of beautiful ceremonial headhunting swords or cutlasses (*parang ilang*). Often the blade incorporates curly fretwork along the top edge comprising spirals and tendrils, with inlaid brass circles. As we have already seen, the smelting methods, which certainly go back to the tenth century, are simple: these are small-scale bloomery smelting operations, using a furnace pit; the ore is roasted and broken into pieces, and then laid in alternate layers with charcoal in the pit; bamboo piston bellows create the draft.

The manufacture of items from brass and silver has not been widely practised among Dayaks. Some groups of central Borneo, like the Kayan, whose women wore clusters of plain, solid brass earrings, did cast ear ornaments in clay or stone moulds. The earrings had a small gap to slot onto the elongated earlobe. Other rings are spiralled or comprise large solid citrons or decorative brass spheres (Hose 1926: 159). Some incorporate stylized hornbill or dragon designs.

Nevertheless, it is the Malohs of West Kalimantan who are well-known specialists in brass- and copper-working, but also in silver, and, to a limited extent, gold. In the past, they generally acquired brassware, and especially brasswire, from Malay and Chinese sources and then melted it down and refashioned it. These skills have now largely disappeared in competition with imported metalware. The main market for Maloh goods was usually Iban communities in Sarawak which itinerant smiths would visit and spend long periods there making items to order. These comprise the distinctive female corsets (*rawai*), as well as armlets, anklets, leg and earrings and other personal ornaments (Hose and McDougall 1912, i: 197). Iban men from the Skrang and Saribas traditionally wore brass or copper ear ornaments, comprising a number of individual rings joined together along the outer cartilage of the ear, with the smallest rings at the top of the ear running down to large rings in the lobe. Sometimes these were decorated with thin, elongated diamond-shaped mobiles (plate 40). Brass bracelets and arm-rings for both males and females were either of plain brasswire, or flattened and incised with abstract motifs. Men would also wear brass leg-rings below the knee to the calf (Low 1848: 178–9). There was a variety of belts and waist decorations too, some of which are still worn today. For example, Iban women wore coils of twisted or braided wire (*sarin*), or a belt 'of short brass tubes threaded on cord-like beads (*sutar*)' (Richards 1981: 358). The *rawai* or small corset comprises small brass rings threaded closely together onto hoops of rattan, fastened parallel to each other by cane and stiffened at intervals with metal wires (plate 41). The ends of the corset can be fastened with interlocking vertical metal plates, or the *rawai* might merely comprise a continuous tube with no fastenings to be slipped on over the

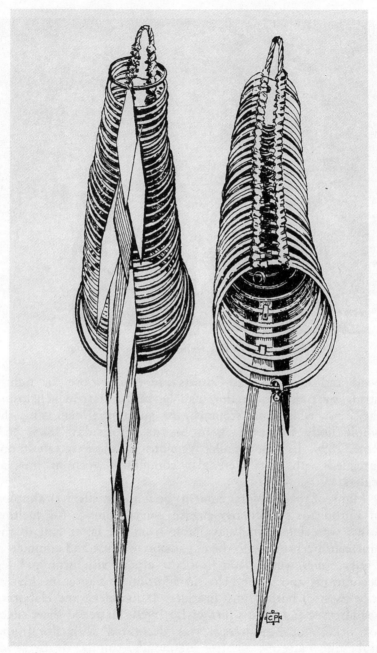

Plate 40   Iban ear ornament

Plate 41   Saribas Ibans wearing the rawai

head and raised arms. Corsets are either loose, or tightly
fitting over the body; they can be rather narrow, enclosing
the hips, waist and stomach, or substantial, encasing the
whole body from thighs to breasts (Hornaday 1885: 462;
Roth 1896, ii: 47). Smaller versions of these rattan hoops
threaded with rings were also commonly worn by men as
leglets.

Many of these objects came to be made in silver as supplies
of European, particularly British, silver coinage for melting
down were increasingly available from the latter half of the
nineteenth century with the expansion of trade and commerce.
Thus, *rawai* were made in silver along with arm and leg
decorations and silver belts, in addition to filigree necklaces,
rope-twist or barley-twist bracelets and anklets, and elaborate
headdresses and combs (Fraser-Lu 1989). Flattened sheet silver
for belts and headdresses was decorated with floral and
arabesque patterns, rosettes, diamonds, spirals, ovals, semi-
circles and lines, as well as human and animal forms in relief

and chased work (King and Bantong 1987). Of course, in coastal areas and in neighbouring regions of the Philippines the local manufacture of silver jewellery appeared sometime in the sixteenth century stimulated by supplies of Mexican silver. Later, Dutch guilders and Indian rupees replaced this source, but silver-working generally in South-East Asia may not be of great antiquity.

The skills in fashioning jewellery and other adornments in metal were very restricted in interior Sarawak. Much of the large brassware sought by Dayaks was acquired from such port centres as Brunei, and increasingly into the twentieth century, Chinese bazaar silver-smiths catered for the Dayak market and Maloh smithing declined. Malay silver-making had been very much directed to the needs of Malay royalty and nobility in the coastal states.

I have argued elsewhere that Maloh skills in working brass and silver were probably acquired relatively recently. Certainly they do not appear to have been involved in silver-working to any extent until at least the end of the nineteenth century, and brass-smithing was probably adopted from a coastal Malay source sometime after the sixteenth century (King 1988a). Maloh techniques were simple. Brass and silver objects were melted down; moulds were used, and a number of different punches, hammers, chisels and pliers were used for decorating and fashioning the metal.

Pottery

Bornean pottery skills go back to early Austronesian settlement. Now pottery manufacture has all but disappeared among the Dayaks. Until recently basic pots and other vessels were still made by such groups as the Ibans, Lun Bawangs, Kelabits and Kenyahs, using the paddle-and-anvil process. Increasingly from the fourteenth and fifteenth centuries imported Chinese jars, used especially in funeral rites, replaced larger locally-made plain vessels, and from the later nineteenth century metal and other imported containers led to an even more rapid decline in pot-making.

Potters were usually females, who undertook all processes

from digging the clay, hand-fashioning the pots, to firing them, and, in some cases, glazing with a finely pounded resin.

As we now know, many of the manufacturing skills of the Dayaks can be traced back to early Austronesian cultures: pottery making, bark-cloth manufacture, plaiting mats and baskets, and presumably also working in natural materials such as wood and bamboo to carve and manufacture everyday utensils as well as ritual objects. Textile weaving and metal-working came into the Dayak repertoire rather later.

Sadly, many of these skills have been rapidly disappearing as a result of competition from imported goods, as well as changes in traditional religious beliefs and practices and in social hierarchies which no longer require the manufacture of large mausoleums and funeral posts, guardian statues, sick-ness-images, masks and religious paintings. One adaptation to new demands has been the production of modified versions of traditional objects for the expanding tourist market. In this connection we shall now turn to examine recent changes in Borneo and their effects on traditional cultures.

10

Modernization and Development

Introduction

We have seen that the island of Borneo, as a result of environmental and other circumstances, had been generally neglected during the European period, even more so in Sarawak where the Brooke Raj had not encouraged the large-scale introduction of private enterprise and capitalist investment. After the Second World War Kalimantan was an economically backward region of the Indonesian Republic, and Sarawak and North Borneo, although experiencing some economic development during the years of British colonialism, entered the Federation of Malaysia as disadvantaged, politically undeveloped and marginal territories. The exception to this situation is the oil-rich Sultanate of Brunei, which enjoys a high standard of living. Even in 1958, for example, when the Sultan was engaged in improving his relations with the newly-independent Federation of Malaya, he made available to it a 100 million Brunei dollar loan as 'a mark of good faith' (Leake 1990: 49). Brunei is one of the world's wealthiest countries in per capita terms, enjoying the same status as such countries as the United Arab Emirates, and having massive foreign reserves and substantial investment income. Nevertheless, there are some hinterland areas of Brunei which remain relatively undeveloped, and the peoples there follow much the same sort of rural lifestyle as Dayaks in neighbouring Sarawak and Sabah.

The Malaysian and Indonesian Borneo territories continue to occupy a peripheral position in relation to the dominant

core-areas of these nations (King 1988b). They are remote
from the centres of power, decision-making and economic
growth. To be sure there have been changes, and some Borneo
communities have benefited from increasing economic opportunities. But, in general terms, Borneo still has a low level of
industrialization and urbanization, and limited infrastructure
and community services such as health provision, piped water,
housing and education. The incidence of poverty is still high,
and this is associated with low income and subsistence agricultural activities, such as rice farming, smallholding rubber
and coconut cultivation and artisanal fishing.

A basic problem which faces government, and which confronted the Europeans and helps to explain the pre-colonial
patterns of commerce and political institutions, is that of
developing intractable coastal swamp and interior rainforest
areas where populations are scattered and difficult of access.

It is this context which helps us to understand the present
plight of Borneo both environmentally and socially. The
island, as in the past, is a zone for the exploitation of natural
resources. Of course, in the period of Asian mercantilism and
in that phase of European expansion which was not driven by
the engine of industrial capitalism, the main interest was in
high-value rainforest products, whose exploitation did not
upset the ecological balance. During the last 30 years the
frontier lands of Borneo have become increasingly subject to
direct exploitation of their most obvious and precious resource: the rainforest itself. If there is one issue which has
captured the attention of the world, and which is having the
most dramatic consequences for local cultures, societies and
economies, it is the large-scale clearance of the rainforests.
Commercial logging operations in Borneo pose the greatest
threat to the ways of life which we have been considering in
this text.

A set of changes which are also related, in part, to the
destruction of the rainforest, but which receive rather less
attention, is rural development by means of resettlement,
large-scale plantation agriculture and the increasing expansion of cash-crop cultivation. In a number of cases, forest
has been cleared specifically to make way for land-development schemes or estate forms of production, or, where log-

ging has made the environment useless for various forms of traditional farming, hunting, gathering and fishing, governments have planted large tracts of land to plantation crops such as oil palm, cocoa and rubber and encouraged shifting cultivators to work these. In addition, in Kalimantan, the Indonesian government has forcefully set itself against the longhouse as a form of domicile and has cajoled or in some cases forced Dayaks to move into single-family dwellings.

The issue which government perceives as crucial, both in Malaysia and Indonesia, and even to some extent in Brunei, is how to develop land and concentrate scattered communities into accessible locations which can be administered and modernized. To an administrative mind the solution seems patently obvious – resettle rural dwellers, clear forests which cannot be worked intensively and plant crops which, theoretically, can provide a regular and continuous yield and which command a price on the world market.

There is a further matter which has special relevance to Kalimantan. Unlike Malaysia, Indonesia faces problems of overpopulation, poverty and shortage of land in its heartlands of Java, Madura and Bali. Again, one of the solutions to this is very clear – 'transmigration'; in other words, the transfer of excess population to those regions of the Republic such as Kalimantan where demographic densities are much lower. It seems to matter little to government that there have been and are obvious environmental constraints on population growth in Borneo, and that the land and soils in many places cannot sustain intensive agriculture. The 'wide open spaces' of the island are an attraction to a government looking for areas for settlement.

It is these issues of forest clearance, land development, internal resettlement and inter-island transmigration on which I shall concentrate in this chapter. There are, of course, other changes currently taking place in Borneo, some of which are related to those above, but they are less general in their impact than those which directly concern the use and exploitation of the environment. I shall examine these too, but in less detail.

As we would expect, certain changes are rather more focused and concentrated in their effects. The exploitation of other natural resources in Borneo has not been widespread, but has, instead, resulted in enclave development. I have in mind, in particular, oil, gas and mineral exploration and production. Aside from timber and forest resources, a major set of exports from both Malaysian and Indonesian Borneo and Brunei has been oil and gas. These activities are confined to a few locations around the coasts, in the zone stretching from the northern parts of Sarawak around Miri, western Brunei, and into the region around Labuan in Sabah. In Kalimantan, the petroleum industry is concentrated on the east coast around Balikpapan. These are very much boom areas, with modern urban-based facilities, infrastructure, housing and good roads; but they are physically confined. They are capital intensive and employ a significant population of immigrant labour. Nevertheless, Dayaks from the interior have migrated to these areas for employment in the oil and gas fields; in some cases settling permanently, in others moving in periodically for shorter periods of work and living in temporary accommodation in shanty towns.

Urbanization too has been limited in Borneo. It has concentrated in the administrative capitals and major ports, in the regional administrative and market centres, and in the few favoured locations for the extraction of minerals. These urban areas have expanded rapidly in recent years and they are the channels by which the cash economy has penetrated rural areas. Availability of money has gradually transformed rural economies, which are now much more affected by the vagaries of the world market, which, in turn, has increased economic uncertainty. This monetization and modernization has also resulted in new social classes emerging: some Borneans have become very wealthy on the proceeds of such natural resources as timber; others have become wage labourers; or white-collar salaried workers. There has been an increase in individualism and acquisitiveness, and an undermining of some forms of mutual reciprocity and sets of obligations stemming from kinship and neighbourhood. One expression of this has been the break-up of longhouses in some communities, and individual families building dwellings closer to their rubber, pepper and cocoa gardens, or moving into towns. Old heirlooms and ritual property have also been sold off in exchange for new consumer goods. Young people especially are now much more physically mobile than previously, moving into towns for work and education, aided by improvements in transport and communications. Young men work in logging, or on road construction, and on building-sites in town. Young girls take up shop-work or work in hotels and bars; some even enter prostitution.

The development which is likely to have an ever-increasing impact on rural areas is the expansion and improvement of communication networks in Borneo. As yet many people in the countryside are still relatively remote from towns, and their contacts with them infrequent. The good roads, and river and air links are still confined to the main urban centres and coastal regions, and most rural dwellers still travel by small river-boats, paddle-canoes and longboats with outboards. Nevertheless, with the exploitation of timber, logging roads are penetrating into the interior, and there have been improvements along the main rivers with express-boats cutting the time needed to travel from the coast to inland destinations. These changes are opening up village societies much more to modern influences from the town, increasing local mobility and undermining village solidarity and the close-knit nature of local social and economic relations.

A further change, which was set in train during the colonial period, has been the expansion of educational facilities and schools into the interior, and the continued influence of the major religions, both Christianity and Islam. Perhaps examples from my own fieldwork in interior West Kalimantan (1985a) will illustrate the point. Secular and mission education, as well as religious conversion to Roman Catholicism, has had an important effect on some Maloh communities during the past 80 years. What is most noticeable is the virtual disappearance of impressive life-crisis rituals such as funeral ceremonies. These latter were intimately interrelated with differences in social rank: aristocrats traditionally enjoyed large-scale funerals; various symbols of rank were displayed; aristocrats' coffins were either placed in large charnel houses (*kulambu*) decorated with elaborate painted and carved motifs, or were placed on high platforms in large communal village *kulambus*. Onerous mourning prohibitions and the display of sacred aristocratic heirlooms while the corpse lay in state also served to reinforce aristocratic positions. During the funeral ceremonies epics were told of the deeds of illustrious aristocratic chiefs and the journey to the Land of the Dead was recounted, which again expressed differences between aristocrats and others.

With Christian burial, these ceremonies have ceased. Oral traditions which are the repository of tribal worldviews and authorize traditional religious practices are gradually being discarded by the young, school-educated generation. With baptism and marriage in church, other traditional rites of passage are also falling into disuse. In particular, Christianity, like Islam before, has offered an alternative set of values for those who are dissatisfied with their own society and culture. This has particularly been so for those of the commoner class who have been generally eager to disavow an ideology which assigned them to a permanent position of inferiority.

Other aspects of traditional religion affected by religious conversion and secular education are agricultural rituals and the belief in the spiritual qualities of rice, omen-taking and the observance of ritual prescriptions and taboos. Along with these changes items of material culture are also no longer made. The more general consequences of Westernization, with the availability of Western clothes and other cultural items and the spread of Christian values, has been the gradual abandonment of traditional costume and bodily adornments and styles which are considered to be a mark of primitivism and paganism: loincloths, tattoos, ear-plugs and heavy brass and copper earrings, and the female practice of wearing a traditional skirt, but without covering the breasts. Now Western blouses, shirts, tee-shirts, shorts, skirts and jewellery are worn, or Malay blouses, skirts and *sarongs*.

Thus, Dayak societies are being quite radically transformed, but this is nowhere more obvious than in economic life.

Land development and resettlement

One can detect a very clear central contradiction in Indonesian and Malaysian government policies towards the relatively poor, marginal territories of their countries. Although there is a desire to 'modernize' the countryside and to alleviate rural poverty and integrate these peripheral populations like the Dayaks into the mainstream of national life, these peripheral regions are also exploited for their natural resources so that national economic growth can be sustained. What is more, models of planned development such as land settlement are often formulated and implemented without taking into account the local circumstances in Borneo (King and Parnwell 1990). These models are usually the product of centralized decision-making, and are based not on the experiences of the peoples of the outlying regions of the nation, but on the circumstances of the economically developed core regions. Thus, the specific requirements of shifting cultivators and forest nomads, their approaches and attitudes to work and labour allocation, their worldviews and cultural practices, and their economic, social and cultural priorities are subordinated to national goals and interests, and are either ignored completely or paid lip-service.

Sarawak

The Malaysian government and the Sarawak state administration have been especially preoccupied with the problems, as they see them, of shifting cultivation. Even in the 1950s the colonial government was anxious about the assumed deleterious environmental and economic consequences of the sustained slashing and burning of interior forest lands. Given these perceptions, the Malaysian government, in its various Five-Year Plans, has linked shifting agriculture to rural poverty, and targetted these farmers as a special category for government development efforts.

The problem of rural poverty in such places as Sarawak has assumed special importance in the Malaysian government's New Economic Policy initiated in 1970. Its principal objective has been to promote and ensure national unity by means of two strategies – the eradication of poverty irrespective of race, and the restructuring of society to eliminate the identification of race with economic function and geographical location. The underlying consideration of this policy has been to rectify the economic imbalance between the generally successful and entrepreneurial Chinese, and to some extent urban Indians, and the disadvantaged indigenous population, comprising the Peninsular Malays and the natives of Borneo, overwhelmingly located in the less productive and remunerative rural and agricultural sectors (King and Nazaruddin 1992).

The contradiction, which I posed earlier in this chapter, between national resource exploitation in the marginal territories of the Federation, and the everyday circumstances of the natives, can be grasped from the following figures on Sarawak. From 1968 onwards Sarawak has generated substantial trade surpluses from oil, gas and timber, amounting to about 40 billion Malaysian dollars. Yet in the mid-1980s about 30 per cent of Sarawak's households were still considered to be below the poverty line, and well over 50 per cent of rural households were in poverty (King 1990: 165).

The Sarawak state authorities, in the context of national planning, have adopted two broad strategies to promote rural development. First, there is a variety of land-development schemes, either *in situ* or on newly cleared land; these are implemented by special statutory bodies established specifically to develop land for estate and cash-crop cultivation (Bugo 1988: 52ff.). Second, there are forms of assistance offered to small farmers to improve, diversify and change existing practices; these include subsidies, credit, extension services, new crops and technologies and improved infrastructure. Such government departments as Agriculture, and Drainage and Irrigation are prime-movers in this strategy.

I wish to concentrate on resettlement and land development here (King 1986b). Stands of cultivated estate crops occupying large tracts of land are now replacing the natural variety of the rainforest. In Sarawak these schemes began some 30 years ago, partly out of a need to promote agricultural development by resettling remote farmers, but also to move communities from what were considered to be unsettled and insecure border areas, arising from the tense relations between Indonesia and Malaysia at that time. A number of Iban villages were therefore moved to more accessible lowland locations near roads.

The first resettlement schemes began in 1964. There were seven land projects in all, totalling some 5,500 hectares and accommodating about 1,200 households. These were planted to high-yielding rubber, and each resettled household was granted approximately 3¼ hectares of land, with just under one hectare of land for fruit, vegetables and other crops. There was also a house-lot provided. Initially the Department of Agriculture supervised the planting of rubber, and after the trees were fully established, the settlers were given responsibility for managing their plots. During the period before the trees began to yield, the subsistence and income needs of the settlers were met by a loan from a special agency, the Sarawak Development Finance Corporation (SDFC), and a mortgage was provided on the newly built family house.

It was envisaged that the income from rubber would be sufficient to meet local household needs to a reasonable level, and release sufficient funds to repay the loan and mortgage. In theory, once the SDFC had been recompensed, the farmers would then be given title to their separate tracts of land. As it turned out titles were issued well in advance of repayment. The advantage of this system, as it was perceived by government development agencies, was that settler households would have a stake in the scheme by being granted a defined part of it, on land which they could call their own. But management, processing and marketing were centralized. The SDFC became responsible for the overall running and organization of the projects in 1968. Farmers would deliver their latex to a purpose-built processing factory; part of their income would then be deducted at source to repay their loans. Each project was also served by a community centre comprising schools, a clinic, meeting halls and access roads.

The schemes were modelled very much on the Federal Land Development Authority resettlement projects in Peninsular Malaysia. Aside from the SDFC projects, there were also resettlement villages, resulting from the regroupment of scattered Iban communities in the lower Rejang area, instituted from the mid-1960s onwards (Masing 1988: 64ff.).

There were three major problems with these projects, which eventually led to the government abandoning them. First, resettlement of shifting cultivators used to operating a mixed economy and combining subsistence production of rice with cash crops such as rubber, supplemented by hunting, gathering and fishing, proved too dramatic a change for the settlers.

They were compelled to concentrate their attention on their rubber gardens, with little opportunity for involvement in other activities, and with no immediate possibility of growing rice, because land was not allocated for it on the scheme. They were not land scarce and therefore not motivated to commit themselves to the project.

Second, the introduction of essentially monocrop schemes, heavily dependent on the price of rubber on the world market, pushed the settlers into a very precarious position within an increasingly monetized economy. Whereas previously they could fall back on subsistence production when prices of agricultural commodities fell, in the land-development schemes their options were severely limited. The outcome was predictable. Rubber prices could not sustain the needs of the settlers to the extent that was originally envisaged. Settlers began to default on their loan repayments, and to ensure that they obtained as much income as possible from their rubber they began to channel it to private rubber processors and dealers off the scheme, and away from the government factories which would have docked some of their income to service their loans. The factories therefore began to run at a much reduced and inefficient level. Settlers also began to sell off land to outsiders.

Third, Sarawak administrative personnel in the SDFC had had little experience in organizing and managing estate enterprises. FELDA officials operating in Peninsular Malaysia were very used to plantation work, since colonial Malaya had an established tradition of large-scale commercial production of such crops as rubber. In Sarawak, with its history of native protection, limited capital investment and lack of large-scale agricultural operations, there was a dearth of expertise in running estates. These were consequently inadequately supervised and organized and financial accounting systems were poor. No clear obligations and regulations had been imposed on the settlers to facilitate the recovery of loans, and no conditions had been established for the proper management of the plantation.

Thus, by the early 1980s the state government had effectively written off the schemes; they had incurred large losses, rubber gardens had been abandoned, some settlers had moved off altogether and only about 20 per cent of settlers had fully repaid their loans.

In 1972 the SDFC was reorganized into two statutory bodies, one responsible for urban projects, the other for rural development. The Sarawak Land Development Board (SLDB) took over the responsibility for the rubber schemes (Hong 1987). The new Board, after having considered the possibility of resettling farmers onto schemes in the newly-established Miri-Bintulu development area, and having already begun with small numbers of settlers, decided against it in 1974. The experience of the rubber projects had been salutary. Instead it paid little attention to the community development approach of the former SDFC, and concentrated on promoting state-run and state-owned plantations using a paid labour force. There was also a change to oil palm, which commanded better market prices than rubber.

By the late 1970s large tracts of land on either side of the main road between Miri and Bintulu had been planted to oil palm. Somewhere in the region of 15,000 hectares had been planted on 12 schemes, employing about 2,500 labourers. Most of the development was undertaken on state land, although some land in the Mukah oil palm scheme had been under native customary tenure, and there was long negotiation and litigation over its use.

As with the rubber schemes, these oil palm estates suffered from poor levels of management, supervision and financial control. More particularly, securing a regular supply of skilled labour used to estate work was a serious obstacle. Many of the labourers were young, male, highly physically mobile workers from surrounding rural areas and from further afield, and turnover was high. Plantation work was considered to be monotonous, too controlled, arduous and low paid. As soon as individuals had earned what they thought to be a sufficient income for their needs and to supplement the household resources in their home village, they would leave. The SLDB had increasingly to resort to employing contract workers brought in from Indonesia. Labour problems and inefficient production methods and management controls meant that productivity was low, overall costs high, and the schemes lost large sums of money. By the 1980s, the Board's debts amounted to about

200 million Malaysian dollars, about 75 per cent of them in the form of federal loans. The Sarawak state government was also having to provide an annual subsidy to meet operating costs. The schemes were eventually turned over to a private, Malaysian-based plantation company on a management contract to staunch the losses and establish them on a sound economic and financial footing (plate 42).

The state government was obviously very conscious of the supreme difficulties in developing land in Sarawak for estate crops. The economy of Sarawak – in which there was not a plentiful surplus supply of labour, nor was labour of the right kind for estate work, and there was not native land shortage as such, in contrast to areas of Peninsular Malaysia – proved very problematical for the implementation of a policy of large-scale land development. The adoption of centralized planning models in a situation different from that which had first generated these models proved to be a very costly mistake for government. It did not set certain rural areas of Sarawak on the road to sustainable economic development, which would be of immediate benefit to local populations.

Plate 42   Palm-oil processing factory

Clearly other strategies were required, and, in fairness to government, these were attempted. In 1976, another state statutory body was established. This was the Sarawak Land Consolidation and Rehabilitation Authority (SALCRA), an agency which was charged with promoting land development *in situ*. Another difficulty Sarawak faced was the existence of large tracts of land under unregistered native customary tenure. Any large-scale estate development was bound to become involved in endless litigation over the use of land which remained unsurveyed, untitled, and which, among some tribes, was subject to complex tenurial arrangements. Among some Bidayuh communities, for example, a large number of individuals and households related by descent could theoretically claim rights in the same areas of land.

To overcome these problems SALCRA, although it was modelled on the Federal Land Consolidation and Rehabilitation Authority, was legally established as a 'native'. In other words, under state law, it was empowered to operate on native land and develop it. Under this arrangement, rights in land do not change hands. SALCRA merely takes over the land temporarily to develop and manage it, but it does not assume ownership rights over it. These remain with the native owners.

The local participants in the scheme agree to make over some of the land to the Authority; it is then planted in a consolidated block. SALCRA has mainly focused on oil palm, although it has also been involved in rubber, cocoa and tea planting on a smaller scale. The landholders are usually employed as labourers on the estate during the development phase. They assist in clearing the land, planting the crops and tending to them. Once the crops begin to yield, the scheme participants then deliver their product to a centralized SALCRA-run processing factory. The income which they received during the establishment of the scheme is treated as part of SALCRA's development costs, and is therefore seen as a bridging loan to participants until they begin to earn an income from the estate crops. Thus, as with the arrangements on the early SDFC rubber schemes, part of their income is held back in order to pay off their loan. In theory, once the scheme is up-and-running, and providing a regular income, and once the loans have been repaid to SALCRA, the Authority gradually withdraws as manager and supervisor, and, in effect, the landholders become smallholding cash-croppers, organized into a large-scale operation and focused on SALCRA's processing facilities and coordinated marketing arrangements. The landholders then get a registered title to the land. In the longer term, therefore, it is envisaged that through the efforts of the Authority, native land is developed and ultimately registered, without government agents becoming involved in the difficult initial processes of negotiating over land rights.

What is more, the perceived advantage of these *in situ* schemes is that development is taken to the local people. They are not forced to resettle, uproot themselves and adjust to an alien environment far from their homeland. The scheme participants can also retain land outside the estate, and continue to cultivate rice, fruit and vegetables. They can also maintain other activities such as hunting, fishing and gathering.

The main focus of SALCRA's efforts has been in the Lemanak and Lubok Antu areas of the Second Division, where many poor Iban shifting cultivators are located. It commenced its schemes there in 1977; these were mainly based on oil palm, and a processing mill was located there. There are other schemes in the First Division of Sarawak, among the Bidayuhs, but there the concentration is on cocoa. There is also a small tea scheme not far from the Bidayuh market town of Serian.

SALCRA has planted a total of about 8,000 hectares of land, involving some 2,250 households or roughly 12,000 people, and it has had a greater degree of success than the SLDB. It is more popular among natives because there is no question that land rights will be lost, forfeited or exchanged. Unfortunately as with other schemes the pace of development has been slow, and the costs are high; about 35,000 Malaysian dollars per household. Yet again, SALCRA has a shortage of personnel with skills in implementing and managing estate enterprises. The Authority has faced a very special problem because it is often developing land *in situ* in relatively remote areas. Costs of infrastructure tend to be high, and delays are caused in getting equipment and staff into the schemes, and getting products out. With any large-scale schemes, there is also the need to ensure smooth coordination between different government departments, and often there are problems of communication between them.

A problem for local scheme participants, and it is seen especially clearly in the Tebakang tea scheme, which is labour intensive, is precisely the allocation of labour between different tasks. Usually farmers welcome the opportunity to continue non-estate activities because it gives them insurance against fluctuations in market prices for cash crops. But it means that household labour is often inadequate to cover all the tasks. In the tea scheme, for example, labour shortage has been a recurrent problem in such work as tea-plucking, especially when the demands on labour are high during certain phases of rice cultivation. On the other hand, farmers become anxious when they feel that they are neglecting their rice farms, pepper gardens and other crops for work on the estate (King 1986a).

Of course, the Authority anticipates that over time the participants will gradually reduce their non-estate work and devote more attention to the cash crops in order that the scheme can pay its way and contribute to the increase in the standard of living of the scheme participants. But because SALCRA's pace of development is slow and expensive it is currently consolidating its projects and not expanding significantly into new schemes.

The state government has also launched other initiatives. In 1981 it established the Land Custody and Development Authority (LCDA), which was, in part, charged with land development. The LCDA, unlike other bodies, attempts to bring capital and expertise in the private plantation sector together with local land and labour to develop large-scale projects. Native farmers have been very wary of entering into agreements with private companies for fear of losing their land or becoming estate labourers working for a company. On the other hand, private companies are cautious of projects on native customary land, with all the problems of determining land rights. Instead, the LCDA has tended to concentrate on joint ventures with estate companies on state land using wage labour, often imported into Malaysia. The Sarawak government has also recently invited into the state the Federal Land Development Authority to accelerate the pace of estate development. But it too is concentrating on state land rather than native land.

A transformation which promises to have dramatic consequences for native farmers is the construction of hydro-electric power projects in Sarawak. At present there has been only one dam scheme established in the state near Lubok Antu. It came onstream in 1985; about 8,500 hectares of land were flooded, affecting some 26 Iban longhouses (King 1986c). Of these communities, 21 were displaced comprising about 3,000 people; they were resettled below the dam site in a purpose-built resettlement scheme incorporating five longhouses already there. The site is equipped with new longhouses made of sawn timber with corrugated iron roofing, glass windows and brick-built toilets, piped water and electricity, and a community centre of shops, schools, health facilities and so on.

The resettled Ibans are to grow cocoa and rubber; each household is allocated a parcel of land for the estate crops, plus a house-lot and garden. The Ibans were also given cash compensation for the loss of their lands, houses and farms in the reservoir area. The resettlement site has been squeezed into areas already occupied by other communities, which were also compensated for surrendering some of their land to the project. Consequently the resettled households received relatively poor, already worked land. There is little room for expansion because the site is cramped and there is virtually no opportunity for hunting, foraging and fishing in surrounding areas. There is also no spare land for rice farming.

Previously the Batang Ai communities had been described as 'traditional' (Kedit 1980). They were predominantly shifting cultivators, although they were only meeting on average 20 per cent to 30 per cent of their annual rice needs, because the area had been subject to sustained swiddening over a considerable period of time. Christian missions, schools and government had not made any significant impact in the Batang Ai, and many Ibans there still practised their pagan traditions. Agricultural rituals to ensure the success of the rice crop were still performed; Ibans still observed bird omenism; they held major festivals or *gawai*; they believed in the importance of dreams as a medium through which humans communicated with the world of spirits.

Following resettlement the Ibans were literally thrown into the marketplace. They could not grow rice, but had to buy it; other goods which they previously collected or cultivated themselves were no longer available and had to be purchased. They received lump sum payments in cash, which they used mainly to purchase consumer goods. They had become more and more dependent on estate work on the project, and ultimately would be expected to survive on the proceeds from rubber and cocoa. They were expected to pay back the development costs of the farm scheme to SALCRA, the agency charged with establishing the estate, along with loans on their new houses; they also had to meet electricity and water bills.

Subsequent studies (e.g. Hew and Kedit 1987) have revealed that the changes have been too rapid and too radical for many Ibans to be able to cope. Ibans are beginning to default on their loans; the estate crops are not realizing the anticipated income. Young Iban men are continuing to undertake labour migration in search of better prospects elsewhere. Some households have moved off the scheme altogether and found areas where they can grow rice again. In short, their future is not an enviable one. Their established ways of life have been so disrupted and transformed that the very integrity of their communities and their ability to meet their subsistence needs have been endangered.

The Batang Ai scheme is obviously relatively localized in its impact. But there may be other larger dam projects in the future. Feasibility studies have been completed for a series of dams along the upper Rejang river. If implemented these would involve the resettling of about 6,000 people, comprising diverse minority groups, some of which are only recently settled forest nomads. For the moment the original plans have been shelved, but they are indicative of the direction of future government policy.

Alongside land development and resettlement the state government is also engaged in promoting a strategy of integrated agricultural development. This has involved the participation of several government departments in a range of rural projects, interconnected throughout a given region. They comprise improvement of drainage and irrigation facilities, land and crop development including estate crops, the upgrading or construction of farm-to-market roads and the introduction of agricultural support services.

It would seem that most of these large-scale schemes have not been markedly successful, dogged as they are by native resistance, and by poor and inappropriate government planning and implementation (King 1986b). It would seem that gradual, *in situ* changes have the greatest chance of success, with emphasis on the introduction of new crops or improved existing crops to individual farms, subsidized inputs such as fertilizers and pesticides, appropriate credit facilities and extension services. However, estate agriculture and large schemes look set to continue, and these will eventually see the further commercialization of agriculture in Sarawak, increasing wage labour, integration of native peoples into the world market and the transformation of established village economies.

Sabah

I will not devote too much time to developments in Sabah; the changes there are broadly similar to those in Sarawak, but there are also some contrasts between the two states.

The British North Borneo Chartered Company, unlike the Brooke Raj, had encouraged commercial agriculture. Concessions of land were granted to private estate companies. In the latter part of the nineteenth century tobacco comprised the main plantation crop, while timber was also an important export. By 1890 there were 61 tobacco estates owned by British, Dutch and German planters (Gudgeon 1981: 191). Tobacco was followed by a boom in rubber cultivation, with large areas again under estate production, and plantation labour was recruited from outside the state even before the Second World War.

It was in 1959–60, well ahead of Sarawak, that Sabah began planting oil palm on estates established by such private companies as Unilever. These were located mainly in the east coast regions, and by 1970 when Sarawak was beginning to move into oil palm cultivation, Sabah already had over 36,000 hectares in production. Other estate crops were coconuts, abaca, and from the 1960s, increasingly cocoa. Sabah is now a large exporter of cocoa.

The Sabah Land Development Board (SLDB) was founded in 1969 to implement FELDA-type schemes, integrating native smallholders into plantation projects. After some initial successes, the Board met several difficulties: native resistance, problems of implementation and management and production inefficiencies. By 1982 the SLDB had decided to stop its settlement activities (Sutton 1988: 46). By the mid-1980s there were 34 schemes, comprising over 50,000 hectares, mainly under oil palm. The estates were taken over by the Federal Land Development Authority and the majority are worked by hired labourers; only a few accommodate settlers.

The problems of organizing an effective resettlement programme to a very large extent replicate those in Sarawak. One major obstacle is the reluctance of rural dwellers to move on to the schemes, their dislike of regular work schedules and problems experienced in loan repayments, and the Board's tardiness in issuing land titles (Sutton, p. 47).

As a commercial venture the Sabah Board was performing relatively well with hired labour from Indonesia and the Philippines. But it was not achieving its social goals of developing native communities. Its commercial orientation was further promoted when private management consultants were brought in to the SLDB following a management and financial crisis in 1980.

FELDA had already been operating in Sabah by the late 1970s. Eventually it hopes to have over 60 schemes in the state, covering over 120,000 hectares (Sutton, p. 53). Yet, it too is experiencing problems of settler recruitment among the numerous different ethnic groups in Sabah. Absenteeism is high among settlers; some have vacated the schemes altogether, or periodically go off to farm rice, hunt and gather.

Despite these difficulties of estate development in general the pace of rural change in Sabah, the decline of shifting cultivation and other forest-related activities, the importation of foreign wage labour and the expansion of estate agriculture and logging have been much more marked than in Sarawak.

Kalimantan

In Kalimantan there is also much evidence of plantation development and resettlement, mainly in the southern and eastern provinces. Some of these schemes have also been integrated into transmigration projects, which from the 1980s began to adopt estate agriculture rather than, as previously, subsistence food-crop strategies (Hurst 1990: 24).

One kind of development model which has been gaining ground in Kalimantan is the 'state corporation'. These were established with the help and encouragement of the World Bank. Examples of this initiative in West Kalimantan involve the concept of 'nuclear estates': in other words, large centralized government-run plantations which generate and link with smaller estates run by smallholders in surrounding areas. The opportunities for this strategy are presented by transmigration: resettled Javanese, Balinese and other transmigrants to Kalimantan are located on plantation projects. Then native smallholders already in the region are 'allocated' a parcel of land for planting to oil palm or other estate crops linked to the government transmigration project so that they can take advantage of the processing and other facilities provided on the scheme.

As Dove has indicated, the assumption of the resettlement agencies is that Dayak shifting cultivators in these regions to which transmigrants are moved have land adequate to their purposes, and that there is sufficient room for new settlers (1985b: 95ff.). Unfortunately the 'empty' land is usually land left under fallow by swiddeners, and is essential for a sustainable system of agriculture. Government has assumed the land to be unused and available for development. Some schemes have then resettled onto the project local Dayaks displaced by transmigrants and left with insufficient land for cultivation. In any case, the pressures on land and all other resources in the area are increased enormously with the influx of migrants. Frequently local people have not been compensated by government for their loss of land. Even Dayaks who, as smallholders on schemes, are provided with 3.5 hectares of land for planting to oil palm, perceive it as unfair that they are not compensated. After all, Javanese transmigrants are granted land which is not their own, while local residents give up substantial areas of swidden land to be reallocated a small plot for oil palm, and they are then subject to the repayment of the loans to meet the development costs of the project (Dove 1986: 3ff.). They therefore argue that, at the very least, they should not have to pay back any share of the projects' capital costs.

Some households consider it more advantageous not to join the schemes at all and become involved in the cultivation of an unfamiliar cash crop, incur debts and risk uncertain returns. Some have even decided to sell all their land for compensation; at least then their rights are recognized and they get an immediate cash return. But as we have seen with the Batang Ai Ibans in Sarawak, a sudden cash windfall is often wasted by people who are not used to handling large sums of money. Dove discovered, in his case-study, that often local people preferred more secure wage labour on the projects to becoming smallholders. They could then continue to live in their own villages, pursue a range of established economic activities outside the scheme and have a relatively secure source of cash income, so that they have a diverse set of pursuits to spread risks. They had a generally poor opinion of transmigration sites, often located in areas of poor soil and terrain, unsuitable for intensive Javanese farming methods, distant from good sources of water, and without income opportunities off the scheme. Many are also suspicious of officials on the scheme who break promises, and issue commands rather than consult participants.

Aside from plantation development both for transmigrants and locals, the Indonesian government has also been engaged in relocating indigenous communities, both swidden farmers and forest nomads, into accessible 'resettlement areas'. It appears that the ultimate goal is to eliminate shifting cultivation, and, in some cases, to move people off land valuable in timber and mineral resources. Furthermore, it is part of a general policy of promoting Islamization among non-Muslim outer islanders, and to extend the presence and influence of the Javanese (Hurst 1990). The first Five-Year Plan (1968) refers to the need for 'the socialization of primitive peoples' and specifically to the importance of 'living in an organized group', like the Javanese (G. Appell 1985). These remarks betray the prejudices of Indonesian officialdom, mainly based in Java, towards the tribal peoples of the rainforest.

From 1970 to the early 1980s, for example, 10,000 local households were resettled in East Kalimantan alone (Fulcher

1983a: 109). Sometimes the resettlement schemes combine settlers from more than one ethnic group and, in some cases, even from different economic backgrounds. Settlers are theoretically provided with materials to construct their own houses, plus a cash grant, or periodic grants to buy specific items such as chainsaws, outboard motors and sewing machines. Relocated households are granted two hectares of land each, and some are provided with fishponds, and poultry farms. The projects are usually equipped with government offices, schools, shops and access roads.

One major problem, as with the situation in Malaysian Borneo, is that there is often insufficient land in the resettlement site for growing rice. Residential densities are also high, resulting in local land exhaustion, the overfishing of rivers and the excessive exploitation of forest resources nearby. There have also been official attempts to prevent Dayaks building longhouses and keeping pigs (G. Appell 1985: 24). For these reasons, Dayak households frequently leave the schemes and return to their home areas, or return there periodically to grow rice.

Another important element in these government efforts physically to uproot people, move them to other sites and 'modernize' agriculture by encouraging plantation enterprises is the change brought about in inter-ethnic relations, which tends also to increase the likelihood of tension and conflict. This is nowhere more obvious than in transmigration projects, where culturally very different Javanese and Balinese are placed in regions inhabited by Dayaks. Indeed, the rationale behind transmigration is not only to redistribute population and promote regional development by assisting transmigrants in establishing 'modern' farming communities, but also to enhance security in territorially marginal and 'empty' areas by spreading the majority Muslim Javanese widely through the archipelago. This is assumed to enhance national identity by Javanizing and Islamizing culturally different tribal peoples and regions.

Transmigration was begun by the Dutch colonial government, and in the 1920s and 1930s small numbers of Javanese were already relocated in southern and eastern Kalimantan (Avé and King 1986: 92). However, following Independence the Indonesian government stepped up the pace of resettlement. From 1950 up to the mid-1970s, around 70,000 people were moved to Kalimantan, but from the commencement of the third Five-Year Plan from 1979–80 transmigration increased rapidly. By 1984, for example, roughly 27,000 families or 150,000 people had been settled in East Kalimantan alone, and about half of these had arrived in the five years covering the Third Plan. Another 110,000 families were targetted to be sent to the province in the Fourth Plan period (Clauss et al. 1988: 79–80). The main concentration has been in the Kutei district of East Kalimantan. In West Kalimantan 37,000 families were relocated between 1971 and the early 1980s, mainly in the Pontianak, Sintang and Sanggau districts, and relocation of a further 10,000 or more families was planned for 1984–9.

Transmigration sites tend, at least initially, to form socially and culturally separate communities or enclaves in the midst of the local Dayak populations (Fulcher 1983a, 1983b). Javanese and Balinese also differ in their resource use. They prefer settled, intensive cultivation and to keep close to their home villages, unlike Dayak shifting cultivators who often live away from the village for a period. Usually transmigrants cannot undertake irrigated wet rice cultivation because environmental conditions preclude it; instead they practise dry field cultivation of rice and other crops such as cassava and maize, and grow garden crops: fruit, vegetables, coffee, cloves, pepper and cocoa. Fields are hoed, clean-weeded and farmed for anything up to seven years, before fallowing. Unlike many Dayaks, Javanese will work land infested by *imperata* grass, using labour intensive techniques (Fulcher 1983a: 110). There is not much interest among the Javanese in forest-related activities. Some who have found it difficult to make ends meet have moved off the schemes altogether and gone into towns, estates or logging camps to find work.

For reasons of cultural and economic contrast, there is often not much interaction between transmigrants and locals. Fulcher says of Javanese-Dayak contact

relations between groups are most often indifferent but are, on occasion, hostile . . . rather than serving the stated purposes of promoting national unity and integration, transmigration presents a situation whereby ethnic status is maintained. (1983a: 109)

A case-study of the Rimbayu transmigration scheme, in the middle Mahakam area of East Kalimantan, reveals a range of inter-ethnic relations. The scheme opened between 1983 and 1986 with 2,500 families initially, comprising East, West and Central Javanese and Sundanese, along with local Kutei Malays, the original inhabitants of the area (Clauss et al. 1988: 81–2). There are cases of Javanese-Kutei marriage; Javanese women sell garden produce in the local markets. Some Javanese men undertake casual work in Dayak villages and for wealthy Kutei Malays (p. 88). Nevertheless, there are conflicts between locals and transmigrants over rights to land, particularly in relation to land which Dayak cultivators have left fallow. Different approaches to agriculture also cause tensions. Some transmigrants claim that locals practise shifting cultivation in the transmigration area, which disrupts their farming, causing erosion and uncontrolled fires, and that fallow fields encourage rats and other pests. Local pigs stray into transmigrants' farms. Natives, on the other hand, complain that impoverished Javanese steal from their lands, fruit gardens and fishponds, and that they transgress local *adat* by clearing locally owned bamboo groves and forest resources, or deliberately kill local animals, particularly pigs (Fulcher 1983a: 111). Not only are there occasions of open conflict; there is generally inter-ethnic antipathy. Transmigrants, for example, say that Dayaks practise 'black magic' against them, pointing to cases of unexplained death, illness and misfortune (p. 113).

Transmigration looks set to continue and to change further the cultural, ethnic and economic landscape of Borneo. Above all, it is one further element in the pressures on lands and forests, on an environment which is exceedingly fragile and easily damaged if not managed with care.

Forest clearance and logging

The issue of commercial logging in tropical rainforests has loomed large in all areas of Borneo, with the exception of Brunei, which, as a result of its oil wealth, has not needed to exploit its timber resources to any extent. The problems have received international attention in two areas in particular –

Sarawak and East Kalimantan – and we shall look in detail at these shortly. However, evidence of the large-scale clearance of forests is widespread on the island (plate 43).

Even in the early 1960s Sabah, for example, was exploiting its hill *dipterocarp* forests by mechanization (Hurst 1990: 105). In 1973, 6.3 million hectares of forest were assumed to be exploitable. By the mid-1980s, this figure had been more than halved (pp. 102ff.). Annual log production increased from 6.5 million cu. metres per annum in 1970 to about 11 million cu. metres annually in 1985. As Walton has noted

In the first half of the 1980s Sabah accounted for 35 per cent of Malaysia's total output of sawlogs whilst the state's export earnings from forest products averaged M$2,000 million per year. (1990: 218).

In 1987 Sabah maintained its log production of over 10 million cu. metres of sawlogs together with about 900,000 cu. metres of sawn timber, serviced by well over 100 sawmills. It has been claimed that by the 1990s all the major lowland forests of Sabah will have been logged, with the exception of small areas of forest reserve.

Plate 43   Transporting logs by river in Sarawak

In Sarawak the increase in logging has been dramatic indeed. Log output rose from 4.4 million cu. metres in 1976 to over 12 million cu. metres in 1985 contributing, as with Sabah, over a third of Malaysia's total output of logs in that year (Colchester 1989: 34; Hong 1987: 125–7). Very roughly, from the early 1960s through to the later 1980s about three million hectares of forest have been cleared, about one-third of the estimated forest resources. A few years ago it was calculated that another third of those resources would have been logged by the mid-1990s. However, with the international attention on Sarawak and the possibility of restrictions being placed on the industry, it is reported that logging has been stepped up recently to clear as much timber as possible as quickly as possible. Figures for the recent annual production of logs suggest something of the order of a staggering 14 to 18 million cu. metres. Now loggers are even clearing areas of the remote hinterlands of the state.

Timber is of enormous financial importance to Sarawak, and indeed Sabah. Although both states are major petroleum producers, most of these benefits are subject to federal control through the national oil corporation, Petronas. However, royalties, duties, premiums and other taxes and fees from logging go into the state coffers, because forests are a matter of state and not federal control. During the 1980s, for example, the Sarawak state government had been receiving annually in excess of 200 million Malaysian dollars. The timber industry is therefore vital in underpinning and resourcing economic development efforts in the state, but it also funds political activity, and has enabled senior politicians to enrich themselves and to build up and sustain political support through patronage (Insan, 1989: 5). The politically powerful and the wealthy obtain timber concessions and licences. As Colchester says

Sadly, the reality is that Forestry Policy in Sarawak has been subverted to serve the interests of the ruling elite, who have used the handing out of logging concessions as political favours and as a source of personal wealth, to ensure their positions. (1989: 35)

The power to grant or deny a licence lies entirely with the Forestry Minister, who since 1966 has come from the ruling political party.

Some state officials and local politicians have attempted to argue that it is not logging which poses the main threat to East Malaysia's forest resources, since the timber industry is subject to various controls. Logging is practised on a 25-year cycle, and the timber companies, so it is said, are regulated so that their operations have to be undertaken on a sustainable basis. On the other hand, it is argued that shifting cultivators are difficult to control; they destroy the forest by burning it, and only produce low-value subsistence crops from the land. The expression of this official view is seen vividly in the report of a workshop on shifting cultivation held in Kuching in 1978 (Cramb 1989: 38ff.; Hatch and Lim 1978). It concluded that, at that time, the net annual loss to Sarawak's economy from farmers burning timber was about 300 million Malaysian dollars; and that shifting agriculture was an inefficient, wasteful and primitive way of using forest resources. The report baldly stated that

shifting cultivation represents probably the greatest single threat to the integrity of Sarawak's natural resources and results in totally unacceptable degrees of human suffering. (Hatch and Lim 1978: 28)

It is this rationale which is used to justify the curtailment of shifting cultivation, and, in certain cases, the resettlement of the farmers concerned.

However, these arguments for commercial logging and against customary farming practices are difficult to support in general. In practice, commercial logging is very little controlled. It is a lucrative source of revenue for politicians and state bureaucrats, and these usually have interests in logging companies and enter into production-sharing deals with timber extraction companies owned by Chinese businessmen. In state land forest, selective logging is not enforced, and, even in protected forests where there are controls, these are often ignored. There is much evidence to demonstrate that where logging is concentrated, there has been a marked increase in soil erosion and water pollution (Colchester 1989: 37ff.; Hong 1987: 152ff.; Hurst 1990: 85).

Chin has pointed out that FAO studies have indicated that

up to 40 per cent of a logged forest consists of open spaces . . . Most of these spaces – including roads, skid trails, log yards and camp areas – are of bare, compacted sub-soil. In such ecologically devastated soil conditions, forest species (especially the valuable dipterocarps) find it very difficult or impossible to regenerate. (1989: 59)

The destruction may be even greater. The World Wildlife Fund (1985) has found damage to about 46 per cent of the forest cover in selectively logged areas because of the use of heavy machinery, damage to neighbouring trees from fallen trees and the opening up of roads and tracks to get the felled timber to a river for transport (Hong 1987: 162ff.). Some estimates in East Kalimantan suggest damage of up to 50 per cent of the trees in a logged area, and one site revealed that 70 per cent of the canopy had been removed.

Hurst has said

Seen from the air, the coasts of Sabah and Sarawak reveal wide fans of red silt spilling from all the river mouths into the South China seas [sic]. (1990: 85)

It is difficult to get hard-and-fast data, but it has been reported that there is now more flooding and erratic water-levels in coastal areas; local climatic disturbances with increased occurrence of drought; and that dredging operations have had to be sustained to keep major river-mouths open to Sarawak's ports, such as Sibu. Even Malaysia's own Fifth Plan reports that, for Sarawak, soil erosion and siltation have become the main source of water pollution, and less than half of the state's rivers remain unpolluted (FMP 1986: 285, 290).

Turning to shifting cultivation, we have seen that under pressure farmers may intensify land use which gives rise to soil erosion and vegetational deterioration. But generally the negative effects of swiddening on the environment have been greatly exaggerated. More recently, Hatch, who worked for the Department of Agriculture in Sarawak, has said

it now seems clear that logging and timber extraction must take a lot of the blame that was previously laid at the door of the shifting cultivator. (1982: 146)

S. Chin further argues that for the whole of Sarawak shifting cultivators, comprising about 30,000 households, are clearing annually much less than commercial loggers, about 72,000 hectares, in comparison with well over 200,000 hectares logged (1985, 1989). State Forestry Department figures suggest areas cleared by shifting cultivators of between 74,000 to 160,000 hectares per annum (Colchester 1989: 48–9), although about 75,000 hectares seems about right (Avé and King 1986: 67; Hong 1987: 135). More importantly Chin maintains that of this amount, only about 5 per cent, or on his figures 3,600 hectares, is valuable primary forest; the rest comes from forest land in fallow (S. Chin 1985: 32–3; 1989: 57–62; Hong 1987: 135–8).

The fact is that Sarawak's steeply sloping terrain and poor soils can only support such activities as shifting agriculture, hunting, gathering and fishing, as well as the production of commercial tree crops such as cocoa, rubber and oil palm. Borneo has been subject to shifting cultivation for a considerable period of time, yet it is only in the last 20 to 30 years, when commercial logging began in earnest, that forest depletion and erosion has taken on very serious dimensions.

The directly negative effects of timber exploitation on local societies and economies are plain for all to see, given the dependence of local people on the forests for their sources of food and raw materials. Shifting cultivation cannot be sustained in some areas, and yet alternative economic activities are difficult to find. Stands of wild sago and forest fruits and vegetables are disappearing. Sources of drinking water are being polluted. Fish spawning-grounds and fish stocks, an important source of protein, are being destroyed. Erratic movements in river levels, flash floods and siltation make river transport more difficult. If changing climatic patterns also occur then this will make farming an even more unpredictable enterprise. Sources of raw materials from the forest such as various woods for building materials and rattans and illipe nut are becoming more difficult to find in heavily logged areas. Above all, stocks of wild animals are disappearing, and hunting pigs and deer is important not only for Dayak agriculturalists, but is especially significant for forest nomads. Therefore, food intakes, and importantly variety in the native diet, and essential protein and other nutrients, are ultimately likely to decrease.

Finally, the Dayaks in Sarawak and elsewhere view logging as an abuse of their rights in land and forest. In some cases, burial grounds and sacred sites have been bulldozed and destroyed. Overall native customary land rights are ignored or overruled. In effect, these rights are only very poorly expressed and represented in formal legal regulations and procedures. In Sarawak, the state government has full claim to all forests and can concession them for logging, even though natives may claim customary rights in the land on which these forests stand. The Forest Department also has full control over permanent forests; these are 'protected' and comprise about 30 per cent of the forest land of the state. Natives do not have legal access to them and have to apply to the Department for a village communal forest to be established there (Hong 1987: 73).

The damaging effects of logging therefore outweigh the advantages for rural dwellers. The benefits are that logging provides revenues for government, some of which are channelled back into rural development, although we have already seen that much money has been wasted on large-scale land-development schemes. Of more immediate benefit is the employment offered to young Dayak men in the logging camps. But even this is a mixed blessing. Figures for workers employed in the industry are very misleading. Hong suggests a labour force of about 30,000 in 1980, two-thirds of which was in timber production and one-third in manufacture, mainly in sawmills (1987: 144). However, local males usually occupy the low paid, dangerous positions – as cutters or sometimes machine operatives. Hong charges that the safety record of the Sarawak timber industry is 'atrocious'. In 1979 there were 1,658 accidents, of which 61 were fatal, in the logging and wood-working industries, comprising about three-quarters of all recorded industrial accidents and about two-thirds of industrial-related deaths (pp. 146–7). From 1973 to 1984 there were 603 logging deaths and 11,648 non-fatal accidents.

It is not surprising then that logging in Sarawak, given its far-reaching and damaging effects on local peoples, without corresponding benefits, has resulted in native resistance and protest. Initially reactions were confined to petitioning and complaining, both to the timber companies and to government officials. Some communities lodged claims for compensation for damage to their homelands; some applied for leaseholds on surrounding forests so that they could be designated as 'communal forests' and protected from logging by outsiders. But as Hurst has said

There are numerous cases in which local communities have tried to obtain compensation for damage to their environment, but very few have had any degree of success. Longhouses attempting to secure rights over Communal Forest areas frequently have their applications rejected . . . At present it takes between six to 12 years for communal forest applications to be heard in court. (1990: 88)

Eventually Dayak communities began more direct kinds of action against logging companies, especially in the areas of intense operations such as the upper Rejang, and the Baram, where in the 1980s about 30 logging companies were working in about 400,000 hectares of forest (Hong 1987: 98). In the early 1980s there had been shows of force by Kenyahs at logging camps, roadblocks set up by Ibans and the destruction of bridges used by loggers. But in 1987 and 1988 natives established 'timber blockades' in the Baram area and the actions quickly spread (Hurst 1990: 90ff.). About 16,000 natives in 40 longhouses in the region had been affected by logging, along with nomadic Penan. The barricades across logging roads were manned by Penans, Kenyahs, Kayans, Lun Bawangs and Kelabits. Various organized protest groups were also involved, including the Malaysian Friends of the Earth (Sahabat Alam Malaysia, SAM), and Survival International. In mid-1987 various of the Dayak leaders of the protest petitioned the federal authorities in Kuala Lumpur; all they achieved were 'vague assurances that the matter would be taken up with the State officials' (Colchester 1989: 42). The state government sent police in; the barriers were dismantled; several natives were arrested and charged with police obstruction and occupation of state lands. The federal government also invoked the Internal Security Act as a means to support the arrest of certain key personnel in protest groups such as Sahabat Alam Malaysia; their activities were designated as contrary to national interests (Insan 1989: v).

Despite these arrests, barricades have continued to reappear across logging roads. But the government has brought in new penalties in a Forest Amendment Bill to fine and imprison individuals obstructing logging operations (Colchester 1989: 43–4). Although the protests have generated more awareness among the international community about the plight of Borneo's forests and natives, at the moment they have only temporarily obstructed logging operations.

Another strategy used by government and timber companies to undermine the strength of protest is to buy off various native communities and individuals. Some village chiefs, tempted by large offers of cash or a share in timber profits, have sold off 'village rights' in land and forest, which are not strictly theirs to dispose of, or have acted as mediators between villagers and companies to keep discontent at a minimum (Insan 1989: 18). Resistance has also been blunted by the collusion of certain local leaders, some of whom have even been granted timber concessions themselves. Some communities have also secured sums of money from logging companies as compensation by negotiating directly with them. These amounts have invariably been small, but they help to defuse some opposition to logging, and where young men have secured employment in companies operating locally, there has been less motivation to obstruct felling. Yet as Colchester argues,

it seems clear that the short-term financial benefits that have accrued to the communities from these deals have been far outweighed by the long-term costs. (1989: 40)

Finally, let us turn to the situation in East Kalimantan, which illustrates extremely well two further aspects of logging: first, the international dimension and second, the dangers to logged forests of fire and drought. In Indonesian Borneo there is a complex interrelationship between local timber companies, and licensees associated closely with influential military personnel and their clients, and Japanese and other multinational companies. An article in *Asiaweek* states

East Kalimantan's timber industry has developed a reputation for being less than entirely above board. The distant, generally unseen end of the vast tangle is Japan . . . . Japanese consume most of the timber shipped from Kalimantan and Japanese interests control, through intermediaries, many of the concessionaires who organise the actual logging . . . On the ground the concessions themselves are a patchwork of intercompany leases, concession swaps, company takeovers and other deals. (in Avé and King 1986: 87)

Although blame can be placed on the greed of local politicians and the unscrupulous actions of Chinese entrepreneurs, one should not ignore the involvement of outsiders, particularly the Japanese. The Japanese market consumes over 50 per cent of the export of saw-logs from East Malaysia, keeping a tight rein on the import of processed wood, which carries high import duties. The Japanese prefer raw timber of high quality, and it is noticeable that when Indonesia placed its own restrictions on the export of raw timber in favour of more value-added wood products like plywood, the Japanese shifted their attention to the less restrictive Malaysian producers who were content to export saw-logs. Japanese trading houses also extend credit to local timber companies to get first refusal on timber. The Japanese have few fixed contracts; they reject much timber of low quality or damaged materials, which are simply left to rot (Hurst 1990: 108).

Large-scale logging did not really get under way in Kalimantan until the establishment of President Soeharto's government after 1965, and the desperate need to generate foreign exchange and promote economic development. Kalimantan has about one-third of Indonesia's forests of just over 120 million hectares, and East Kalimantan has nearly half (17 million hectares) of Kalimantan's total forested land of over 40 million hectares and supplies about 30 per cent of Indonesia's timber (Avé and King 1986: 83). By 1982 more than 31 million hectares of this forest had been concessioned, mainly in the eastern and central provinces.

The main early foreign concession holders in East Kalimantan were Weyerhauser and Georgia Pacific of the USA, and then the Japanese multinationals Mitsubishi, Sumitomo, Shin Asahigawa and Ataka. Weyerhauser went into partnership with various top Indonesian generals to form the International Timber Corporation of Indonesia, which in 1977 produced 1.6 million tons of logs on concessions of 386,000 hectares. In

1984 Weyerhauser withdrew from its operations, apparently under pressure from the Indonesian government to reinvest more of its profits on local processing facilities, and perhaps because of the destruction by fire of large areas of its timber concessions (see below). It switched its attention to more profitable operations in East Malaysia (Hurst 1990: 34). Georgia Pacific had joint ventures with wealthy Indonesians, including the close ally of President Soeharto, the Chinese businessman, Bob Hasan. Hasan's joint venture company had a concession of 357,000 hectares in East Kalimantan, of which 10,000 hectares, following logging, was to become a transmigration site.

One major event in East Kalimantan, which so aptly illustrates the dangers facing Dayak communities, and the devastation which is being wrought in the rainforests of Borneo, was the Great Fire of 1982–3. Serious fires were also reported in East Malaysia. There were severe droughts in East Kalimantan, commencing in June 1982, which clearly contributed to the intensity and extent of the fire. Overall, more extreme weather conditions and other environmental changes have been reported. Flash floods have been more widespread, and since the late 1970s it has been reported that the Barito river has become more flood-prone, destroying crops and farms near the river. As to drought conditions, Hurst reports that

Scientists are now linking it [drought] with a change in the Pacific air current known as the El Nino Southern Oscillation Event. A team from the University of Hamburg think forest destruction may play a central role because it affects the turbidity of the South China Sea, which in turn may affect the intensity of El Nino. (1990: 5)

The drought also proved devastating to farmers in East Kalimantan operating lowland rainfed and irrigated agriculture; many farms produced no crops at all.

In late 1982 fires broke out in many places in East Kalimantan and by March–April 1983 had grown into a vast sea of flames concentrated in the middle and lower Mahakam basin, along the coasts from Balikpapan to Sangkulirang, and in forest reserves in Kutei and near Samarinda (Mackie 1984). It has been estimated that 3.5 million hectares of timber were destroyed, representing about one-fifth of the forests of East

Kalimantan (Avé and King 1986: 85–6; Hurst 1990: 36–7). The impact on local economies was devastating. Drought and then fire resulted in dramatic decreases in food supplies, and transport systems were disrupted.

Although it is difficult to blame forest clearance directly, it has been suggested that it is contributing to more erratic weather patterns, and it is clear that, where logging had been undertaken, the fire, once started, burned more intensely (Mackie 1984: 65). According to reports, the fire spread rapidly through the thick organic deposits of the peat-swamp forests, which had been dried out to a depth exceeding 0.5 metre (Avé and King 1986: 85ff.). It travelled along timber trails littered with wood debris. Aerial surveys of the affected areas estimated that 800,000 hectares of unlogged *dipterocarp* forests were destroyed, 550,000 hectares of swamp and peat forest, 750,000 hectares of secondary forest and farmland and 1.4 million hectares of logged forest. It is clear that the fire burned most fiercely in the more open logged-over forests and adjacent unlogged forest, which had dried out more thoroughly. The dry felled timber and debris provided excellent kindling, and the timber trails provided ideal wind tunnels. In the closed canopy of the primary forest, more dense and damp, the fire burned less well. It would appear that logged forest is especially vulnerable to fire.

The fire may well have been started by shifting cultivators during the burning period prior to sowing, but its devastating effects were in no small way the result of logging. What is more, Dayak farmers are being augmented by settlers from other parts of Indonesia and transmigrants who are slashing and burning the forest for farming, and putting down cash crops such as pepper. East Kalimantan is, then, a booming frontier region, based on oil, gas, timber and plantations; it is experiencing large increases in population and the local rural-dwellers and their environment are suffering accordingly. There is also much illegal felling in the province, often in areas already selectively logged by licensed companies. Illegal loggers may have links with licensed operators or work for urban-based entrepreneurs and sawmill owners. Even licensed loggers often fell more timber than is legally permitted, to pay for government levies, fund corruption and make quick profits.

As Mackie has said

All of the lowland rainforests in East Kalimantan within reach of waterways have been the site of frantic, frontier-style, logging since the late 1960's. (1984: 66)

Epilogue

What does the future hold for the native populations of Borneo? Unless something is done to halt or considerably reduce rainforest clearance, then the prospects for the Dayaks must be bleak indeed. The very resources upon which they have depended for centuries – the land, forests and rivers – will no longer be able to sustain them. The present-day descendants of the Austronesians, who, over the course of four thousand years or so, have adapted to the natural environment, used it and protected it, will have been transformed into marginal peasants, estate workers and urban wage labourers, in the space of about 40 years. This seems to be the ultimate destiny which governments probably more consciously than unconsciously have marked out for them. The main thrust of government policies is likely to continue to be the promotion of estate agriculture, resettlement and amalgamation of communities and forest clearance.

These development programmes have been conspicuously unsuccessful, and it is now clear that policies towards resettlement, in particular, need urgent rethinking. What is more, the moves to establish large-scale plantations need to be modified. When they are asked, local people generally want the benefits of development, but they want to be consulted, and they want to retain some links with their traditions. They want government help in the form of community facilities, education, health services, new and appropriate agricultural methods and crops and a rising standard of living, but they want more freedom of manoeuvre to adjust to change. Rather than the transformation to plantation forms of production, native communities usually prefer to retain a mix of subsistence activities, cash crops and sometimes wage work to spread risks, and to retain the variety of life. Small-scale, *in situ* forms of agricultural development would seem to be ideal.

However, none of this will be possible unless and until commercial logging is dealt with. In this regard, governments must be made to recognize indigenous rights. There has to be a formal legal system instituted which ensures the status and rights of indigenous people to live in, work on, farm and use particular areas of land. This in turn, requires effective native political representation. It has been very much missing up to now. But signs of an increasing self-awareness of Dayak identity are emerging. This was initially much more obvious in Kalimantan, and it demonstrates what an increase in ethnic identity and political strength can do, if channelled in the right direction.

As we have seen, in 1957 the separate province of Central Kalimantan was finally established as a Dayak-run province, after a struggle against the central government. The Ngajus then continued to press for the national recognition of their traditional religion, and in 1980 Kaharingan was officially accepted by the Indonesian government as a religion proper. Without a local power base, without the efforts of Dayak leaders with that power, working genuinely for Dayak interests, these gains would not have been made. Nevertheless, it has been difficult for the Dayaks to get their voice heard on such matters as forest destruction and resettlement programmes.

More recently in Sabah the Parti Bersatu Sabah (PBS: the Sabah United Party), an ostensibly multiracial party, although dominated by Christian Kadazans, won a victory in the state elections in 1985. Previously Sabah had been controlled by Muslim politicians for some 20 years, when Islam and the Malay language were specifically promoted. Since 1985 a Kadazan has been Sabah's Chief Minister, and there has been a persistent tension between the federal authorities representing Muslim-Malay interests and PBS's goals of securing resources, education and political influence in the state on behalf of Dayaks, as well as the wider recognition of the cultural values, traditions and distinct identities of the non-Muslim peoples.

In Sarawak the story is somewhat different. After some initial Dayak success in government from 1963 to 1970, their voice has since been muted, and Muslim interests have been promoted vigorously by Muslim political leaders. Dissatisfaction with their status led the Dayaks to found a new party – Parti Bansa Dayak Sarawak (PBDS) in 1983. The Dayaks, especially the Ibans, have felt that they are not receiving a sufficient share of the benefits of economic growth and the wealth derived from the timber industry, yet their homelands and livelihoods are threatened by forest destruction. However, the new party has not made a significant impact.

These political developments demonstrate the importance of access to power and influence for the Dayaks. But they also serve to show that the natives of Borneo do perceive themselves to be neglected and marginalized by central governments. What they are demanding is a recognition of their rights and identity. This does not mean that they wish to return to the traditional ways of life and culture which I have examined in this book. As we have seen these have been in a process of constant change throughout history. But they wish to retain some of their traditions, and be given a breathing space to adjust and seek an appropriate synthesis of the old and the new. It would be a tragedy if through human greed and arrogance the rich cultural and natural resources of this great island were lost forever.

References

Abbreviations

BKI   Bijdragen tot de Taal-, Land- en Volkenkunde
BMJ   The Brunei Museum Journal
BRB   Borneo Research Bulletin
JMBRAS   Journal of the Malaysian Branch of the Royal Asiatic
           Society
SMJ   The Sarawak Museum Journal

Adelaar, Sander 1990: Borneo as a cross-roads for comparative Austronesian linguistics. *The Austronesians in History: Common Origins and Diverse Transformations.* Unpublished conference paper, Australian National University, Research School of Pacific Studies.

Alexander, Jennifer 1989: Culture and ethnic identity: the case of the Lahanan of Ulu Belaga. *SMJ*, 40, Special Issue No. 4, pt I, 51–9.

Andaya, Barbara Watson and Andaya, Leonard Y. 1982: *A History of Malaysia.* London: Macmillan.

Anon. 1984: Wound in the world. *Asiaweek*, 13 July, 34–55.

Appell, Amity C. P. 1986: The *Bulusu'* language of East Kalimantan: ethnographic profile and basic word list. *BRB*, 18, 166–75.

Appell, G. N. 1968a: The Dusun languages of northern Borneo: the Rungus Dusun and related problems. *Oceanic Linguistics*, 7, 1–15.

—— 1968b: Ethnographic profiles of the Dusun-speaking peoples of Sabah, Malaysia. *JMBRAS*, 41, 131–47.

—— (ed.) 1976: *The Societies of Borneo: Explorations in the Theory of Cognatic Social Structure.* Washington, DC: American Anthropological Association.

—— 1978: The Rungus Dusun. In Victor T. King (ed.), *Essays on Borneo Societies*, Oxford/Hull: Oxford University Press, 143–71.

—— (ed.) 1985: Resettlement of peoples in Indonesian Borneo: the social anthropology of administered peoples. *BRB*, 17, 3–31.

Avé, Jan B. n.d.: The Dayak of Borneo. In W. Stöhr (ed.), *Art of the Archaic Indonesians*, Geneva: Musée d'Art et d'Histoire, 93–117.

—— 1972: Kalimantan Dayaks. In Frank M. Lebar (ed. and comp.), *Ethnic Groups of Insular Southeast Asia. Indonesia, Andaman Islands and Madagascar*, Vol. 1, New York: HRAF Press, 185–7.

—— and King, Victor T. 1986: *The People of the Weeping Forest: Tradition and Change in Borneo*. Leiden: National Museum of Ethnology.

——, King, Victor T. and Wit, Joke G. W. de 1983: *West Kalimantan: A Bibliography*. Dordrecht, Cinnaminson: Foris.

Baring-Gould, S. and Bampfylde, C. A. 1909: *A History of Sarawak Under its Two White Rajahs 1839–1908*. London: Henry Sotheran.

Barth, F. 1952: The Southern Mongoloid migration. *Man*, 52, 5–8.

Bassett, D. K. 1971: *British Trade and Policy in Indonesia and Malaysia in the Late Eighteenth Century*. Switzerland: Inter Documentation Company AG Zug.

—— 1980: *British Attitudes to Indigenous States in South-East Asia in the Nineteenth Century*. University of Hull: Centre for South-East Asian Studies.

Beccari, Odoardo 1904: *Wanderings in the Great Forests of Borneo*. London: Archibald Constable.

Beeckman, Captain Daniel 1718: *A Voyage to and from the Island of Borneo in the East-Indies*. London: T. Warner and J. Batley.

Bellwood, Peter 1978: *Man's Conquest of the Pacific: The Prehistory of Southeast Asia and Oceania*. Auckland, Sydney, London: Collins.

—— 1985: *Prehistory of the Indo-Malaysian Archipelago*. Sydney, Orlando, London: Academic Press.

—— (ed. and comp.) 1988: *Archaeological Research in South-Eastern Sabah*. Kota Kinabalu: Sabah Museum.

—— 1989: Archaeological investigations at Bukit Tengkorak and Segarong, southeastern Sabah. *Bulletin of the Indo-Pacific Prehistory Association*, 9, 122–62.

—— 1990: The Tingkayu industry of Late Pleistocene Sabah. In Ian and Emily Glover (eds), *Southeast Asian Archaeology 1986*, Oxford: BAR International Series 561, 1–10.

—— 1991: Fils du Pléistocène. In Antonio Guerreiro and Pascal Couderc (eds), *Bornéo. Des Chasseurs de Têtes aux Ecologistes*, Paris: Autrement, 164–71.

—— and Koon, Peter 1989: 'Lapita colonists leave boats unburned!'

The question of Lapita links with island Southeast Asia. *Antiquity*, 63, 618–22.

—— and Matussin bin Omar 1980: Trade patterns and political developments in Brunei and adjacent areas, A.D. 700–1500. *BMJ*, 4, 155–79.

Black, Ian 1983: *A Gambling Style of Government: The Establishment of Chartered Company Rule in Sabah 1878–1915*. Kuala Lumpur: Oxford University Press.

—— 1985: The 'Lastposten': Eastern Kalimantan and the Dutch in the nineteenth and early twentieth centuries. *Journal of Southeast Asian Studies*, 16, 281–91.

Blume, C. L. 1843: Toelichtingen aangaande de nasporingen op Borneo van G. Müller. *De Indische Bij*, 1, 103–76.

Blust, R. A. 1976: Austronesian culture history: some linguistic inferences and their relations to the archaeological record. *World Archaeology*, 8, 19–43.

—— 1977. The Proto-Austronesian pronouns and Austronesian subgrouping: a preliminary report. *Working Papers in Linguistics*, University of Hawaii: Dept of Linguistics.

—— 1980: Early Austronesian social organization: the evidence of language. *Current Anthropology*, 21, 205–47.

—— 1982: The linguistic value of the Wallace line. *BKI*, 138, 231–50.

—— 1988: The Austronesian homeland: a linguistic perspective. *Asian Perspectives*, 26, 45–67.

Bock, Carl 1881: *The Head-Hunters of Borneo: a Narrative of Travel up the Mahakkam and down the Barito; also, Journeyings in Sumatra*. London: Sampson Low, Marston, Searle and Rivington.

Bouman, M. A. 1924: Ethnografische aanteekeningen omtrent de Gouvernementslanden in de Boven-Kapoeas, Westerafdeeling van Borneo. *Tijdschrift voor Indische Taal-, Land- en Volkenkunde*, 64, 173–95.

—— 1952:Gegevens uit Smitau en Boven-Kapoeas. *Adatrechtbundels*, 44, 47–86.

Brace, C. L. and Hinton, R. J. 1981: Oceanic tooth-size variation as a reflection of biological and cultural mixing. *Current Anthropology*, 22, 549–69.

Bronson, B. 1978: Exchange at the upstream and downstream ends: notes toward a functional model of the coastal state in Southeast Asia. In K. Hutterer (ed.), *Economic Exchange and Social Interaction in Southeast Asia*, Ann Arbor: University of Michigan, Centre for South and Southeast Asian Studies, 39–52.

Brooke, Sylvia 1972: *Queen of the Headhunters: The Autobiography of H. H. the Hon. Sylvia Brooke, Ranee of Sarawak.* London: Sidgwick and Jackson. First published 1970.

Brooks, S. T., Helgar, R. and Brooks, R. H. 1977: Radio-carbon dating and palaeoserology of a selected burial series from the Great Cave of Niah, Sarawak, Malaysia. *Asian Perspectives*, 20, 21–31.

Brothwell, D. R. 1960: Upper Pleistocene human skull from Niah Caves, Sarawak. *SMJ*, 9, 323–49.

Brown, D. E. 1970: *Brunei: the Structure and History of a Bornean Malay Sultanate*. Brunei: Brunei Museum Monograph.

—— 1976: *Principles of Social Structure: Southeast Asia*. London: Duckworth.

Bugo, Hamid 1988: Economic development since Independence: performance and prospects. In R. A. Cramb and R. H. W. Reece (eds), *Development in Sarawak: Historical and Contemporary Perspectives*, Monash University: Centre of Southeast Asian Studies, 49–55.

Cator, W. J. 1936: *The Economic Position of the Chinese in the Netherlands Indies*. Oxford: Blackwell.

Cense, A. A. and Uhlenbeck, E. M. 1958: *Critical Survey of Studies on the Languages of Borneo*. The Hague: Martinus Nijhoff.

Chadwick, Neil J. and Courtenay, P. P. 1983: *Punan Art and Artefacts*. James Cook University: Centre for South-East Asian Studies.

Chatfield, Godfrey A. 1972: *Sabah: A General Geography*. Singapore: Eastern Universities Press, 4th revised edition.

Cheng, Te-K'un 1969: *Archaeology in Sarawak*. Cambridge: W. Heffer and Sons.

Chew, Daniel 1990: *Chinese Pioneers on the Sarawak Frontier 1841–1941*. Singapore: Oxford University Press.

Chhabra, B. Ch. 1965: *Expansion of Indo-Aryan Culture during Pallava Rule (as evidenced by inscriptions)*. Delhi: Munshi Ram Manohar Lal.

Chin, John M. 1981: *The Sarawak Chinese*. Kuala Lumpur: Oxford University Press.

Chin, Lucas 1980: *Cultural Heritage of Sarawak*. Kuching: Sarawak Museum.

Chin, S. C. 1985: Agriculture and resource utilization in a lowland rainforest Kenyah community. *SMJ*, 35, Special Monograph No. 4.

—— 1989: Shifting cultivation and logging in Sarawak. In *Logging Against the Natives of Sarawak*, Petaling Jaya: Insan, 57–62.

Chong Chin Seng 1987: *Traditional Melanau Woodcarving (Bilum) in Dalat, Sarawak*. Kuching: Persatuan Kesusasteraan Sarawak.

Christie, Jan Wisseman 1985: On P'o-ni: the Santubong sites of Sarawak. *SMJ*, 34, 77–89.

—— 1988: Ironworking in Sarawak. In J. W. Christie and V. T. King, *Metal-working in Borneo: Essays on Iron- and Silver-working in Sarawak*, University of Hull: Centre for South-East Asian Studies, 1–28.

—— 1990: The Sanskrit inscription recently discovered in Kedah, Malaysia. In Gert-Jan Bartstra and Willem Arnold Casparie (eds), *Modern Quaternary Research in Southeast Asia*, Rotterdam, Brookfield: A. A. Balkema, 39–53.

Clauss, Wolfgang, Evers, Hans-Dieter and Gerke, Solvay 1988: The formation of a peasant society: Javanese transmigrants in East Kalimantan. *Indonesia*, 46, 79–90.

Coedès, G. 1968: *The Indianized States of Southeast Asia*. Canberra: Australian National University Press.

Colchester, Marcus 1989: *Pirates, Squatters and Poachers: The Political Ecology of Dispossession of the Natives of Sarawak*. London: Survival International; Petaling Jaya: Insan.

Collins, Mark 1990: *The Last Rainforests*. London: Mitchell Beazley.

Coon, C. S. 1962: *The Origin of Races*. London: Jonathan Cape.

—— 1966: *The Living Races of Man*. London: Jonathan Cape.

Crain, Jay B. 1978: The Lun Dayeh. In Victor T. King (ed.), *Essays on Borneo Societies*, Oxford/Hull: Oxford University Press, 123–42.

Cramb, R. A. 1989: Shifting cultivation and resource degradation in Sarawak: perceptions and policies. *BRB*, 21, 22–49.

—— and Reece, R. H. W. (eds) 1988: *Development in Sarawak: Historical and Contemporary Perspectives*. Monash University: Centre of Southeast Asian Studies.

Crawfurd, J. 1856: *A Descriptive Dictionary of the Indian Islands and Adjacent Countries*. London: Bradbury and Evans.

Crisswell, Colin N. 1978: *Rajah Charles Brooke: Monarch of All he Surveyed*. Kuala Lumpur: Oxford University Press.

Deen, Abdul Rahman 1989: The coming of Indian Muslim merchants to Sarawak. *SMJ*, 40, Special Issue No. 4, pt IV, 217–23.

Domalain, Jean-Yves 1974: *Panjamon*. St Albans: Panther Books. First published 1972.

Dove, Michael R. 1985a: *Swidden Agriculture in Indonesia: The Subsistence Strategies of the Kalimantan Kantu'*. Berlin, New York, Amsterdam: Mouton.

—— 1985b, 1986: Plantation development in West Kalimantan I: extant population/lab. balances, *and* II: the perceptions of the indigenous population. *BRB*, 17 and 18, 95–105; 3–27.

Dungen Gronovius, D. J. van den 1849: Bijdrage tot de kennis der binnenlandsche rijken van het westelijk gedeelte van Borneo. *Tijdschrift voor Nederlandsch-Indië*, 11, 338–56.

Dunselman, P. Donatus 1949, 1950: Bijdrage tot de kennis van de taal en adat der Kendajan Dajaks van West-Borneo. *BKI*, 105 and 106, 59–105, 147–218 (1949); 321–73 (1950).

—— 1952: Strafrecht en huwelijksrecht van de Kendajan-Dajaks van Sungai-Ambawang. *Adatrechtbundels*, 44, 168–81.

—— 1955: *Kana Sera, Zang der Zwangerschap*. The Hague: Martinus Nijhoff.

Dyen, I. 1965: *A Lexicostatistical Classification of the Austronesian Languages*. International Journal of American Linguistics Memoir, 19.

—— 1971: The Austronesian languages and Proto-Austronesian. In T. Seboek (ed.), *Linguistics in Oceania*. 2 vols, The Hague: Mouton, Vol. 1, 5–54.

Elshout, J. M. 1923: *Over de Geneeskunde der Kenja-Dajak in Centraal-Borneo in Verband met hunnen Godsdienst*. Amsterdam: Müller.

Enthoven, J. J. K. 1903: *Bijdragen tot de Geographie van Borneo's Wester-afdeeling*. 2 vols, Leiden: Brill.

Fidler, Richard C. 1976: Sarawak and the study of plural societies: an outline. *SMJ*, 24, 173–84.

Fisher, Charles A. 1967: *South-East Asia: A Social, Economic and Political Geography*. London: Methuen. First published 1964.

FMP 1986: *Fifth Malaysia Plan, 1986–1990*. Kuala Lumpur: National Printing Department.

Fraser-Lu, Sylvia 1989: *Silverware of South-East Asia*. Singapore: Oxford University Press.

Freeman, J. D. (Derek) 1955: *Iban Agriculture: A Report on the Shifting Cultivation of Hill Rice by the Iban of Sarawak*. London: HMSO.

—— 1960: The Iban of western Borneo. In George P. Murdock (ed.), *Social Structure in Southeast Asia*, Chicago: Quadrangle Books, 65–87.

—— 1961: On the concept of the kindred. *Journal of the Royal Anthropological Institute*, 91, 192–220.

—— 1970: *Report on the Iban*. London: Athlone Press.

—— 1975: The Iban of Sarawak and their religion – a review article. *SMJ*, 23, 275–88.

—— 1979: Severed heads that germinate. In R. H. Hook (ed.), *Fantasy and Symbol*, London: Academic Press, 223–46.

—— 1981: *Some Reflections on the Nature of Iban Society*. Australian National University: Dept of Anthropology, Research School of Pacific Studies.

Fulcher, Mary B. 1983a: Avoidance and ambiguity in inter-ethnic relations: population resettlement in East Kalimantan. *BRB*, 15, 108–13.

—— 1983b: *Resettlement and Replacement: Social Dynamics in East Kalimantan, Indonesia.* Unpublished Ph. D. thesis, Northwestern University.

Galvin, A. Dennis 1966: 'Mamat': Leppo Tau-Long Moh. In Tom Harrisson (ed.), Borneo Writing and Related Matters, *SMJ*, Special Monograph No. 1, 296–304.

—— 1968: Mamat chants and ceremonies, Long Moh (Upper Baram). *SMJ*, 16, 235–48.

Geddes, W. R. 1954: *The Land Dayaks of Sarawak.* London: HMSO.

Geertz, Clifford 1963: *Agricultural Involution: The Processes of Ecological Change in Indonesia.* Berkeley and Los Angeles: University of California Press.

Gill, S. H. S. 1968: *Selected Aspects of Sarawak Art.* Unpublished Ph. D. thesis, Columbia University.

Glover, I. C. 1979: The late prehistoric period in Indonesia. In R. B. Smith and W. Watson (eds), *Early South East Asia: Essays in Archaeology, History, and Historical Geography*, New York and Kuala Lumpur: Oxford University Press, 167–84.

—— 1989: *Early Trade Between India and South-East Asia: A Link in the Development of a World Trading System.* University of Hull: Centre for South-East Asian Studies.

Goldman, Philip 1975: *The Divine Gifts: Dayak Sculpture from Kalimantan.* London: Gallery 43.

Goodenough, Ward H. 1955: A problem in Malayo-Polynesian social organization. *American Anthropologist*, 57, 71–83.

Graham, Penelope 1987: *Iban Shamanism: An Analysis of the Ethnographic Literature.* Australian National University: Dept of Anthropology, Research School of Pacific Studies.

Greenwood, James 1869: *The Adventures of Reuben Davidger: Seventeen Years and Four Months Captive among the Dyaks of Borneo.* London, New York, Melbourne: Ward Lock. First published 1865.

Groeneveldt, W. P. 1880: Notes on the Malay Archipelago and Malacca compiled from Chinese sources. *Verhandelingen van het Bataviaasch Genootschap van Kunsten en Wetenschappen*, 39, 1–144.

Groot, J. J. M. de 1885: *Het Kongsiwezen van Borneo. Eene Verhandlingen over den Grondslag en den Aard der Chineesche Politieke Vereenigingen in de Koloniën, met eene Chineesche Geschiedenis van de Kongsi Lanfong.* The Hague: Martinus Nijhoff.

Gudgeon, Peter Spence 1981: Economic development in Sabah 1881–

1981. In Anwar Sullivan and Cecilia Leong (eds), *Commemorative History of Sabah 1881–1981*, Kota Kinabalu: Sabah State Government, 183–360.

Guerreiro, Antonio J. 1985: An ethnological survey of the Kelai River area, Kabupaten Berau, East Kalimantan. *BRB*, 18, 106–20.

Haddon, Alfred C. and Start, Laura E. 1936: *Iban or Sea Dayak Fabrics and their Patterns*. Cambridge: Cambridge University Press.

Haddon, Ernèst B. 1905: The dog-motive in Bornean art. *Journal of the Royal Anthropological Institute*, 35, 113–25.

Hall, D. G. E. 1968: *A History of South-East Asia*. London: Macmillan, 3rd edition. First published 1955.

Harrisson, Barbara 1967: A classification of Stone Age burials from Niah Great Cave, Sarawak. *SMJ*, 15, 126–99.

—— 1986: *Pusaka: Heirloom Jars of Borneo*. Singapore: Oxford University Press.

Harrisson, Tom 1955: The first British pioneer-author in Borneo. *SMJ*, 6, 452–69.

—— 1957: The Great Cave of Niah. *Man*, 57, 161–6.

—— 1958a: The Great Cave, Sarawak; a Ship of the Dead cult and related rock paintings. *Archaeological Newsletter*, 6, 199–202.

—— 1958b: Niah: a history of prehistory. *SMJ*, 8, 549–95.

—— 1959a: New archaeological and ethnological results from Niah Caves, Sarawak. *Man*, 59, 1–8.

—— 1959b: Radio carbon – C.14 datings B.C. from Niah: a note. *SMJ*, 9, 136–8.

—— 1959c: *World Within: A Borneo Story*. London: Cresset.

—— 1963: 100,000 years of Stone Age culture in Borneo. *Journal of the Royal Society of Arts*, 112, 74–91.

—— 1965: A stone and bronze tool cave in Sabah. *Journal of the Sabah Society*, 4, 151–9.

—— 1970: *The Malays of South-West Sarawak before Malaysia: A Socio-Ecological Survey*. London: Macmillan.

—— 1971: Niah Cave double-spouted vessels. *SMJ*, 19, 367–73.

—— 1972: The Borneo Stone Age – in the light of recent research. *SMJ*, 20, 385–412.

—— 1984: The prehistory of Borneo. In Pieter van de Velde (ed.), *Prehistoric Indonesia: A Reader*, Dordrecht, Cinnaminson: Foris, 298–326. First published in 1970 in *Asian Perspectives*.

—— and Harrisson, Barbara 1969–70: *The Prehistory of Sabah*. Kota Kinabalu: Sabah Society.

—— and O'Connor, Stanley, J. 1967: The 'Tantric Shrine' excavated at Santubong. *SMJ*, 15, 201–22.

—— 1969: *Excavations of the Prehistoric Iron Industry in West Borneo*. 2 vols, Ithaca: Cornell University Press.

—— 1970: *Gold and Megalithic Activity in Prehistoric and Recent West Borneo*. Ithaca: Cornell University Press.

Hatch, T. 1982: *Shifting Cultivation in Sarawak – A Review*. Kuching: Dept of Agriculture.

—— and Lim, C. P. 1978: *Shifting Cultivation in Sarawak*. Kuching: Dept of Agriculture.

Healey, Christpher 1985: Tribes and states in 'pre-colonial' Borneo: structural contradictions and the generation of piracy. *Social Analysis*, 18, 3–39.

Heekeren, H. R. van 1957: *The Stone Age of Indonesia*. The Hague: Martinus Nijhoff.

—— 1958: *The Bronze-Iron Age of Indonesia*. The Hague: Martinus Nijhoff.

Heine Geldern, R. von 1932: Urheimat und früheste Wanderungen der Austronesier. *Anthropos*, 27, 543–619.

—— 1937: L'art prebouddique de la Chine et de l'Asie du Sud-Est et son influence en Océanie. *Revue des Arts Asiatiques*, 11, 177–206.

—— 1966: Some tribal art styles of South-East Asia: an experiment in art history. In D. Fraser (ed.), *The Many Faces of Primative Art: a Critical Anthology*, Englewood Cliffs, NJ: Prentice-Hall, 165–221.

Heppell, Michael 1975: *Iban Social Control: The Infant and the Adult*. Unpublished Ph. D. thesis, Australian National University.

Hew Cheng Sim and Kedit, Flora 1987: The Batang Ai Dam, resettlement and rural Iban women. In Noeleen Heyzer (ed.), *Women Farmers and Rural Change in Asia: Towards Equal Access and Participation*, Kuala Lumpur: Asian and Pacific Development Centre, 163–219.

Hirth, Friedrich and Rockhill, W. W. 1966: *Chau Ju-Kua: his Work on the Chinese and Arab Trade in the 12th and 13th Centuries, entitled Chu-Fan-Chi*. New York: Paragon.

Hitchcock, Michael 1985: *Indonesian Textile Techniques*. Princes Risborough: Shire Publications.

Höevell, W. R. Baron van 1852: Onze roeping op Borneo. *Tijdschrift voor Nederlandsch-Indië*, 14, 187–94.

Hoffman, C. L. 1983: *Punan*: Unpublished Ph. D. thesis, University of Pennsylvania.

Hong, Evelyne 1987: *Natives of Sarawak: Survival in Borneo's Vanishing Forests*. Pulau Pinang: Institut Masyarakat.

Hornaday, William T. 1885: *Two Years in the Jungle: The Experiences of a Hunter and Naturalist in India, Ceylon, the Malay Peninsula and Borneo*. London: Kegan Paul, Trench and Co.

Horton, A. V. M. 1984: *The British Residency in Brunei, 1906–1959*. University of Hull: Centre for South-East Asian Studies.

Hose, Charles 1926: *Natural Man: A Record from Borneo*. London: Macmillan.

—— and William McDougall 1912: *The Pagan Tribes of Borneo*. 2 vols, London: Macmillan.

Howells, W. W. 1973: *The Pacific Islanders*. New York: Scribner's.

Hudson, A. B. 1966: Death ceremonies of the Padju Epat Ma'anyan Dayaks. In Tom Harrisson (ed.), Borneo Writing and Related Matters, *SMJ*, 13, Special Monograph No. 1, 341–416.

—— 1967a: *The Barito Isolects of Borneo: a Classification based on Comparative Reconstruction and Lexicostatistics*. Ithaca: Cornell University Press.

—— 1967b: *Padju Epat: the Ethnography and Social Structure of a Ma'anjan Dayak Group in Southeastern Borneo*. Unpublished Ph. D. thesis, Cornell University.

—— 1970: A note on Selako: Malayic Dayak and Land Dayak languages in Western Borneo. *SMJ*, 18, 301–18.

—— 1972: *Padju Epat: The Ma'anyan of Indonesian Borneo*. New York: Holt, Rinehart and Winston.

—— 1977: Linguistic relations among Bornean peoples with special reference to Sarawak: an interim report. In Mario D. Zamora, Vinson H. Sutlive and Nathan Altshuler (eds), *Sarawak: Linguistics and Development Problems*, Virginia: Boswell, 1–44.

—— and Hudson, Judith M. 1978: The Ma'anyan of Paju Epat. In Victor T. King (ed.), *Essays on Borneo Societies*, Oxford/Hull: Oxford University Press, 215–32.

Hunt, J. 1812: *Sketch of Borneo or Pulo Kalamantan*. Bencoolen; rpt. in J. H. Moor (ed.), *Notices of the Indian Archipelago and Adjacent Countries*, pt 1, Singapore, 1837, appendix, pp. 12–30.

Huntington, Richard and Metcalf, Peter 1979: *Celebrations of Death: The Anthropology of Mortuary Ritual*. Cambridge: Cambridge University Press.

Hurst, Philip 1990: *Rainforest Politics: Ecological Destruction in South-East Asia*. London and New Jersey: Zed.

Hüsken, Frans and Jeremy Kemp (eds) 1991: *Cognation and Social Organization in Southeast Asia*. Leiden: KITLV Press.

Hutton, J. H. 1938: *A Primitive Philosophy of Life*. Oxford: Clarendon Press.

Insan, 1989: *Logging Against the Natives of Sarawak*. Petaling Jaya: Insan.

Ipoi Datan and Bellwood, Peter 1991: Recent research at Gua Sireh (Serian) and Lubang Angin (Gunung Mulu National Park), Sarawak. *Indo-Pacific Prehistory Association Bulletin*, 10, 386–405.

Irwin, Graham 1967: *Nineteenth Century Borneo: A Study in Diplo-*

matic Rivalry. Singapore: Donald Moore Books. First published 1955.

Izikowitz, K. G. 1985: Fastening the soul: some religious traits among the Lamet (French Indochina). In Göran Aijmer (ed.), *Compass for Fields Afar: Essays in Social Anthropology, Karl Gustav Izikowitz,* Goteborg: Acta Universitatis Gothoburgensis, 212–57. First published 1941.

Jackson, James C. 1968: *Sarawak: A Geographical Survey of a Developing State.* London: University of London Press.

—— 1970: *Chinese in the West Borneo Goldfields: A Study in Cultural Geography.* University of Hull: Dept of Geography.

Jay, Sian 1991: *Shamans, Priests, and the Cosmology of the Ngaju Dayak of Central Kalimantan.* Unpublished D. Phil. thesis, Oxford University.

Jayl Langub 1987: Ethnic self-labelling of the Murut or Lun Bawang of Sarawak. *Sojourn,* 2, 289–99.

Jayum A. Jawan 1990: The Dayak in Sarawak: politics and participation in national development. In Victor T. King and Michael J. G. Parnwell (eds), *Margins and Minorities: The Peripheral Areas and Peoples of Malaysia,* Hull: University of Hull Press, 147–62.

Jensen, Erik 1974: *The Iban and their Religion.* Oxford: Clarendon Press.

Jones, L.W. 1966: *The Population of Borneo: A Study of the Peoples of Sarawak, Sabah and Brunei.* London: Athlone Press.

Josselin de Jong, P. E. de (ed.) 1977: *Structural Anthropology in the Netherlands: A Reader.* The Hague: Martinus Nijhoff.

Kedit, Peter 1980: *Modernisation among the Iban of Sarawak.* Kuala Lumpur: Dewan Bahasa dan Pustaka.

King, Victor T. 1976a: Cursing, special death and spirits in Embaloh society. *BKI,* 132, 124–45.

—— 1976b: Migration warfare and culture contact in Borneo: a critique of ecological analysis. *Oceania,* 46, 306–27.

—— 1976c: The peoples of the middle and upper Kapuas: possible research projects in West Kalimantan. *BRB,* 8, 86–105.

—— 1978a: Introduction. In Victor T. King (ed.), *Essays on Borneo Societies,* Oxford/Hull: Oxford University Press, 1–36.

—— 1978b: The Mualang of Indonesian Borneo: neglected sources for Iban studies. *BRB,* 10, 57–73.

—— 1978c: 'Revitalization movements' in Kalimantan (Indonesian Borneo). *Indonesia Circle,* 17, 14–27.

—— 1980: Structural analysis and cognatic societies: some Borneo examples. *Sociologus,* 30, 1–28.

—— 1982: Ethnicity in Borneo: an anthropological problem. In

Victor T. King and W. D. Wilder (eds), *Ethnicity in South-East Asia*, Singapore: Southeast Asian Journal of Social Science, 23–43.

—— 1983: Aspects of sugar manufacture in Borneo. *BMJ*, 5, 81–103.

—— 1985a: *The Maloh of West Kalimantan: An Ethnographic Study of Social Inequality and Social Change among an Indonesian Borneo People.* Dordrecht, Cinnaminson: Foris.

—— 1985b: Symbols of social differentiation: a comparative investigation of signs, the signified and symbolic meanings in Borneo. *Anthropos*, 80, 125–52.

—— 1986a: Land development in Sarawak, Malaysia: a case study. *Land Reform, Land Settlement and Cooperatives*, 1/2, 263–98.

—— 1986b: Land settlement schemes and the alleviation of rural poverty in Sarawak, East Malaysia: a critical commentary. *Southeast Asian Journal of Social Science*, 14, 71–99.

—— 1986c: *Planning for Agrarian Change: Hydro-electric Power, Resettlement and Iban Swidden Cultivators in Sarawak, East Malaysia.* University of Hull: Centre for South-East Asian Studies.

—— 1988a: Maloh, Malay and Chinese: silversmithing and cultural exchange in Borneo and elsewhere. In J. W. Christie and V. T. King, *Metal-working in Borneo: Essays on Iron- and Silver-working in Sarawak*, University of Hull: Centre for South-East Asian Studies, 29–56.

—— 1988b: Models and realities: Malaysian national planning and East Malaysian development problems, *Modern Asian Studies*, 22, 263–98.

—— 1989a: Editor's introduction. In H. F. Tillema, *A Journey Among the Peoples of Central Borneo in Word and Picture*, ed. V. T. King, Singapore: Oxford University Press, 1–27.

—— 1989b: What's in a name? Ethnicity and the problems it poses for anthropologists. *SMJ*, 40, Special Issue No. 4, pt I, 235–45.

—— 1990: Why is Sarawak peripheral? In Victor T. King and Michael J. G. Parnwell (eds) *Margins and Minorities: the Peripheral Areas and Peoples of Malaysia*, Hull: University of Hull Press, 110–29.

—— 1991a: Cognation and rank in Borneo. In Frans Hüsken and Jeremy Kemp (eds), *Cognation and Social Organization in Southeast Asia*, Leiden: KITLV Press, 15–31.

—— 1991b: Collectionneurs et objets. In Antonio Guerreiro and Pascal Couderc (eds) *Bornéo. Des Chausseurs de Têtes aux Ecologistes*, Paris: Autrement, 104–17.

—— and Bantong Antaran 1987: Some items of decorative silverware in the Brunei Museum ethnographic collection. *BMJ*, 6, 52–103.

—— and Nazaruddin Mohd. Jali (eds) 1992: *Issues in Rural Development in Malaysia.* Kuala Lumpur: Dewan Bahasa dan Pustaka.

—— and Parnwell, Michael J. G. 1990: The peripheral areas of Malaysia: development problems, planning and prospects. In Victor T. King and Michael J. G. Parnwell (eds), *Margins and Minorities: the Peripheral Areas and Peoples of Malaysia*, Hull: University of Hull Press, 1–23.

Koenigswald, G. H. R. von 1958: Remarks on the prehistoric fauna of the Great Cave. *SMJ*, 8, 620–6.

Komarusamy, T. 1989: South Indians in Sarawak. *SMJ*, 40, Special Issue No. 4, pt IV, 237–52.

Leach, E. R. 1950: *Social Science Research in Sarawak*. London: HMSO.

Leake, David Jr 1990: *Brunei: The Modern Southeast Asian Islamic Sultanate*. Kuala Lumpur: Forum.

Lebar, Frank M. 1972a: Dusun. In Frank M. Lebar (ed. and comp.), *Ethnic Groups of Insular Southeast Asia, Indonesia, Andaman Islands and Madagascar*, Vol. 1, New York: HRAF Press, 148–50.

—— 1972b: Kedayan. In Frank M. Lebar (ed. and comp.), *Ethnic Groups of Insular Southeast Asia, Indonesia, Andaman Islands and Madagascar*, Vol. 1, New York: HRAF Press, 176.

Lee, Edwin 1976: *The Towkays of Sabah: Chinese Leadership and Indigenous Challenge in the Last Phase of British Rule*. Singapore: Singapore University Press.

Lee Yong Leng 1965: *North Borneo: A Study in Settlement Geography*. Singapore: Eastern Universities Press.

Leur, J. C. van 1955: *Indonesian Trade and Society – Essays in Asian Social and Economic History*. The Hague, Bandung: W. van Hoeve.

Lijnden, D. W. C. Baron van (and J. Groll) 1851: Aanteekeningen over de landen van het stroomgebied der Kapoeas. *Natuurkundig Tijdschrift voor Nederlandsch-Indië*, 2, 537–636.

Lindblad, J. Thomas 1988: *Between Dayak and Dutch: The Economic History of Southeast Kalimantan, 1880–1942*. Dordrecht, Cinnaminson: Foris.

Linklater, Andro 1990: *Wild People*. London: John Murray.

Low, Hugh 1848: *Sarawak: Notes during a Residence in that Country with H. H. the Rajah Brooke*. London: Richard Bentley.

Luhat, Henry O. 1989: Some aspects of Belaga Kajang ethnohistory. *SMJ*, 40, Special Issue No. 4, pt III, 49–56.

Lumholtz, Carl 1920: *Through Central Borneo: An Account of Two Years' Travel in the Land of the Head-Hunters between the Years 1913 and 1917*. 2 vols, New York: Scribner's.

Mackie, Cynthia 1984: The lessons behind East Kalimantan's fires. *BRB*, 16, 63–74.

MacKinnon, John 1975: *Borneo: The World's Wild Places*. Amsterdam: Time-Life.

318   *References*

Mallinckrodt, J. 1928: *Het Adatrecht van Borneo*. 2 vols, Leiden: Dubbeldeman.

Marryat, Frank S. 1848: *Borneo and the East Indian Archipelago*. London: Longman, Brown, Green and Longman.

Martinoir, Brian de 1974: Notes on the Kajang. In Jérôme Rousseau (ed.), The Peoples of Central Borneo, *SMJ*, 22, Special Issue, 267–73.

Masing, James 1988: The role of resettlement in rural development. In R. A. Cramb and R. H. W. Reece (eds), *Development in Sarawak: Historical and Contemporary Perspectives*, Monash University: Centre of Southeast Asian Studies, 57–68.

Matussin bin Omar 1981: *Archaeological Excavations in Protohistoric Brunei*. Brunei: Brunei Museum.

McKinley, Robert 1976: Human and proud of it! A structural treatment of headhunting rites and the social definition of enemies. In G. N. Appell (ed.), *Studies in Borneo Societies: Social Process and Anthropological Explanation*. Northern Illinois University: Center for Southeast Asian Studies, 92–126.

Medway, Lord 1959: Niah animal bone: II (1954–8). *SMJ*, 9, 151–63.

—— 1977: *Mammals of Borneo*. Kuala Lumpur: Malaysian Branch of the Royal Asiatic Society.

Meilink-Roelofsz, M. A. P. 1962: *Asian Trade and European Influence in the Indonesian Archipelago between 1500 and about 1630*. The Hague: Martinus Nijhoff.

Metcalf, Peter 1975: The distribution of secondary treatment of the dead in central north Borneo. *BRB*, 7, 54–9.

—— 1976: Who are the Berawan? Ethnic classification and the distribution of secondary treatment of the dead in central north Borneo. *Oceania*, 47, 85–105.

—— 1982: *A Borneo Journey into Death: Berawan Eschatology from its Rituals*. Philadelphia: University of Pennsylvania Press.

Miles, Douglas 1970: The Ngadju Dayaks of Central Kalimantan with special reference to the Upper Mentaya. *Behavior Science Notes*, 5, 291–319.

—— 1976: *Cutlass and Crescent Moon: A Case Study in Social and Political Change in Outer Indonesia*. Sydney: Sydney University Press.

Molengraaff, G. A. F. 1900: *Borneo-Expeditie: Geologische Verkenningstochten in Centraal-Borneo (1893–94)*. Leiden: Brill.

Morris, H. S. 1953: *Report on a Melanau Sago Producing Community in Sarawak*. London: HMSO.

—— 1974: In the wake of mechanization: sago and society in Sarawak. In Robert J. Smith (ed.), *Social Organization and the Applications of Anthropology*, Ithaca, London: Cornell University Press, 273–301.

—— 1977: Melanau sago: 1820–1975. In K. Tan (ed.), *Sago – 76*, Kuala Lumpur: Kanji, 121–42.

—— 1978: The Coastal Melanau. In Victor T. King (ed.), *Essays on Borneo Societies*, Oxford/Hull: Oxford University Press, 37–58.

—— 1980: Slaves, aristocrats and the export of sago in Sarawak. In James L. Watson (ed.), *Asian and African Systems of Slavery* Oxford: Blackwell, 293–309.

—— 1982: How an old Sarawak society was undermined. *The Sarawak Gazette*, 108, 51–7.

Munan, Heidi 1989: *Sarawak Crafts, Methods, Materials and Motifs*. Singapore: Oxford University Press.

Murdock, George P. (ed.) 1960: *Social Structure in Southeast Asia*. Chicago: Quadrangle Books.

Needham, Rodney 1966: Age, category and descent. *BKI*, 122, 1–35.

—— 1972: Punan-Penan. In Frank M. Lebar (ed. and comp.), *Ethnic Groups of Insular Southeast Asia, Indonesia, Andaman Islands and Madagascar*, Vol. 1, New York: HRAF Press, 176–80.

—— 1976: Skulls and causality. *Man*, 11, 71–88.

Nicholl, Robert 1975: *European Sources for the History of the Sultanate of Brunei in the Sixteenth Century*. Brunei: Brunei Museum.

—— 1980: The medieval cartography of Borneo. *BMJ*, 4, 180–218.

Nieuwenhuis, A. W. 1900: *In Centraal Borneo: Reis van Pontianak naar Samarinda*. 2 vols, Leiden: Brill.

—— 1904–7: *Quer durch Borneo: Ergebnisse seiner Reisen in den Jahren 1896–97 und 1898–1900*. 2 vols, Leiden: Brill.

Nimmo, A. H. Arlo 1972: *The Sea People of Sulu*. London: Intertext Books.

Nothofer, Bernd 1991: Current interpretations of Western Malayo-Polynesian prehistory. *Indo-Pacific Prehistory Association Bulletin*, 11, 388–97.

O'Connor, Stanley, J. 1977: Tom Harrisson and the ancient iron industry of the Sarawak river delta. *JMBRAS*, 50, 4–7.

—— and Harrisson, Tom 1964: Western Peninsular Thailand and West Sarawak – ceramic and statuary comparisons. *SMJ*, 11, 562–66.

Ozinga, J. 1940: *De Economische Ontwikkeling der Westerfadeeling van Borneo en de Bevolkingsrubbercultuur*. Wageningen: Zomer and Keuning.

Padoch, Christine 1982: *Migration and its Alternatives among the*

Ibans of Sarawak. The Hague: Martinus Nijhoff.

Peranio, Roger D. 1972: Bisaya. In Frank M. Lebar (ed. and comp.) *Ethnic Groups of Insular Southeast Asia, Indonesia, Andaman Islands and Madagascar*, Vol. 1, New York: HRAF Press, 163–6.

Porter, A. F. 1967: *The Development of Land Administration in Sarawak from the Rule of Rajah James Brooke to the Present Time (1841–1965)*. Kuching: Land and Survey Department.

Pringle, Robert 1970: *Rajahs and Rebels: The Ibans of Sarawak under Brooke Rule, 1841–1941*. London: Macmillan.

Pusat Penelitian Purbakala dan Peninggalan Nasional 1976; *Survai di Daerah Kalimantan Selatan*. Jakarta: Dept Penelitian dan Kebudayaan.

—— 1977: *Survai di Daerah Kalimantan Barat*. Jakarta: Dept Penelitian dan Kebudayaan.

Ras, J. J. 1968: *Hikajat Bandjar: A Study in Malay Historiography*. The Hague: Martinus Nijhoff.

Rees, W. A. van 1858: *Montrado. Geschied- en Krijgskundige Bijdrage betreffende de Onderwerping der Chinezen op Borneo. Naar het Dagboek van een Indisch Officier over 1854–1856*. 's Hertogenbosch: Muller.

Reid, Capt Mayne 1892: *The Castaways: A Story of Adventure in the Wilds of Borneo*. London: T. Nelson. First published 1870.

Richards, A. J. N. (compiler) 1963: *Dayak Adat Law in the Second Division*. Kuching: Government Printing Office.

—— 1981: *An Iban-English Dictionary*. Oxford: Clarendon Press.

Ricklefs, M. C. 1981: *A History of Modern Indonesia: c. 1300 to the Present*. London: Macmillan.

Rienzi, G. L. Domény de 1836: *Océanie ou Cinquième Partie du Monde*. Vol. 1, Paris: Didot, 236–83.

Riwut, Tjilik 1958: *Kalimantan Memanggil*. Jakarta: Engang.

Roth, Henry Ling 1896: *The Natives of Sarawak and British North Borneo*. 2 vols, London: Truslove and Hanson.

Rousseau, Jérôme 1974: *The Social Organization of the Baluy Kayan*. Unpublished Ph. D. thesis, Cambridge University.

—— 1975: Ethnic identity and social relations in Central Borneo. In Judith A. Nagata (ed.), *Pluralism in Malaysia: Myth and Reality*, Leiden: Brill, 32–49.

—— 1978: The Kayan. In Victor T. King (ed.), *Essays on Borneo Societies*, Oxford/Hull: Oxford University Press, 78–91.

—— 1979: Kayan stratification. *Man*, 14, 215–36.

—— 1980: Iban inequality. *BKI*, 136, 52–63.

—— 1988: Central Borneo: a bibliography. *SMJ*, 38, Special Monograph No. 5.

—— 1990: *Central Borneo: Ethnic Identity and Social Life in a Stratified Society*. Oxford: Clarendon Press.

Rutter, Owen 1929: *The Pagans of North Borneo*. London: Hutchinson.

St John, Spenser 1862: *Life in the Forests of the Far East*. 2 vols, London: Smith, Elder and Co.

Sandin, Benedict 1967: *The Sea Dayaks of Borneo before White Rajah Rule*. London: Macmillan.

Sargent, Wyn 1976: *My Life with the Headhunters*. St Albans: Panther Books. First published 1974.

Sather, Clifford 1971: *Kinship and Domestic Relations among the Bajau Laut of Northern Borneo*. Unpublished Ph. D. thesis, Harvard University.

—— 1972: Tidong. In Frank M. Lebar (ed. and comp.), *Ethnic Groups of Insular Southeast Asia, Indonesia, Andaman Islands and Madagascar*, Vol. 1, New York: HRAF Press, 167–8

—— 1975: Bajau Laut. In Frank M. Lebar (ed. and comp.), *Ethnic Groups of Insular Southeast Asia, Philippines and Formosa*, Vol. 2, New York: HRAF Press, 9–12.

—— 1978: The Bajau Laut. In Victor T. King (ed.), *Essays on Borneo Societies*, Oxford/Hull: Oxford University Press, 172–92.

Saunders, Graham 1986: James Erskine Murray's expedition to Kutei, 1843–1844. *BMJ*, 6, 91–115.

Schärer, Hans 1963: *Ngaju Religion: The Conception of God among a South Borneo People*. The Hague: Martinus Nijhoff.

Schneider, William M. 1978: The Selako Dayak. In Victor T. King (ed.), *Essays on Borneo Societies*, Oxford/Hull: Oxford University Press, 59–77.

Sellato, Bernard 1986: *Les Nomades Forestiers de Bornéo et la Sédentarisation: Essai d'Histoire Economique et Sociale*. Unpublished doctoral thesis, EHESS, Paris.

—— 1987: Notes on the Kebahan of West Kalimantan. *BRB*, 19, 94–107.

—— 1989a: *Hornbill and Dragon: Kalimantan. Sarawak. Sabah. Brunei*. Jakarta and Kuala Lumpur: Elf Aquitaine (republished under the title *Hornbill and Dragon: Arts and Cultures of Borneo*, Singapore: Sun Tree, 1992).

—— 1989b: *Nomades et Sédentarisation à Bornéo. Histoire Economique et Sociale*. Paris: École des Hautes Études en Sciences Sociales.

Singh, D. S. Ranjit 1984: *Brunei, 1839–1983: The Problems of Political Survival*. Singapore: Oxford University Press.

Skipwith, T. 1875: Men with tails. In Crocker, W. M. (ed.), *Waiting for the Tide or Scraps and Scrawls from Sarawak*, Kuching: Crocker and Chapman.

Solheim, Wilhelm G. II. 1959: Two major problems in Bornean (and Asian) ethnology and archaeology, *SMJ*, 9, 1–5.

—— 1977a: The Niah research program. *JMBRAS*, 50, 28–40.

—— 1977b: Tom Harrisson and Borneo archaeology. *BRB*, 9, 3–7.

—— 1981: Notes on 'Malay' pottery in East Malaysia and neighbouring areas. *SMJ*, 29, 3–16.

—— 1983: Archaeological research in Sarawak, past and future. *SMJ*, 32, Special Issue No. 3, 35–58.

——, Harrisson, Barbara and Wall, Lindsey 1958: Niah 'three colour ware' and related prehistoric pottery from Borneo. *Asian Perspectives*, 3, 167–76.

—— 1961: Niah 'three colour ware' and related prehistoric pottery. *SMJ*, 10, 227–37.

Spencer, J. E. 1966: *Shifting Cultivation in Southeastern Asia*. Berkeley and Los Angeles: University of California Press.

Stöhr, Waldemar 1959: *Das Totenritual der Dajak*. Köln: Brill.

Strickland, S. S. 1986: Long term development of Kejaman subsistence: an ecological study. *SMJ*, 36, 117–71.

Sutlive, Vinson H. 1978: *The Iban of Sarawak*. Arlington Heights, IL: AHM Publishing Corp.

Sutton, Keith 1988: Land settlement in Sabah: from the Sabah Land Development Board to the Federal Land Development Authority. *Malaysian Journal of Tropical Geography*, 18, 46–56.

Tarling, Nicholas 1963: *Piracy and Politics in the Malay World: A Study of British Imperialism in Nineteenth-Century South-East Asia*. Melbourne, Canberra, Sydney: F. W. Cheshire.

Tillema, H. F. 1934: Apo-Kayan, the heart of Borneo. *The Nederland Mail*, 1, 1–4.

—— 1938/1989: *Apo-Kajan. Een filmreis naar en door Centraal-Borneo*. Amsterdam: Munster's. New English edition, *A Journey among the Peoples of Central Borneo in Word and Picture*, ed. V. T. King, Singapore: Oxford University Press.

Tregonning, K. G. 1965: *A History of Modern Sabah (North Borneo 1881–1963)*. Singapore: University of Malaya Press.

Treloar, F. E. 1978: Chemical analysis of iron, iron slag and pottery remains of the prehistoric iron industry of the Sarawak river delta. *SMJ*, 26, 125–33.

Tromp, J. C. E. 1879: De Rambai en Sebroeang Dajaks. *Tijdschrift voor Indische Taal-, Land- en Volkenkunde*, 25, 108–19.

Turnbull, C. Mary 1988: *A Short History of Malaysia, Singapore and Brunei*. Singapore: Graham Brash. First published 1980.

Tuton Kaboy 1965: The murder of Steele and Fox: two versions. *SMJ*, 12, 207–14.

Veth, P. J. 1854–6: *Borneo's Wester-afdeeling: Geographisch, Statistisch, Historisch, voorafgegaan door eene Algemeene Schets des Ganschen Eilands*. 2 vols, Zaltbommel: Noman.

Vredenbregt, Jacob 1981: *Hampatong: The Material Culture of the Dayak of Kalimantan*. Jakarta: P. T. Gramedia.

Vroklage, B. A. G. 1936: Das Schiff in den Megalithkulturen Sudostasiens und der Sudsee. *Anthropos*, 31, 712–57.

Wallace, Alfred Russel 1869: *The Malay Archipelago: The Land of the Orang-Utan and the Bird of Paradise. A Narrative of Travel with Studies of Man and Nature*. 2 vols, London: Macmillan.

Walton, John R. 1990: The economic structure of Sabah. In Victor T. King and Michael J. G. Parnwell (eds), *Margins and Minorities: The Peripheral Areas and Peoples of Malaysia*, Hull: University of Hull Press, 208–26.

Warren, James Francis 1981: *The Sulu Zone, 1768–1898*. Singapore: Singapore University Press.

Waterson, Roxana 1990: *The Living House: An Anthropology of Architecture in South-East Asia*. Singapore: Oxford University Press.

Weinstock, Joseph Aaron 1983: *Kaharingan and the Luangan Dayaks: Religion and Identity in Central-East Borneo*. Unpublished Ph. D. thesis, Cornell University.

Whittier, Herbert L. 1973: *Social Organization and Symbols of Social Differentiation: an Ethnographic Study of the Kenyah Dayak of East Kalimantan (Borneo)*. Unpublished Ph. D. thesis, Michigan State University.

—— 1978: The Kenyah. In Victor T. King (ed.), *Essays on Borneo Societies*, Oxford/Hull: Oxford University Press, 92–122.

Willigen, P. C. van der 1898: Mededeelingen omtrent een reis door Borneo van Pontianak naar Bandjermasin, langs Melawi en Kahajan, in 1894: *Tijdschrift van het Koninklijk Nederlandsch Aardrijkskundig Genootschap*, 15, 365–443.

Wolters, O. W. 1967: *Early Indonesian Commerce: a Study of the Origins of Srivijaya*. Ithaca: Cornell University Press.

World Wildlife Fund 1985: *Proposals for a Conservation Strategy for Sarawak*. Kuala Lumpur: WWF Malaysia.

Wright, L. R. 1970: *The Origins of British Borneo*. Hong Kong: Hong Kong University Press.

Zaharah Hj. Mahmud 1976: Spatial prognosis of the rural population. In Khoo Soo Hock, Lam Thim Fook, Voon Phin Keong and Zaharah Hj. Mahmud, *Brunei in Transition: Aspects of its Human*

Geography in the Sixties, Kuala Lumpur: University of Malaya, Dept of Geography, 1–51.

Zainie, Carla 1969: *Handcraft in Sarawak*. Kuching: Borneo Literature Bureau.

Zuraina Majid 1982: The West Mouth, Niah, in the prehistory of Southeast Asia. *SMJ*, 31, Special Monograph No. 3.

Government publications

Annual Bulletin of Statistics, Sabah

Annual Statistical Bulletin, Sarawak

Brunei Statistical Yearbook

Fifth Malaysia Plan, 1986–1990, FMP (National Printing Department, Kuala Lumpur, 1986)

Statistik Indonesia. Statistical Yearbook of Indonesia

Index

Bintarti, D. D. 100
Bintulu 5, 6, 144, 277
binua (Bidayuh village) 206
Bisaya 57, 121
Blust, R. A. 79–80, 82–3, 91–2
Bock, Carl 13
Bongkissam 113
Boyan river 132
Brace, C. L. 77
Britain *see* colonialism; Europeans
British Malayan Petroleum
    Company 155
British North Borneo Company
    146, 284
Brooke, Sir Charles 144, 146, 149
Brooke, Sir Charles Vyner 9
Brooke, Sir James 9, 18, 27–8, 30,
    143–9, 152, 155, 158–62, 188,
    203, 267, 284
Brooke, Sylvia 9
Brooke Raj 267, 284
Brown, D.E. 136, 226, 228
Brunei 5, 6, 24–6, 34–6, 49, 57, 96,
    107, 110, 113, 118, 120–5, 127–
    8, 227–8, 256, 270
    Sultan of 128, 139, 143–6, 225,
        227, 267
    Sultanate 8, 18, 27, 125, 136–7,
        140, 144, 146, 154, 156, 161,
        163–4, 188, 224–31
Brunei Darussalam 4–5, 19, 62
Brunei Malays 32, 191, 225, 227
Brunei-Muara 6
Brunei river 225
Buddhism 55, 107, 119
Bugau 49
Bugis 9, 25–6, 33, 48, 81, 125, 138–
    9
Bukat 40
Bukat-Ukit 40
bukit (hill) 40
Bukit 40
Bukit Tengkorak 95
Bukit Tilung 234
Bukitan 40
Bulungan, Sultanate 139, 147, 152
Bulungan river 57

Bulusu 57
Bungan movement 150
Bunut 126, 130, 133, 154
Busang 41
Büttikofer, J. 151

camphor 18, 105, 109, 119, 121,
    125, 136
carving 256–61
cash crops *see* agriculture
cassava 170
cattle raising 33, 48, 55, 69
Cense, A. A. 130
Central Borneo groups 41–8
    Badang 44
    Bahau 41, 44
    Berawan 46, 86, 170, 243, 256
    Busang 41
    Embaloh *see* Malohs
    Kajangs 44, 46–7, 170, 212, 257
    Kanowits 9, 44, 46, 144
    Kayans 29, 32, 40–2, 44, 46–8,
        54, 86, 100, 104, 116–17,
        121, 144, 151, 159–60, 164,
        167, 208–18, 220, 225, 227,
        230, 239–41, 243–4, 250,
        252, 254–61, 297
    Kejaman 44
    Kelabits 47–8, 93, 116, 219,
        252, 255, 261, 265, 297
    Kelabits-Muruts 47
    Kenyahs 30, 40, 42–7, 86, 94,
        128, 144, 167, 170, 208–18,
        220, 240–4, 249, 251–2,
        254–61, 265, 297
    La'anan 44
    Lepo' Pu'uns 46
    Lepo' Tau 44
    Lepo' Time 44
    Long Tutoh 46
    Malohs 29, 31, 48, 81, 86, 128–
        9, 132–3, 149, 157, 167, 174,
        177–9, 209, 220, 239–41,
        249, 256, 262, 265, 271
    Melanaus 44, 46, 144, 168, 188,
        191, 209, 215, 225, 251, 257,
        259